The Scottish Highland Estate

Preserving an Environment

The Scottish Highland Estate

Preserving an Environment

Michael Wigan

Photographs by Glyn Satterley

SWAN·HILL
PRESS

*"Wildlife conservation will best be promoted by the encouragement
of legitimate sport; of scientific interest in natural history; and
by building up the public opinion to make and enforce wise laws."*
Charles Sheldon, 1915 Chairman of the Game Preservation Committee
of the American Boone and Crockett Club.

Copyright © 1991 Michael Wigan (text) and Glyn Satterley (photographs)

First published in the UK in 1991 by
Swan Hill Press, an imprint of Airlife Publishing Ltd.

British Library Cataloguing in Publication Data
Wigan, Michael
   The Scottish highland estate : preserving an environment.
  1.   Scotland. Environment. Conservation. Role of
      agricultural industries
  I.   Title II. Satterley, Glyn
     333.7209411

  ISBN 1 85301 162 1

Printed by Kyodo Printing Co (Singapore) Pte Ltd

Swan Hill Press
An imprint of Airlife Publishing Ltd.
101 Longden Road, Shrewsbury SY3 9EB, England.

Contents

Author's Note

Technically speaking, the Highlands is constituted by the crofting counties of Argyll, Caithness, Sutherland, Invernesshire, Orkney, Rosshire and Shetland. However, when referring to the Scottish Highlands I include the whole area popularly thought of as the Highlands, which incorporates all of the Grampians and the high country in Perthshire, Stirlingshire and Dunbartonshire. Similarly, I have stuck to popularly understood spellings and measurements.

The views expressed are the author's only.

Preface

On an October afternoon three years ago I waited at the Kinbrace railway station in Sutherland for the Inverness train arriving at 2.40. The wind was of a strength even locally to qualify as a gale, sweeping across a county in which force eights are obdurately referred to as breezes. An American couple alighted from the train. It looked as if only the bags they held prevented them from being blown flat on the platform. The man and I supported his wife, a psychotherapist from Chicago, to the car. The breath had been knocked out of them.

I thought it worth a drive, before the light drained out at teatime, to nearby Badanloch, a large sheet of water in a flat expanse of empty flow country with the humped shoulders of Ben Armine and the 3,157 feet-high top of Ben Klibreck behind. Battling through extraordinary air turbulence we got to the road above Loch Achnamoine, just east of Badanloch. Around us the air was a blur of driven fine moisture and small objects — twigs, wool, bits of heather. On the loch's face we could see water being pushed up and propelled along the surface in vertical sheets about the height of a man. At the tail of the loch these flurried into spinning cones which disappeared when they hit the heather.

The two Americans, at first muted, became excited and thrilled witnesses of the wind and water spectacle. We drove home, and exchanged tales sitting around a crackling fire as the storm did its worst outside. The lodge is sheltered by trees but down the chimney we could hear the gale in a cadence of moaning overhead. Next morning presented the rinsed and gleaming look the Highlands have after heavy rain. Views into the distance were pellucidly clear and birds were singing noisily. There was no wind at all. The American pair gazed around in wonderment, hardly able to believe the previous afternoon had really occurred. The freshness of the hill, resplendent in deep autumnal colours, seemed to belong to a different world from the terrible tumult of the previous afternoon. They ask still, when we speak on the telephone, if the wind hasn't blown all the water out of Scotland's lochs yet.

What they saw and revelled in was, in dramatic degree, what all visitors to the Scottish Highlands appreciate — a mixture of temperamental extremes and fast-changing moods that brings nature to life as an independent force. And it is what imbues native Highlanders with a passionate love of their country. Often called an 'unspoiled' landscape, or even worse a 'wilderness', the Highlands of Scotland have a natural beauty which man's activity has changed but not reduced. Many parts of the world possess physical beauty, shapely hills and blue water, but few are charged with the atmosphere peculiar to the Highlands and felt by all who spend time there, a feeling perhaps generated by its long and troubled history. It is a landscape chastened by the huge span of geological time in which formerly mighty mountains have been gradually eroded to the stumps that form the mountain ranges today; a landscape chastened too by its fierce human history.

Being the son of a Highland mother, and a father whose line has owned property in the Highlands for three generations, I used to suppose my birth-right predisposed me towards Scotland's hills. But over the twelve years I have lived at Borrobol in Sutherland I have heard echoed in so many different individuals responses to the Highlands which are the same as my own. What-ever the chemistry of the matter, few people today would endorse Dr Johnson's comment on the Highlands: 'The best thing — the road south!'

Indeed, the Highlands are attracting greater interest from the nation as a whole as congestion tightens its grip on other parts of Britain. Rising interest in wildlife, country sports, and the conservation of open country directs attention to Scotland's Highlands where the population is considerably less dense than in any area of Europe. This interest crystallised in the ongoing debate about afforestation and the northern flow country.

At the centre of this debate, though often only as a rather ghostly presence, is that strange entity, both redolent of the past and blessed with the germ of future hopes, the Highland estate. The argument about whether conifer plantations are a right and proper use of deep peat flow country is usually carried out in the abstract. It is as if, having proved their case to the Secretary of State for Scotland, the planting companies could suddenly mobilise their moorland ploughs and commence combing through the topsoils of the straths and flows in preparation for immediate planting. Of course, the planting programme depends on the provision of land. This comes from farmers, crofters and estate owners, but mainly from the latter. Which accounts for the concern, strange at first sight, expressed by the open-land conservationists, such as the Royal Society for the Protection of Birds (RSPB) and the Nature Conservancy Council (NCC), for the quality of the grouse nesting season, or the price of venison. Impoverished Highland landlords, or landlords agree-able to releasing portions of land for money out of all proportion to their sporting or farming value, have provided forestry companies with a steady supply of land.

Only a short time ago estates in the Highlands were bought or sold purely as sporting assets. The value of the estate was the total game bag, the fish, birds and mammals which could be had for sport annually, multiplied by the going rate for each species. A nominal value was attached to the farm, possible land for tree-planting, and a premium was put on the charms of the lodge and its access to good roads and airports.

We are now entering a new era in regard to estate ownership; fresh perceptions are working. Increasingly those willing to spend the considerable sums necessary to buy a Highland estate seem aware that ownership has brought with it the custodianship of a precious asset in the lists of Scotland's capital. Even the business development groups which have suddenly forged their way into Highland estate ownership ardently stress in their first press briefings, close on the heels of their strong Highland connections, their concern for the environment and preservation. Lairds in the past generally acknowledged the duties of their patriarchal position; now, too, it is consciously as guardians of the environment that newcomers appear on the scene. Technology has put at man's disposal the ability to change his environment fast and in far-reaching ways. We now understand better how these impacts will be felt, not only locally on the home patch, but throughout an environment which is closely interconnected.

When the Forestry Commission began its planting programme after the First World War, and indeed until recent times, it did not assess what effects conifers would have on water quality, what soil conditions would be like after one rotation of trees, and what effect fencing red deer out from their low-ground winter shelter would have. When public utility companies impounded Highland loch waters for power generation or water supply it was not realised what the long-term impacts might be. The loss of sport fishing was not a primary reason advanced against this form of development. Hopefully, the search in the Scottish Highlands by the Government for a long-term nuclear waste disposal site is not another in a series of initiatives that has seized on this area for experimental measures that would be too strongly opposed by powerful and residential lobbies elsewhere.

The future of the Highlands is now poised for radical changes (the same might have been said 250 years ago when, strangely enough, the Highland population of 230,000 was approximately what it is today). The sheep which succeeded the small black cattle of the pre-Clearance crofting communities are now themselves going, herded for the last time to the mart to become breeding stock for the burgeoning sheep farms south of the Highland line. Stalking the red deer continues, but the sport is increasingly beleaguered by the necessity to operate amongst phalanxes of hill walkers; and both of these groups are squeezed into smaller compartments by the advance of conifers. The red grouse persists, but cyclically, as this notoriously erratic breeder has always done. In the troughs of the cycle impatient proprietors have often been forced into land sales for interim cash, particularly on the periphery of the Highlands, now sprouting its first crops of spruce, pine and fir. The cries of alarm from salmon fishers, fearful that their quarry's survival is imperilled, have been heard before in the annals of rod-fishing, but are they more scientifically based now; is the spring salmon really depleted for ever? A plethora of new interests are claiming their say in the development of the Highlands, often espousing incompatible rights — skiers, bird-watchers, developers, botanists, tourist promoters and so on. In the centre of the mêlée is the sporting estate, comprising a tiny social unit, often in a relatively faraway location, its owners strangely muted in the turmoil of the debate.

The sporting estate has, I contest, with reasonable success, kept in good heart that large part of the Highlands given over to deer forest and grouse moor for well over a hundred years. Exactly 200 years ago the Old Statistical Account records that there were only nine deer forests in the Highlands. In

1912 there were around 200, now there are over 300. Yet the area inhabited by deer has actually shrunk. What happened in these areas? More to the point, what happens now? Glyn Satterley's photographs will hopefully put flesh on to the bones of my explanations. Whatever happens in the future, and I shall attempt to chart a direction we might take, his photographs will give some idea of the values of the present and recent past, and the personal lives of those who live and work in that part of the kingdom described as 'God's Country'.

Chapter One
The Long History

In geological terms, as in human terms, the Highlands have been subjected to violent transformations. The strange shapes of the north-western mountains protruding statuesquely from level plains are accentuated starkly by their isolation. They are of Lewisian gneiss, the oldest rock in Europe, exposed by the tremendous scraping of successive glaciations. The clear faces of this most beautiful native stone are pale pink. The Lewisian gneiss was formed 2,800 million years ago; by 1,000 million years ago it had been eroded to near the present level. At a rate of erosion of one millimetre every twenty years, it will take another twenty million years for the high mountains in Sutherland to have been ground away by wind and rain to sea-level. The geology of Scotland, subjected to notoriously rough weather, is inching through its own evolution. In a different time-frame, the social evolution of its people is forging great changes, changes which often have radically altered the country in one lifetime.

From man's earliest presence in the Highlands, the main human concentrations were on the coast near sea-level, as they are now. It is a curious thing to consider that the area now known and cherished for its wildness and open spaces was comparatively heavily populated. The density of early man's surviving habitations on Orkney exceeds anything in Britain. Perhaps elsewhere Neolithic and Bronze Age civilisation has been obliterated or covered over; although population numbers have not been computed, remains tell us that the Highlands supported a considerable population around the coast. An inspection of Skara Brae on Orkney, a seaside village buried by a sandstorm 4,500 years ago, shows stone-built homes complete with utility rooms separated by hinged doors, equipped with shelving, and serviced by functional drainage.

It appears that small communities were often wiped out by sudden catastrophe. Estimates of early man's numbers are therefore difficult. This was an ominous precursor: the Highlands were to become notorious for population movements of a dramatic type. After a population peak in the Strath of Kildonan around 1811, when sheep came north to replace the small black cattle, the human population had dropped from 1,574 to 257 in twenty years. Today the population of Sutherland (around 13,000) is still shrinking. In the rest of the Highlands the small current rise in population is due to expansion in the towns. In one recent year Inverness, the capital town, was the fastest-growing town of its size in Britain. However, in the glens and straths the picture has been one of houses going empty or being occupied seasonally. The last few years have registered a general population movement northward, but for the most part newcomers have infilled houses on the coast deserted by younger folk seeking work further south.

The present landscape, often referred to as natural, is in fact the end-product of 6,000 years of human occupation and utilisation. As the whitened root protruding from the peat bank testifies, the Scottish hills were once partially tree-clad; the rotations of the old woodlands were determined by fires and hurricanes. The great majority of trees in the primeval forest, sprouting from a glaciated soil far more fertile than today's, was deciduous. Oak, ash, elm and alder woodlands grew on the wetter, low-lying areas around the coast and up the valleys. Birch replaced ash and elm where it was driest. Oak dominated the fertile, low, sunny ground, with an understorey of holly and hazel. Higher up the hillsides more stunted birch, alder, rowan, willow, aspen and hazel formed a lower forest cover. Wind-wracked birch and willow virtually disappeared above 2,000 feet or, exceptionally, 3,000 feet in the eastern Highlands. Scots pine, despite its name, was a small part of the tree-cover and not a strong competitor among these vigorous hardwoods, occupying the tops and sides of moraine mounds in the central and western Highlands and climbing higher up the granite-based slopes in the drier east. Later on, as peat spread over degraded soil types, the opportunity arose for Scots pine to extend its range.

An idea of what the primeval forest looked and felt like can be gleaned from the wooded islands in lochs which have escaped the hands of men and the champing jaws of deer, cattle and sheep. Often the highest tree is in the middle, the scrub around it growing lower and lower towards the shoreline. These little islands today are idyllic spots, tranquil and sheltered, carpeted in soft and varied vegetation, and also filled with birds; all congregating in the wooded oases in a landscape denuded of trees. However, the primeval Highlands should not be envisaged as completely continuous woodland. Swamps and bogs and bare peat plains were interspersed.

The Highland wildlife which seems noble and majestic today is the remnant of an order of mammals that was altogether mightier. The giant elk bore aloft antlers which weighed five or six times those of a contemporary hill stag. Its peat bog remains conjure up a behemoth of tremendous dimensions, which probably passed into history before the advent of man. The brown bear, a bigger type than the European bear, lasted until well into the tenth century, so was presumably exterminated by man. The reindeer squeezed into the diminishing area of wood, retreated northwards, then probably succumbed to hunting pressure by man in Caithness or Sutherland in the twelfth or thirteenth century. Wild boar, beaver and lynx all disappeared within historic time, as did the great wild ox or aurochs, whose blood is thought to run still in the shaggy West Highland cattle. Wolves clung on until more recently, and to flush them the woodland was extensively burnt. The last wolf was killed in Invernesshire in 1743. With it went the last of a grand order of earlier mammals not dissimilar to those of Canada today. Were it not for its sporting role, the red deer itself would certainly have disappeared also. The moorland red deer's present size is in any case a shadow of the potential physique it develops in a protected environment with access to scrub and forest for browsing. The achievement of deer farmers in rearing red stags of thirty to forty stones shows that the potential for growth survives in our own hill deer, if nurtured or sheltered.

If man's presence in the Highlands has killed off the giants and reduced the stature of the survivors, some species have been added by his efforts. Fallow deer, rabbits, squirrels and pheasants are not native to Scotland. In the case of the rabbit, the introduction took place in the twelfth century, the purpose being the provision of fur. In the reign of Alexander II (1214–49) the royal warrens were protected by statute, with a penalty of death for poachers, followed, vindictively it might seem, by confiscation of property. When the rabbit's predators had been decimated by Victorian gamekeepers, numbers of this unremitting breeder rose so fast it actually led to a desperate government order authorising anyone, anywhere, to kill rabbits to protect crops. The more recently introduced sika deer is becoming a problem, with the interbreeding of red and sika deer on the woodland edge where their territories overlap. Reintroductions, like that of the capercaillie (gaelic for 'old man of the wood'), doggedly pursued by Lord Breadalbane at Taymouth Castle in 1837, the polecat, and more recently the white-tailed eagle, have had no complications, at any rate biologically. For some birds, however, such as the bittern and common crane, the disappearance of correct habitat makes reintroduction impossible.

The difficulty of reintroductions in today's pressurised land area is that they are not always accepted by people in the spirit they were intended. A scheme some years ago to establish a wild boar presence in the woods around Beauly led to an animal being shot before young witnesses as it charged around the village playground. I had always disbelieved press stories about predatory big cats pacing the moors and savaging lambs until a feral black panther was actually captured in the central Highlands and photographed with its proud captors.

Early Scottish history was the story of animals, woodlands and, of course, the instigator of rapid change, man. Until around 2000 BC early hunters and fishermen made little impact on their untutored surroundings. However, the new Stone Age farmers, who grew barley in woodland clearings, felled and ring-barked small trees around the coast for their cultivations. The Bronze Age, which lasted until around 250 BC, produced more telling changes. More permanent settlements needed larger areas of cultivation; cleared areas helped keep wild animals at bay. Light, higher-altitude scrub woodland was cleared for grazing stock. The Iron Age and the period of Roman occupation until the fifth century saw further felling and clearing of the upper timber line and the middle woodland zone.

When it was found that the woodlands were a source of game, hides and skins began to be used for clothing, and timber as a building material. The axe was applied to the last untouched, and richest, tree zone — the valley bottom. Deer and trees became valuable property and the woodlands offered shelter to the growing hordes of domesticated cattle, horses and sheep, a use which accelerated their disappearance. Early-age browsing also accounts for the poor stature and shape of some of the woodland relicts from this time.

By the time of the Stuarts, as deer in the royal forests in the Borders had been replaced by sheep, large areas of the Highlands were set aside as replacement reserves. The Highland forests supplied venison, timber, furs and grazing, and were protected by law from graziers and woodcutters. However, in the sixteenth century in England so much timber had gone into charcoal production for smelting iron in the manufacture of guns that further felling was prohibited. Over the next 250 years the iron workers migrated to Scotland and Ireland, where vast volumes of wildwood were turned to charcoal and fed to the smelter. Far out on the deer forest in central Sutherland I have found coke deposits which presumably date from this time. Also, in the sixteenth century oak bark became a valuable asset for use in tanning. Boat building began to be organised on a national scale and wood fuel was needed for salt-making. With their growing usefulness forests were being administered by a complex hierarchy of foresters, whose functions ranged from policing to impounding stray cattle. By the end of the eighteenth century woodlands were an extremely valuable asset and source of income for landowners. The coppiced oak alone on 700 acres in the parish of Luss was worth £7,600. Meantime, agriculture was pushing the surviving woodland further into the hills and there was a steady trade in grants of land by clan chiefs to new freeholders and tenants. Additional woodland clearance resulted from road-making and the creation of an open border beside the road as protection from brigands.

Although no national statistics exist, it would appear that by the end of the eighteenth century tree cover in Scotland as a whole was considerably less than it is today. Much of the land must have presented a bleak and rugged aspect, with patches of the primeval woodland surviving and all around them the beginnings of new uses of land. This impression is reinforced when the extraordinary energy of a few private individuals to restore sylvan beauty to the hills is considered. The fourth Duke of Atholl, who succeeded to the title in 1774, continued a family tradition of planting with a programme of astonishing ambition. Its best results can still be seen today in the big trees around Dunkeld and Tummel and the area along the Tay. Duke John bequeathed to Perthshire the legacy of over twenty-seven million planted trees, covering an area of 15,500 acres. His championing of pioneer experiments in planting larch resulted in many Scottish-grown ships being constructed, amongst them some from wood he had planted in his own lifetime. The Atholl case stands as a glowing, though rare, example of an enlightened attitude towards tree cover and a flexible use of land suited to particular local conditions. This was amidst a general picture, true up to recent times, of neglect and opportunistic exploitation of native woodlands, and a disinclination to have regard for the future. Concern for tree cover, however, was a negligible theme when considered beside the process which started in the late eighteenth century to transform agriculture in the Highlands from small scale to large scale production, from low to high productivity, from high population to low population, from cattle to sheep; a process known as the Clearances.

No subject in Scottish history excites such passionate feelings as the Clearances does. Even for those who admit that the flows and straths of the Highlands could not forever escape the pace of agrarian change which had been sweeping the rest of Europe since 1500, typified in England by the enclosures period, the Highland Clearances can become a matter of intense resentment.

For political nationalists the Clearances are still a powerfully emotive *cause célèbre* and a scapegoat for a general sense of grievance. The Clearances have become a historian's hardy perennial, partly because documentation at the time was poor and eye-witness accounts were mostly written much later; because the very complexity and confused nature of the subject leaves more room for creative interpretation; and because the lives of the pre-Clearance clansmen living simply in their beautiful land have the same romantic appeal for latter-day historians as they had for the Gaelic poets, who celebrated the pastoral existence at the time.

Although painful agrarian change was forced on every Western nation at some stage in its history, the process in the Highlands was dressed in a peculiar drama, was conducted more haphazardly and with less institutional restraint, and was given a special vividness because of the vast gulf in means and lifestyle between tenant and landlord. To this unhappy situation the evocative Highland landscape lent a soulful backdrop. It is an inescapable and sad fact that in some areas entire glens were emptied of their native inhabitants, often against their will, and often to pathetic, ill-prepared existences on the coast, in the English cities, or abroad. If the ancient way of life was an anachronism, so too were the immense discretionary powers which survived in the hands of the Highland landlords. The problem was compounded by a population rapidly growing as the means of support in a more modernised population dwindled. The potato became a staple diet, supporting a top-heavy population which then suffered the more cruelly when potato blight struck. Poor relief was inefficient, the people were unprepared, and some lairds bankrupted themselves on relief programmes that should have been provided by central government.

Into this unstable and outmoded system arrived an energetic, persuasive, financially-aware breed of stockmen, mostly from other parts of Scotland, who pressed on the landowners the benefits of a more modern and productive stock farming system, and the allurements of rents out of all proportion to the erratic pittance which traditional smallholding was able to supply.

The Clearances advanced pastoral farming and consolidated extensive areas into sheepwalks under single managements. The traditional Highland sheep, a poor small-bodied, fine-fibred animal descended from the Soay sheep of St Kilda, which had lived cheek by jowl with its owners, was replaced by selectively bred blackface hill sheep and woolly North Country Cheviots developed in the Borders. The first blackfaces entered the Highlands in Dunbartonshire before 1760; by 1782 they had reached Rosshire. Much of the remaining woodland was burnt and cleared for grazing, an environmental degradation from which the Highlands suffers still today.

The old Highland communities, clusters of houses which cultivated around them small patches of soil for their oats, potatoes and barley, were vacated. With the tenantry went their small black (more accurately brindled) cattle, kept in roughly equal numbers with the sheep, and the few goats. Their rude black-houses, with spaces in the stones for windows, or window-less in which case the peat-smoke filtered through the turf thatch, backing onto the byre-wall from which the animals gave them warmth, tumbled down. In the open hill country of Borrobol, my home in Sutherland, it is easy today to see where the clachans were, for the hillsides they built on are green still, testifying to the hand-ploughed pastures well-manured by the stock in winter. The grass-covered humps of the fail-walls, or enclosed fields, mark out the field systems, and drains run diagonally, high up, across the slopes in much the same way as they do across the much earlier settlements of the Iron and Bronze Age. These are smaller in area, with round ruins instead of long rectangular ones. The benefits of the old pre-Clearances communities are enjoyed yet by the deer and sheep which graze their greens, and by grazing and manuring them help keep them verdant.

When flockmasters from the south arrived in the Highlands they saw at once the potential for organised stock management of land that had only been utilised in a haphazard way. The wandering black cattle had furthermore bequeathed high fertility in the hills and this provided capital off which large numbers of sheep lived for many years. At the same time, cattle prices were moving up more slowly than those of sheep and wool. In the eighteenth century, and up until the slump of the 1830s, when Australian sheep-farmers broke into the market, wool values had risen, latterly very fast. Sheep and wool played a major part in Britain's rise to commercial greatness in the nineteenth century. The proportion of British wool supplied by the whole of Scotland by 1841 was a quarter, and principally that output came from the two sheep-rearing areas of the Borders and the Highlands.

Although sound statistics are few and far between, the quoted stock numbers for some of the Highland counties tell the expansionary tale them-selves. From 250,000 in 1800, sheep numbers in Argyll had risen meteorically to over a million in 1880; in Invernesshire about 50,000 multiplied to 700,000. The figure in Sutherland, the county classically associated with the larger scale Clearances, rose from a paltry 15,000 in 1811 to 204,000 a mere forty-five years later. Those increases were spectacular, and although records do not exist which tell the whole story, it is awesome to consider the scale and speed of this change at a time when the country barely had any roads and only rudimentary communications, and when probably a quarter of all the stock died annually in bad winters. Grazing regimes had altered radically.

Considerable profits were made in sheep farming, and a few private fortunes, the golden years being the early part of the nineteenth century, and the thirty-five years after 1840 following the revival of the wool price. Thus the tacksman, the middleman and land-tenant who collected the landlord's rents under the old system, gave way to the flockmaster from the south. Emigrating with the tacksman, some say, went the Highland's nascent middle class, the people who might have helped moderate the speed and nature of sweeping change. The folk from the glens made way for sheep, scornfully christened 'four-footed clansmen'. Emigration of the native people had been a continuous process which famine had advanced long before the Clearances. In those parts where traditional landlords doggedly observed their roles as providing patriarchs, the people still drifted away, often to end up in the industrial power-houses of Victorian Britain. Good intentions seemingly could not save the occupants of the straths and glens from the engine of agrarian and social change that was crossing Europe. If the reaction of many landlords to their tenants' destitution was lackadaisical, the convening of a government board for famine relief resulted in prompt action and the despatch of large quantities of meal. Nonetheless, at the close of the nineteenth century the parts of the Highlands, such as the Grampians, largely unaffected by the Clearances resembled the rest: the turf roofs of the clachans had fallen and the dykes had started to crumble. The Clearances with their bitter legacy were a calamity. However, had they not taken place it seems certain that famine for a growing population unable to sustain itself would have been inevitable; the purses of landlords providing relief would have emptied anyway. The anguish of the cleared people had about it an awful predictability.

Highland depopulation was offered temporary reprieves by such alternative industries as linen production, fishing and kelp. Linen production quickly faded out and the hillmen initially showed little enthusiasm for the sea: often foreign boats plied the coastal trade. Kelp production which boomed and collapsed in the period 1796–1825 shone the brightest star in the shaky firmament of options. With kelp began the start of crofting and the movement of the hill people into smallholdings on the coast close to the new source of labour. The Highlands suited the kelp industry because the seaweed-gathering coastline was extensive, labour was plentiful and the interior population was moving anyway to the coast where the seaweed grew profusely. Rocks were moved offshore for the seaweed to colonise. It was harvested in midsummer with metal hooks, and incinerated in kilns till the molten slag cooled, forming a brittle bluish material which contained valuable industrial chemicals including salt. The economic value of kelp to Highland communities can be calculated in the figure for Orkney. In the decade to 1800, kelp was worth over £30,000 annually; this was nearly four times the rental of all the land on the islands. In the early nineteenth century, the Hebrides were exporting up to 20,000 tons of kelp worth around £70,000 a year. Most of the west Highland estates earned good revenue from kelp, although some islands were better suited to trapping seaweed than others. Although kelp production on a small scale limped into the twentieth century, it was largely destroyed by the repeal of the tax on imported salt in 1825. The consequences for both the kelpers and their landlords, for whom kelp had provided an economic lifeline, were profound. Furthermore, the harvesting of kelp had stolen a traditional fertiliser from use on the land, so soils had become impoverished. Kelpers had bought meal for their cattle with their wages and enlarged their stock, which was now forced back onto small areas of poorer land for sustenance. Kelping, which was labour-intensive, had propped up a top-heavy population which it was beyond the agricultural capacity of the land to feed.

So many Highland endeavours have gone this way, boom then bust industries sprouting from the desire to put far-flung communities to productive use, industries amassing around them a large imported workforce which suddenly finds itself without a purpose, rootless, and stranded. Highland history is littered with their failures, and legacies.

The aluminium smelter at Invergordon and the pump-mill at Fort William are two examples of large government-led industrial initiatives in the Highlands in recent time which have collapsed with embarrassing speed. This book concerns itself with land uses rather than industries, although some industries have land use implications. A timber mill processes forestry's end product; distilleries situated in the Highlands utilise arable-belt barley; the products of west Highland salmon farming and salmon ranching entail on-shore processing and are generated from on-shore hatcheries; weaving and yarn industries employ woolly fleeces from the hills. The industrial future of the Highlands is, however, another subject.

Chapter Two
Sporting Use in the Highlands

After around 1850, and in particular the highly controversial Clearances at Greenyard in Easter Ross in 1854, no large-scale Clearances took place. Clearances had aroused wide public interest in the nation, and frequently intense indignation. Through local newspapers a movement started, spearheaded by the religious revivalists known as 'Evangelicals' who were to form the breakaway Free Church of Scotland, which publicly questioned the right of the landlords to evict tenants without legal restraint. For three decades the situation simmered until the appointment of the Napier Commission in 1883, which investigated the causes of the problems of the Highland economy in great detail. The Napier Report of 1884, published at a time of growing rural unrest and agitation, sometimes running to lawlessness, recommended radical alterations in the organisation of the Highlands and set in train ideas which were to culminate in the Crofters Act of 1886. Ever since then, and up to the present time, the status of crofts and crofters has been consolidated through legislation.

As a solution to the problem of the emigration of the Highland population this has been a controversial thing. Some Scottish historians believe that tying up small uneconomic parcels of land in impregnable tenancies has insulated the crofter's life entirely from normal economic trends. Arguably, the cast-iron protection offered to crofters by administrators motivated by the emotional belief that small scattered patches of land were the minimal basic birthright of Highlanders, has also choked off the possibility of flexible responses to a changing world. The crofting system has the look of a palliative sop, a gesture rather than a solution, to mitigate the effects of restlessness for a landless people. It is a fraught issue: suffice it to say at this point that the Crofters Acts of the 1880s were the first steps in curtailing unrestricted private property rights, and as a result a considerable area of the Highlands was set aside into a specially protected category. Whilst not instrumental in determining what happened elsewhere, the fact that this arable ground, and the further large hill area on which crofters acquired grazing rights, was taken out of the equation of the Highland's potential for competitive production, is nonetheless important. Today there are around 17,600 registered crofts occupying an area of two million acres, of which just over half is held in common grazings. This is a quarter of the agricultural land area.

Before the Clearances ever began, a development of a different type was quietly taking place in the Highlands, like the Clearances in a piecemeal fashion. This was the development of interest in sport, especially the formation of deer forests. The phrase 'deer forest' derived from the time of earlier royal hunting preserves or 'forests'; it came to signify any area, usually devoid of tree cover, in which pursuit of deer was the main activity. In the sixteenth and seventeenth centuries the spread of sheep farming in the Scottish Lowlands had divided up the old royal hunting forests, the dispersed denizens of which had then succumbed to poachers. Royal hunting moved to the Highlands and established such forests as Mar and Cluanie.

Deer had been hunted in the Highlands from the earliest time and statutory protection for young calves existed in 1474. In deer hunting's most organised form, deer were driven by hundreds, even thousands, of men in a process sometimes lasting a few days, towards a defile where the hunters and their hounds lay in wait. Where the provision of venison exceeded the importance of exciting sport, deer were driven into walled bottleneck enclosures or tinchels. In a bedlam of murderous fury hardly palatable to modern-day sensibilities they were despatched by the Highlanders at close quarters, the mightier participants supposedly being able to split the animals in two with one blow from their enormous Lochaber axes. Anyone wishing imaginatively to recreate these bloody scenes should try lifting one of these cumbrous weapons off the ground.

More civilised management of deer is discernible in the tradition, also very early, of deer parks. These systems ranged from a herd of deer kept in a confined area around the landowner's house for the provision of venison, to much larger enclosed areas set aside for deer and often planted with trees for their benefit. On Loch Lomond Sir James Colquhoun and his neighbour across the loch, the Duke of Montrose, established deer parks on islands in the loch. The parks maintained by the wealthier landowners form a link between the ancient hunting forest and the modern unenclosed deer forest.

In 1745 the Battle of Culloden sealed the fate of the clan system. The broken ties between the chief and his clansmen made the landholders look to new ways to utilise their sprawling domains. The period 1750–1850 can be seen as the first in three phases of deer forest development. The major changes took place after 1811, at which time only six deer forests contained large numbers of deer. These were Atholl, Black Mount, Glenartney, Glen Fiddich, Invercauld and Mar. It is interesting to note that the hostility of the High-landers to sheep-farming in this period was partly because it interfered with their informal right over much of the area to take their own venison. This right was eventually curtailed in the deer forests, with the same reaction.

By the middle of the eighteenth century, news of the sporting charms of the moors had percolated throughout high society. Bird shooting, already a popular sport in England, was experiencing an excess of demand over supply. Poor harvests in the south had led to landowners cropping woodlands to raise money; shipbuilding demand depleted woodlands too. The invention of the threshing machine in the 1790s led to the disappearance of the long stubble loved by gamebirds, and other habitat was lost as more rough ground was turned to cultivation. English rivers were being systematically choked to extinction by the effluents of early industrial production and the salmon disappeared from the Thames in 1821. The Scottish Highlands offered an extensive and beautiful countryside brimming with fish and game, which was increasingly accessible, at least to those willing to endure the discomforts of the long distance stage-coach. By 1820 thirty coaches were travelling to Edinburgh daily, and Britain led the world in the efficiency of coaching services. By the 1840s rail travel had arrived and the Highlands was opened up for the road construction which swabbed up labour in the aftermath of the awful potato blights of 1846–8. The first Highland gamebook had appeared at the end of the eighteenth century; refinements in the design of guns and rifles coincided to improve the tools of the sporting man's craft immeasurably.

The 'heather lairds', as they were called, accustomed to the roller-coaster of the agricultural economy, and chastened by the social disruptions of the Clearances, were only too delighted to receive money for letting people dangle baits for fish and shoot some birds and deer. That people would pay to do such things might have surprised them, for in the old times the landlords had employed a 'sealgair' (hunter), whose job was to provision the larder with venison and game. The lairds themselves had never thought to make such efforts for the sheer fun of it. For this reason Scottish sport was cheap. Lord Malmesbury, the proprietor of Harris, offered the whole sporting rights of the island, including grouse moor, stalking and fishing for £25 in 1833; only fifty years later that rental value was to grow to £2,000. A noted deer forest commanded a rent of £300 in the early days; by the 1880s this figure had moved to £4,000. All over the Highlands today's famous forests appeared on the lists as letting properties, early rents finding their level in a tentative market. Gaick (probably the first) was open to tenders in 1812; Black Mount (emptied of sheep for the purpose) in 1820; Coignafearn in 1824; and the forest of Mar in 1826. In the far north, landowners were slower to realise the possibilities and were more involved with the creation of sheepwalks.

The traditional Lowlander's distaste for all things Highland made a remarkable turnaround, and so popular did Highland deer forests and moors become that by the 1840s many sportsmen from both south Scotland and England, wandering the countryside in the hope of securing tenancies on the spot, straggled south again unable even to locate accommodation. This was at the time when inns were a rarity; most shooting properties were enjoyed striking out from a heather couch in a shepherd's house or the modest dwelling of a Highland fox-hunter.

The visit by Queen Victoria and her consort Prince Albert to Atholl took place in 1844; they stayed with the Duke of Argyll at Inverary in 1847. Their delight with the Highlands and subsequent lease of Balmoral set in motion a fashion for Highland sport across the nation. The vivid paintings of Landseer, imbued with the awesome spirit of unbridled nature, and the rapturous reception given to the deerstalker William Scrope's writings, captured the public imagination and the Highlands became all the rage. Highland sport, with its strong overtones of hardiness and fresh-air athleticism, chimed with the self-confident late Victorian mood of 'muscular' Christianity.

Britain was now the pre-eminent world power. Fortunes lay in the hands of industrialists looking for a socially acceptable way of spending them. If sporting leases could be had rather too cheaply to confer sufficient distinction on the spender, then building shooting lodges carried with it more substantial prestige. Victoria and Albert bought Balmoral from the Earl of Fife's trustees in 1852 and work on a new house began the next year. So started the programme of lodge construction by proprietors and sometimes even tenants, which has furnished the Highlands with some of its most distinctive buildings. This was when life in the lodges could be tough. W. A. Adams records that 100 years ago a morning bath for a Caithness shooting party was taken standing in line outside being douched by the ghillies with buckets of spring water. In the autumn, at the same latitude as southern Alaska, this would fairly put a man on his mettle, surely? Mr Adams' accounts of trudging over the Caithness and Sutherland flows in rainstorms that seemed determined to outlast all other rainstorms, with ghillies who lost their lochs, laden with all the old-fashioned heavy fishing tackle, gives a taste of the fun, the slog, and the sheer sporting richness which the early pioneers experienced. The rewards were tangible too. By the 1880s 4,500 stags were being shot in the Highlands and the grouse bag, obtained from moors as small as sixty acres upwards, was then estimated at around 500,000 birds. The rental worth of these was considered to be £250,000 and £500,000 respectively, demonstrating the size of the cash injection this constituted for the Highland economy. By the mid-nineteenth century the balance between the economics of sheep and sporting rents was delicately poised: by the 1860s sporting returns had overtaken graziers' rents.

Meanwhile in the larger perspective of human affairs things were happening that were accelerating the utilisation of the Highlands for sport. The wool price collapsed in the face of competition from imports in 1874. The temporary respite offered by the loss in England of 2.8 million sheep from liver-rot, and consequent demand for Scottish breeding stock, could not offset the effects of a further collapse of the wool price in 1880. The meat value of sheep made the same nose-dive when Australia, New Zealand and the Argentine used the new refrigerated transport to undercut British mutton, affecting the Highland producers severely. By 1885 importers were building cold storage facilities for New Zealand lamb in Britain. Yet again, movements in the world economy and a technical invention had a stunning effect on a part of the British Isles that was economically undeveloped and dependent on a tenuous use of marginal land. Between 1880 and 1906 sheep and wool prices declined and the sheep population in Scotland fell thirty per cent. As the demand for Scottish sheep dropped and stock numbers declined, rents fell. Concomitantly the area referred to as deer forest, although much of it still contained grazing sheep and cattle, increased from a figure of under two million acres in 1883, accounting for a total of ninety-nine deer forests, to a huge three-and-a-half million acres in 1912, spread over 202 forests. This transformation in the context of the large numbers of landless cottars was unpopular. It was to go into reverse in the First World War with a sea blockade, the renewed need for more intensive meat production from the hills, and agricultural restocking of the major deer forests. Some 83,000 sheep and

8,000 cattle were reintroduced to deer forests and in 1922 the deer forest area had actually dropped by 150,000 acres.

The conversion of a sheepwalk into a deer forest might appear a more difficult exercise than in fact it was. As the mixed stock of the pre-Clearance glens had left a herbage which was in good heart for sheep grazing, so the sheepwalks, which had benefited from rotational heather-burning, when cleared of sheep were suited to rapid colonisation by deer. The red deer is a strong, regularly breeding animal, generally untroubled by disease, and it was by this time free of predators. Deer will move readily onto ground cleared of sheep, providing it has not been too overgrazed and degraded. The pressures of hunting from the pre-Clearance Highlanders had gone, and with the reduction in numbers of shepherds another regular predator declined. These human pressures, in combination with those of traditional medieval hunting, were severe, and had eliminated the red deer altogether by the sixteenth century from its range in the Scottish Borders and Fife. Now, for the first time in many years, as the twentieth century dawned, much of the Highlands was used for the maximisation of red deer. Gone were the mixed populations of roe, red, fallow and sika which profited in the old deer parks with their scrubland and protective plantations. Here the red deer alone was being nurtured, partially in harness with a reduced population of sheep, and almost invariably on open moorland and hillside where shelter lay along the burns. When the nineteenth century writer-sportsman Charles St John eventually killed the Muckle Hart of Benmore, an epic, vividly-narrated deer-chase lasting a week, embracing all-night revelling in 'whisky-bothies' illumined with burning bog-firs, the animal is said by this reliable reporter to have weighed thirty stone. The red stag today, competing for food with much larger numbers of his fellows, mostly fenced out of the shelter of woodland, never attains this weight. The hill stags weighing over twenty stone in a stalking season today are few.

The creation of a deer forest with the attendant lodge-construction and furnishing, road and bridge building, and general estate outfitting (ponies, dogs, guns, carts), brought employment and money to areas that had enjoyed few direct benefits from sheep pasturing. Victorian economists calculated that sporting estates generated more money and were a better asset locally than sheepwalks; although this calculation took no account of the nation's benefit in mutton and wool. In *Monarchs of the Glen*, Duff Hart-Davis has quoted at length the minutely-recorded activities of the fifteenth Lord Elphinstone in his creation of a sporting estate at Coulin in 1866. Employment was generated to a horde of local contractors in lodge and road building. Fencers, gardeners, woodcutters, horse and cart hauliers continued to benefit from the new laird's energetic plans, aside from permanently employed stalkers, after the main constructions were completed. Disputes with neighbours about boundaries (known in the Highlands as 'marches'), sporting rights, rights of access and so on, beefed up the portfolios of local solicitors. Nor were estate workers employed for a pittance: the bounties paid for vermin which it was the stalker's duty to control could amount to a fair portion of his salary paid over again.

Lodge construction itself was the largest item of expenditure. Some astonishing figures for these costs are recorded — £40,000 on Inverlochy House in the 1880s; £70,000 on Duncraig; £12,000 each on Balmacaan and Torridon; £10,000 at Rosehall. Comparative values are hard to state precisely. However, a contemporary head keeper's wage at Ardtornish was £79, a head shepherd's £71. Using these wages as a base, and assuming a head keeper today might receive an annual wage of around £7,500, the cost of building Duncraig today, assuming equivalent cost increases, would be over £6 million. (A teasing comparison is the £24 James II is recorded as spending on his wooden hunting lodge at Loch Freuchie in the fifteenth century.) Surviving sporting lodges testify to the lavishness of the new lairds' ambitions. Lodges like Ardverickie, Langwell and Wyvis stand as magnificent constructions in their own right. Excepting the considerable number which have gone up in smoke, these buildings are often still the natural focal point in small communities to which they attract the life-blood of custom in the season.

The scale of development was sometimes of an order to compare with colonial pioneering overseas. Sir John Ramsden spent £180,000 in twelve years at Ardverickie on roads, drains and pony paths. The contribution by the Sutherland family to the public railway which opened up their sporting holdings north of Helmsdale was £301,000. These examples of capital expenditure are not representative of an average; smaller landholdings obviously would not have justified it. However, they give some indication of the economic stimulus the estate owners provided in a general economy which had been so long undernourished.

It is a testament, too, to the quality of workmanship. Most of the roading laid down then services sporting estates still. Pony paths for extraction of deer carcases, laid in stone or dug down to the bedrock, threaded along the floors of the glens and zig-zagged up the more benign slopes, assiduously skirting or bridging soft spots where a heavily-laden pony might stumble. Culverted roads were constructed, either to the ends of glens where the lodges arose, commanding a view of the approach, or branching out into corners of the ground that would otherwise have remained unworked. At least one corner in most deer forests repelled practical access. These areas were safe ground for deer which became resident there, and were known as sanctuaries.

No practical alternative to sporting use had materialised. Where resettlements of small agricultural tenants were assisted by government, results were patchy. When government investigations into land use in the Highlands were carried out in the 1880s, it became clear the landless crofters wanted restoration of their tenancies, not to own the land itself. The root cause of the crofters' grievance was that some areas on which they had traditionally grazed sheep had been cleared for deer; their grazings had been unfairly disenfranchised. The problem of their restricted grazings, and the inevitable conflicts about deer doing damage to their crops, were not resolved by the palliative of estate gifts of venison. However, the sheer magnitude of the boom in sporting values, combined with the conspicuous absence of any economical way acceptable to government of satisfying crofters' demands on a national scale, meant the development of deer forests was bound to continue.

From the accounts of such early sportsmen/writers as John Colquhoun, W. A. Adams, Osgood MacKenzie and Charles St John, it appears some Highlanders in any case understood and sympathised with the roving sportsmen whom they now encountered, and found the sporting era more acceptable than the regime of sheep grazers it replaced. Sportsmen brought benefits to a wider range of people and sought pleasure rather than profits. Moreover, the sporting era left a bulky legacy of informative and lively literature, as good a record of social conditions and attitudes, and the natural history in the Highlands at the time, as exists.

In the period from around 1880 up to the First World War the Highlands was carved up by the large hereditary landowners into sporting blocks or estates in which, approximately, they remain today. The majority of estates were rented by a sporting tenantry composed of the English upper classes, to whom game-hunting was a natural pastime, and of the prominent people in the country wishing to establish themselves socially. The summer season in the Highlands became a major social event. In the process, the land set aside as deer forest underwent many of the modifications which remain now.

As far as tree cover was concerned, most of the uses for native timber disappeared when Scandinavian supplies could be ferried by steamships more cheaply than Scottish timber could be moved across country, a state of affairs which says something about the dearth of good standing timber in commercial quantities. By 1905 hardwoods were being imported in quantity from America, and birch from Canada and Finland. Forest cover by the turn of the twentieth century had been severely depleted. The construction of railways in particular, and the need for sleepers and wooden wagons, had carved huge tracts out of what was left of Scotland's high trees. The nineteenth-century decay of the charcoal and tan-bark industries, crushed by cheaper imports, had led to surviving coppice-woods, previously protected, being used as wintering quarters for grazing stock. This put paid to any natural regeneration of primeval forest-cover as the smaller trees were chewed and the saplings grazed off. An untimely spread of the rabbit halted the process of regeneration finally. The denuding of the nation's timber had not been accompanied by any serious effort, apart from a few individual cases, to repair the stock of trees. The use of the hill country for deer forests discouraged landowners from setting aside land for planting, and sporting tenants obviously had little interest in long-term ventures. Plantings to shelter deer at Ardverickie, Corrour, Mar, Flowerdale, Caenlochan, Balmacaan and Braemore were noble exceptions. Rates were imposed on woodlands, and the ravages of several years of particularly severe gales from 1860 onwards were compounded by the problems of the railways sending sparks into adjacent scrub and causing stupendous forest fires. The railway companies were not held liable for the damage. Not surprisingly, tree cover over Scotland declined between 1800 and the First World War. The hills became barer, the stock lacked for shelter, and fertility in the hills entered a new phase of long-term decline. The chronic shortage of native timber, emphasised by the submarine blockade of the First World War, was officially recognised in the creation in 1919 of the Forestry Commission, a state-controlled body set up to replenish native woodlands.

Much planting has since taken place, mostly with evergreens of foreign provenance, and therefore of an experimental nature. The sad thing from the point of view of the Highlands is that the natural scrub cover at high elevations has made a once-and-for-all disappearance. The protective functions of high-altitude native trees in shielding soil from the elements can only be appreciated in hindsight. The high pastures would have been richer and more productive had a realisation existed long ago that shelter potentially had a beneficial effect on stock, on vegetation, and in modifying a harsh climate. Erosion in the Highlands has accelerated in the last 200 years since natural birch vanished under the incisors of the sheep.

Since the First World War the Highlands has been the site of an inexorable national tree-planting programme, started by the Forestry Commission in Lochaber, and more recently taken up by private sector tree-growing bodies in the much more silviculturally marginal region of the Sutherland and Caithness flows. Almost exclusively the trees planted have been spruce, pine and fir — varieties of evergreen. Symbolically, the Commission's headquarters is now in Scotland, and in 1988 Scotland could boast for the first time in centuries a forest cover of more than one million hectares, or around two-and-a-half million acres.

This has altered the landscape in major overt and covert ways. The scenery has been completely changed. It is possible to drive through large parts of Argyll surrounded on both sides by conifers, blocking from view the landscape beyond. High mountains behind poke above the faraway tree-line here and there, and sporadically rise above the trees which hug the roadside. In most practical terms these hillsides are impenetrable; the only access is along forest roads and paths, from which, also, the view is often blocked by the trees. The high blocks stretch up the hillsides in the most favourable growing environments to 2,000 feet, the trees becoming manifestly more stunted with every 100 feet of altitude.

Unseen by the naked eye, these plantations have widespread hidden effects — climatologically, on the water table, on water purity, on the physical body of valley-bottom river beds, on the soil, and on wildlife. They create inside them a new environment altogether, an environment which changes with phases of growth; and they substantially alter the environment on their peripheries. As the amount of land under trees in the Highlands grows, with a national forestry policy set on constant and continual expansion at a rate of about 30,000 acres a year, much research into the impact of this relatively new land use is busily going on. For these are not the aesthetically-pleasing, mixed deciduous plantations of forestry's eighteenth-century private patrons in Scotland. These are commercial crops for use in pulp for paper or board, chips for compound hardboard construction, and planks and poles for building and agricultural use. By and large the older plantations are monocultures, row by row of similar-looking trees all the same age.

Obviously the removal from farming and sporting use of such a large area of the Highlands has a big impact. In the hills on the periphery of the Highlands in Perthshire, Stirlingshire, Dunbartonshire, Aberdeenshire, Moray, Banff and Nairn, farmers nestle into corners of the dark green blanket which undulates over the surrounding countryside. The whole ecosystem of these hill farms has been changed and, whilst benefiting in bad weather from the shelter, encircled sheep farms can no longer practise the old extensive stock-rearing system, pushing the sheep out on to the higher ground in summer. Of the crofting counties, Argyll has been most heavily planted and trees form a continuous mantle in very large areas. In places there is effectively no other land use aside from forestry.

In the higher hills and further north, forestry has been planted on grouse moors and deer forests. Where estate owners found themselves in the financial doldrums a sale to forestry has been an easy way out of trouble. Unlike other land disposals, a forestry-land sale need only be a part of an estate, a corner here or there which, it is hoped, might not be missed. The tragedy here is where continuous aprons of trees have been planted at the bottoms of high hills. Deer, undernourished and desperate, have found their traditional winter avenue of escape to lower ground and shelter blocked by wire. In the winter of 1988/9 this predicament resulted in severe mortality in parts of the west Highlands. Forestry, again and again, has been the butt of blame, not because it is there but because of the way it is planted, with scant regard for existing uses round about. To have left rides and access down the hills would, in hindsight, have been so easy, for the price of a little more fencing.

Grouse moors have, hitherto, provided the bulk of ground for forestry because the cyclical nature of grouse populations has found many moor owners at the bottom of the cycle also at the bottom of their pockets. They have not been able to wait for the upturn of bigger bags and higher rents. The modern practice of letting moors by the week, or by the day, has exacerbated this dilemma. The old-fashioned shooting tenant took a lease for ten years or for life, and if the grouse slumped for two or three years he knew, or hoped, the stock would bounce back. The source of revenue for proprietors, whilst smaller, was at least constant. Grouse are tricky birds and the weather at nesting can determine whether a season is a triumph or a calamity. The precariousness is telling on the nerves of a landowner who must make his year's earnings in six weeks of the late summer, and land-hungry forestry companies have learnt the value of bad weather in June and keeping a close eye on grouse bags. So too have neighbours of moors which underperform. For forestry is an insidious land use beside a moor. The environmental effects of forestry, and the economic case, are looked at in Chapter 9.

The other land uses which have changed the face of the Highlands since the two wars are smaller and more localised than forestry. The growing cost of labour had induced many hill farmers to improve and fence moorland pasture, compressing flock management in a continual process which has waxed and waned since post-war inducements to increase production and national self-sufficiency. Whilst typically in some of the milder west Highland valleys stock fencing for sheep, enclosing a greener sward, climbs higher up the hill to near the ridge, in the straths (flat-bottomed glens) of the east the improved pasture on hillsides is selective and generally low-down. In the steep-sided sharp defiles of the wildest Highland glens the small patches of fenced-off greens on the haugh dwindle away altogether as ground rises, and in high corries permanent pasture improvements have never been worthwhile. Most of these pasture enhancements and 'reseeds' have occurred during times of high capital grants. For the treatment is expensive, involving long stretches of deer or stock fencing, liming to eliminate old heather and enrich the soil, fertilising, and seeding with grasses and clover.

A sheep farmer's troubles are not over when he has turned the pasture green and increased his stock numbers. As valleys all over the Highlands poignantly attest, improved pastures are prone to regress, sprouting rough grasses and rushes which smother the tender artificial strains. The Great Glen cattle ranch experiment at Fort William in the 1960s is today one of several sad testimonies to grand plans for large-scale ranching which ignored the basic low productivity of such ground when forced to intensive single-purpose use. The colonisation of the western Highlands, Rosshire, Perthshire, Caithness and Sutherland with sheep during the Clearances may be seen as one concerted effort in this direction on a national scale. Even if sporting use had not arisen to mitigate the effects of this exclusive type of pastoral farming, it is doubtful if the sheep numbers in the Highlands would be any higher than they are today. At the end of 1989 the sheep population of the Highland Regional district was only 1.25 million, approximately what the county of Argyll alone contained 110 years earlier. Sheep farming in the Highlands is presently in a state of crisis, subsidies are being withdrawn, and the Clearances may be coming full circle with the quickening of a long-term swing into sheep clearance.

Peat-digging is an extractive land use which ultimately may be seen as the preparation of ground for commercial forestry. This has happened in Caithness. The peat is sliced off the top ground layer, often in trenches six to eight feet deep, exposing the lower subsoils and minerals required by foraging tree roots. Peat-digging is small-scale in the Highlands and fortunately we have never gone in for the large-scale scalping of the blanket bog that Ireland engaged in for fuel in firing power stations. Turbary, or peat-digging rights, were preserved in the crofting acts for most crofters, and estate workers have been allowed free peat as a perquisite. No market for local sales of peat has ever grown to a big industry in the Highlands.

Manipulation of the water table has been going on for a long time. As far back as 1830 Loch Leven was lowered by nine feet, reducing its surface area by nearly a quarter. More recently, hydro-schemes to produce electricity and provide water supplies have raised water levels often with dramatic results. On Loch Quoich a shooting lodge was actually submerged in the process of raising water levels in a drowned valley. In low water conditions the upper casements of the house eerily appear again, forlorn and dripping with weeds. Other hydro-schemes in the Highlands, even where they have no ill effects on salmon and sea trout fisheries in blocking off the spawning redds, nonetheless dry up downstream river beds in a way which has an invariably depressing effect. A dammed river seems to have had its life stolen away. At a barrier like the dam at Loch Mullardoch above Cannich the effect of the unnatural water level, the stark and stony shore-line combined with the dam's massive dark ramparts ending in watchtowers, give the scene a foreboding air and the stage-set appearance of a spy thriller denouement. Dams are prone to siltation, and many schemes in America have become redundant from silting up long before schedule. Closer to home the Dunoon No. 3 reservoir, impounded in 1920, showed that extremely fast siltation from adjacent forestry could be fatal. Run-offs from a small nearby planting managed to fill the entire storage basin in fifteen years, leading to the removal of the dam in 1982. If any more water impoundments are to disfigure the Highlands they should be subjected to more powerful scrutiny than hitherto, and to a complete environmental analysis by ecologically-aware scientists trained in hydrology, watershed and wildlife management, and river fluctuations.

My grandfather, Sir Iain Colquhoun, fought the Highlands' first hydro-scheme project at Loch Sloy by Loch Lomond, and went to final arbitration in the House of Lords. However, his case was based on simple scenery considerations and the objection that damming would interfere with his stalking, a standpoint that looks quaintly old-fashioned only a short time later. A scheme to place a dam on the other side of the loch on Ben Lomond itself, in the central massif of the Highlands' most famous beauty spot, has been shelved, hopefully permanently. The overblown, so-called Craigroyston scheme, although it was to have been the biggest pump storage station in Britain, was only to have been used when power from other supplies had run short. Its justification was predicated entirely on forecasts of escalated growth in demand. Fortunately the public outcry drove this late 1970s concept out.

Chapter 3
Grouse and Management for Grouse

The Highland estate today is improperly understood and dogged by old-fashioned stereotyping. The sporting laird is an old stand-by of cartoonists and social satirists, and often estate owners and their employees have found it simpler to quietly accept these woeful, half-comic characterisations rather than make a serious case for what they are doing. The whisky-soaked, tweed-draped buffer of the comic-strip, backed up by his rough Highland band of forelock-tugging keepers, belongs firmly inside the covers of comic novels and the skits of perishable periodicals.

During the 1980s the Highlands developed more openly into what it is fated soon to become — the central arena within Europe for tussles between conservationists and developers. Its beauty is famous, its population extremely small, its ecological richness is not in doubt, and there is the added *frisson* of its established reputation as the site of one major land use change which has, fairly or unfairly, entered the annals of history as an outrageously ill-judged foray into social engineering.

It is an astonishing proof of the fringe nature of some of the bodies which have mushroomed as the self-appointed custodians of the Highlands that they seem not to wish for contributions from, or involvement with, those who still own the bulk of the land they champion — the Highland lairds. Political transformations aside, it is on the shoulders of these individuals, or syndicates, companies, national bodies and charities which are fast replacing them, that the direction of the future lies. An understanding of how the estates work, what they are trying to achieve, and their significance as guardians of a spectacular part of our contemporary heritage is therefore vital.

The popular image of the Highland estate still draws almost entirely on sporting events at the height of the season. The most famous annual event is the Glorious Twelfth, known amongst sporting people even in Europe and America as the day the red grouse shooting season commences. Every year, with unfailing zest, the national papers make an effort to incorporate the Twelfth into the news as a surviving part of our heritage, confirming that things never change. Even in the Scottish dailies the grouse is still mis-represented as a reared bird. Considering that it is difficult to raise grouse in captivity, and that it has never been attempted for sporting purposes, it seems extraordinary such a fallacy persists.

Yet so it does, seemingly representing some stolid refusal to contemplate the possibility that game shooting is a natural thing and its practitioners acceptable people. This is at a time when shooting is the fastest growing hobby in Britain, at a time also when an interest in wildlife information is sweeping the country. The reason for this wilful perpetuation of untruth is partly to do with the failure, uniquely the case in Britain, of sporting organisations and hobby birdwatching bodies, such as the RSPB, to see that they complement, rather than oppose, each other as preservers of our avian heritage.

The simple-minded idea that because one man is shooting birds and the other watching them they are on opposite sides of the fence must be broken down. The great majority of bird-shooters in Britain are bird-lovers and students of the species they seek to shoot. Often they need to be. To use the simplest example, wildfowlers not conversant with the habits of duck at dusk would have a lean time. Grouse moor management is a specialised management activity, in the process of becoming a science.

The future of the Highlands and existing land uses, which are favourable to species diversity, depends on a properly-informed rapprochement between nature lovers and sporting people. Routine misrepresentation of the Twelfth of August on basic factual grounds impedes better understanding.

The Twelfth of August is only the best known day of a year-round season. It is, in any case, only a date enshrined in statute (in 1773), when grouse can start to be shot. On many grouse moors, under seasonal conditions which have delayed nesting, or resulted in a second nesting, birds are really too young to be shot on the Twelfth. Grouse moor owners may postpone the start of the season if they wish, a decision made more difficult in the present day because shooting tenants have booked a long way ahead, probably for a day or a week, very rarely for a whole season. The nesting in early June is the first time a shooting proprietor and his keeper will know how grouse stocks will be in August. It is a late date for shifting shooting parties.

The Twelfth should be seen as the culmination of a keeper's season and the beginning of the management of the grouse stock for future seasons. Enough has been written elsewhere about the scientific management of grouse, organising a driven grouse moor, placement of butts, the classic days of record grouse bags, and the astonishing excellence, taken close to perfection, of some of the old-time shots who devoted their lives to shooting. Quite simply, to the grouse's abilities as a flier, whirring and jinking from view with the wind under its wing, is owed a whole tradition in British sport and land use. It is a classic fast-flying game bird, supposedly capable of reaching speeds of 70 mph, which has chosen for its home some of Britain's loveliest countryside.

This habitat used to be different. Centuries ago grouse occupied only one stratum of the hillside, that between the high tops frequented by its cousin the ptarmigan, and the edge of the tree-line at around 2,000 feet. The high woodland belt had a population of blackgame, still of the same family as grouse, and further down in the big pines dwelt another family member, the capercaillie. The adaptation of the grouse to moorland habitat at almost all except the highest altitudes is a phenomenon of comparatively recent times, and it is instructive to note in the gamebooks of a hundred years ago that where good moors were recording five hundred or a thousand brace of grouse, there were seasonal bags of a hundred or two hundred blackgame. This is no longer a possibility. The blackgame is a beautiful, somewhat esoteric species with its fan-tail and matador-like display dance or 'lek', which is suffering a long-term decline. Game Conservancy research has identified the cause of blackgame's decline principally as habitat loss. The spread of bracken and loss of young woodland-edge birch and pine habitat has reduced blackgame's feeding, and also the supply of invertebrates favoured by blackgame chicks. Despite the incidence in young commercial forestry plantations of more open clearings which approximate to blackgame habitat, the species' decline continues.

Grouse, meanwhile, have also changed radically in the last hundred years, disappearing almost altogether from the western Highlands and islands, and exhibiting erratic population movements in the eastern Highlands. The best grouse moors in Britain are now on all-heather terrain in the Pennines in northern England, where keepers and landowners have taken to high levels the management art of producing very heavy concentrations of birds. Those parts of the Lowlands still unafforested come second in the grouse moor numbers league, and the moors of the east Grampians next. As ever in shooting, the quality of a day is not ultimately measured by the bag, and the Highland scene offers surroundings of a type that on a clear day outclasses anything else. The most memorable days are complete outdoor experiences made up of the company, the surroundings, and the quality of the sport.

This quality depends, as I have mentioned, on weather, the incidence of disease, and that part of management over which man has some control. It is intimately tied up with heather-burning, a subject which rouses strong differences of view even amongst the keepers required to conduct the operation. Heather-burning takes place in spring up to the closing date of 16 April or, in exceptional conditions, in early winters which have escaped the customary October downpours. The purpose is to rejuvenate ling heather, which is technically a dwarf-shrub, by incinerating the old twigs and flowers and reducing the stem to near ground-level. If burning is done when the ground is too dry the fire will burn down, not along, and may smoulder in the peat for days; if the roots themselves get burnt only seeds in the ground will bring the heather back. Too light burning will at most do little good, leaving leggy blackened stems which will gradually sprout new shoots. It is now certain, which was not known when 'muirburn' was erratic and conducted over too-large areas in the nineteenth century, that in soil chemistry terms potassium is lost to the ground in smoke, and there is a tendency to lose small quantities of phosphates in leaching if the burn is followed by heavy rainfall. In theory this could lead over a hundred years to long-term depletion of minerals. The dangers of over-grazing newly-burnt ground and the consequent risk of permanent soil erosion are widely known, but remain a problem in the west Highlands where the heather-burning on estates is for deer, whose movements cannot be controlled. Uncontrolled fires ignited by crofters are still a particular problem in the west Highlands and have led to the proliferation of that doughty, exclusive, nutritionally-worthless colonist, bracken, a development deplored by all.

Opposite: The laird of Invercauld, in kilt, going to the hill on the first morning butts.

Top: Deeside grouse butt with left-handed lady gun, loader and retriever. Strip-burnt heather background.

Bottom: Lunch at Cabrach, Aberdeenshire, on the Glorious Twelfth.

Opposite: Grouse butts at Invercauld. Flanker up hillside on left to keep grouse flying straight.

Overleaf: Pointer change-over during family dogging day at Langwell, Caithness. Scaraben range of hills in background.

Top: A pair of guns on Caithness flows.

Bottom: David Woodley with home-bred peregrine falcon on Gartymore, Sutherland. Hunting grouse with falcons pre-dates gun-shooting by several centuries.

Opposite: Robert Howden, the factor at Langwell, head keeper Ack Sutherland and another gun, in front of Morvern.

The differences of opinion about heather-burning have largely arisen because it has not been sufficiently understood that a rotation of heather lasting ten years in one place should, under different climate and geographical conditions, be twenty years somewhere else. The aims of heather management also differ depending on whether the heather is meant primarily to serve the interests of deer, sheep or grouse. All of these depend at some time or another on protected corners where the heather is left as long as possible without dying away, for in stormy, snowy weather it provides shelter and the stems may be shaken to expose the bushy tops. Usually in the western Highlands, where sedges and bent grasses are more dominant plants, heather burning should be much less frequent. Conversely, in the eastern Highlands, where good patches of heather form an uninterrupted carpet, heather needs to be burnt regularly, ideally in controlled strips twenty metres wide, to promote a mosaic of different age classes of herbage for grouse feeding. At Borrobol the situation is dramatically illustrated by the growth potential of the north-facing side compared to the south-facing side of the same hill. The south-facing slope, assuming a similar mineral distribution and peat-depth, will benefit from the far longer hours of sunlight over a year, and grow heather quite briskly. Ground two hundred feet higher up and six miles further west in the lee of the wetter climate of the Ben Armine range grows new heather at half the speed.

Except on the stonier dry slopes, in most of the Highland area heather-burning is in any case very difficult to manage; it is rare to get the conditions which permit it. Allied to the problems of fogs and haars, high ground snow, dews which don't disperse until afternoon, winds which are too strong or in the wrong direction, ground too wet or too dry, are the difficulties of getting sufficient labour on the ground at short notice. At Borrobol we reckon on one year in ten giving us the opportunity for perfect burning, and even then the wind direction limits possibilities. Every hill fire under responsible organisation requires to be aimed either towards a burn, drain or river which will stop its progress, or to a strip previously 'back-burned' for this purpose. Older keepers have learnt to their cost the devastation a fire can do if the wind swivels in the middle of burning, whereupon the burning team must run along the fire-edge beating out the flames with brooms and trying to direct the leading edge to an area in which it will fizzle out. Blackened faces and singed whiskers are not an unknown sight tramping home on an early April evening. Heather-burning can be wearisome and frustrating. On firm ground it is sometimes possible to break heather areas by thrashing with a flail operated by tractor. This enables heather-burning controls to be built up, even in wet weather.

The major role played by heather-burning needs stressing. It is the only practical method of moorland management, hill draining aside, that exists. In that unrivalled compendium of general knowledge, the 1911 report 'The Grouse in Health and Disease', the authors estimate the value of burning as potentially increasing the food-bearing capacity of the moor ten-fold. Grouse principally live in heather, and at various stages during the year sheep and

Opposite: Picking up after a drive.

deer can expect succour from no other quarter. The heather maintains some nutritional value for almost the whole year, although with desiccated winter stalks grouse need to consume three or four times the volume which suffices in summer. Without its regular removal the stocking rates for all these species and the productivity of the ground would sharply decrease. What appears to the eye of the Highland tourist a natural untutored landscape is, in fact, the product of burning over the ages. Fires were regulators even before the days of heather moorland in the ancient woodland. Without burning, the claret-red colours of the August hills remembered in so many songs and poems, and so familiar from calendars, shortbread tins, and the radiator-grilles of holiday traffic heading south, would gradually give way to the ubiquitous green of the west Highlands. Heather moorland once covered north-west Europe's hills; Scotland's moors are the last survivor, a debt to sporting use which is seldom acknowledged. However, the heather area is shrinking, partly because of grazing pressure from increasing numbers of deer, and partly because disillusionment on hill farms has led to a relaxation of traditional disciplines keeping stock off newly-burnt ground. Heather has already shrunk so far that an organisation has been created to save it.

The last twenty-five years have shown a slow change in the heather ecology of deer forests which corresponds meaningfully with the period of a burgeoning red deer population. In the east and central Highlands low-lying heather moorland has suffered from overgrazing by hungry deer and, combined with their dunging and trampling, has produced an increase of short grasses. On poor gravelly soils over hard rock, and on thick peat, the bared ground may not grow any new cover. Large deer numbers and their tendency to pluck out young heather saplings whilst grazing are responsible. The keeper's duty in these situations is to press for a higher cull to reduce grazing pressure, an argument that may be supported by the common experience recently of finding grouse mainly on the high ground, which is too exposed to hold deer in winter. Heather is the heart of the hill ecology; its astonishing capacity to provide all-year nutrition must not be pushed too far.

The Highland keeper is not concerned only with habitat management and the operation of shooting, fishing and stalking days. In his role as controller of vermin he has acquired a fixed image in the perception of the public as unrepresentative as that of the laird. Perhaps all that is true of it is that by and large Highland keepers have the manners and natural courtesy which Queen Victoria so liked in her keeper at Balmoral, John Brown. The image of an unselective decimator of wildlife with which so many keepers are falsely tarnished originates with the activities of their predecessors in Victorian times, who arrived on a scene infinitely richer in wildlife than what is left today. They were instructed by their employers to improve the environment for grouse, and protect lambs and deer calves; in the process they eliminated large numbers of birds which are now rare, and therefore especially cherished.

Early nineteenth-century vermin bags make awesome contemplation. It is very hard even in hindsight to imagine our familiar Highland environment being able to support the numbers of large birds and other animals which evidently abounded. There is a record of the seven-year vermin bag on the Sutherland and Caithness properties of Langwell and Sandside over the period 1819–26. In this time, if the records are to be believed, 1,115 assorted hawks were killed; 355 eagles, carefully recorded under old or young; and 6,408 members of the crow family. The effort and man-hours that went into this grand-scale obliteration, over a bleak, unroaded tract of country, is stupefying to imagine. It is worth also keeping in mind that the Sandside/ Langwell area would have looked much as it does now, barring the new conifer plantations of the last twenty years. In other places huge population increases of animals, leading to monumental culls, owed something to land use changes. The bag of 51,932 rabbits in the period 1844–53 on a Perthshire estate coincided with a spread of agricultural use of land in the same area. But over much of the Highlands wildlife in Victorian times was more varied, vigorous and numerous than ever since.

The Highland keeper today is prohibited from shooting all birds of prey, and amongst the crow family protection is extended to the raven. Of other animals which were once decimated because of their predilection for game meat, the otter and badger are protected, and soon the pine marten and wildcat will be too. The protection afforded to raptors has certainly had its effect, and the hen harrier has extended its range from Orkney right through the Highlands, just in the post-war period. The legislation of today makes it clear that single-species game bird management, to the exclusion of various other species, is no longer publicly acceptable. The fact that in the past many species were killed which did not threaten grouse stocks or lambs has given contemporary orders extra force. It has also meant that even a build-up of raptors which threatens to exterminate grouse, or reduce the shootings to an unviable level, cannot be redressed. In a future state of affairs which acknowledges the conservation value of grouse moors as a moorland management practice, and their value for protecting cherished breeding birds such as golden plovers, it is to be hoped that special orders to reduce a proliferation of predators could be granted after consultations on a case by case basis. The structures to permit this have not yet been created.

It is unfortunate that the inevitable shift of focus towards protection for raptors, itself laudable, has brought division between game shooters and keepers and the conservationists. Just as local Highland newspapers relish dramatic deer or fish poaching episodes, often phrased to recall and inflame historic grievances about public rights to game, so they relish too tales of keepers themselves breaking the Countryside and Wildlife Act. The truth is that keepers by and large adhere to its code for fear of the law and respect for natural variety. Birds such as the eagle and the peregrine are admired and left alone. If there are occasional offenders among keepers, their impact on the full spectrum of bird life is negligible; the rare species are mostly increasing in numbers, not the reverse. The healthy British red grouse stocks owe their existence in large part to keepers, and it would be a step in the right direction if the grouse could be removed from the RSPB list of 116 threatened species. Its presence there, alongside the red kite of which there are only a handful of individuals, prejudices those laymen against grouse shooting who naturally assume shooters are persecuting a rare species.

The real offenders reducing our avifauna are egg collectors. Egg collectors are a strange group of people from all walks of life for whom the collection becomes an obsession. Unlike the falconry traders who rob falcon nests to sell young tiercels, there is usually no financial motive for egg collecting; some collectors start as keen birdwatchers. No wonder the gamekeepers resent the bad press they get when, as happened at Dartford magistrates court in 1989, an egg collector was convicted of possessing 23,000 eggs, including many rare ones. It is the collectors rather than the gamekeepers in whom the spirit of the indiscriminate and indefatigable Victorian keepers survives.

The arch enemy of a grouse moor, and a legitimate target, is the fox. The hill fox is a different customer altogether from the low-ground town or 'cur fox' as John Colquhoun dismissively refers to it in *The Moor and the Loch*. Large, strong, broad-headed, the hill fox is formidably cunning and formidably destructive, consuming in addition to carrion in winter, lambs, grouse, ptarmigan, and even the wariest of birds such as duck. The hill fox may not be hunted with all the panoply of ceremonial importance as in Leicestershire, but for all that the day of his capture means more to a true keeper than most others in the year. It is, as it were, the keeper's own sport.

Some fox culling is opportunistic, patrolling likely areas by night in a vehicle with powerful searchbeams from a lamp, looking for foxes out hunting. The open-ground fox cull on the hill is a different sport, more a one-to-one battle of wits. Each spring, in April, the keeper checks the known fox-dens on his ground. Foxes return to the same dens, though not always in consecutive years. Once the presence of a fox is confirmed by the terriers, the long chilly night vigils commence, waiting within rifle-shot of the den for the return of the adults to their cubs. Frequently the purpose is frustrated because the fox senses his enemy's presence; its ability to do this is uncanny. It might alternatively return just before first light by which time April frosts may have immobilised beyond useful action the patient keeper. During the interim, the keeper will play at loud volume tape recordings of yapping fox cubs which ring out spookily over the vacant landscape. His powerful lamp-beam at intervals will cross again and again over the terrain, searching for the tell-tale glowing eyes zigzagging across the distance. When and if the adult is killed, the terriers are let into the den for the cubs. It sounds a raw, savage combat, and it is.

You might suppose the foxes would be reduced to elimination. Not a bit of it. Every year without fail the keeper walks fresh snow with a faint sense of trepidation. For there, despite his laborious fox cull and its hard-won successes, are the tracks of the redoubtable, inextinguishable foxes, criss-crossing the pristine snow. Compared to controlling crows and gulls, and the amazing breeding dynamic of the rabbit, the fox shooting season is particularly arduous, satisfaction particularly elusive.

There is a phrase in use now to describe a keeper who works alone on an estate: it is 'one-handed'. It implies, correctly, such a man is at an insurmountable disadvantage. It is a sad thing that many smaller, less well-situated estates are unable to maintain more than one employee, but it is a fact of modern Highland economics that this is often so. Such a man may have farm stock to look after also, sheep and a few cattle. Even if, by way of an inducement, they belong to him and substantially supplement his income, it is a rare man today, with a rare wife, who will take on a hard isolated posting. Satisfaction must lie in the job itself.

Not long ago, on the better estates, there was a team of keepers; on the big estates there still is. In the hey-day of shooting, and after the last war, one man might have had responsibility for some 5,000 acres. That was reckoned the area limit that could be competently managed, just as 600 ewes was the stock limit a hill shepherd was expected to tend. Now some single-handed keepers are wearing themselves to the bone on 30,000 acres and over, far too exhausting a burden. Only a generation ago, a head keeper on a medium-sized estate ran his dogs in the grouse season, or organised his beaters, took the more important guests out for a stag, and generally supervised his department otherwise. On smart deer forests the head stalker was accompanied by a rifleman whose sole function was bearing the weapon. The ponyman had his own ghillie and the stalking guest would depart for the hill with a veritable entourage. The old timers remember these days fondly, and particularly the social amusement they brought with them. They lament the new method, the stalker and guest forming a lonely pair as they set off for the hill; and frequently the guest departing abruptly at day's close when previously a long dram and general blether had been enjoyed by all in the deer-larder or gunroom.

The keeper now has a full and overflowing calendar of duties. The upkeep of paths, roads, hill bridges, outbuildings, kennels, sluices, dams, vehicles and all his equipment are part and parcel of the job. Only the big estates employ an estate handyman. As often as not, the keeper might have to attend to anti-poacher patrols, river ghillieing, drain clearing, timber cutting, peat digging, gardening, boat and fence maintenance as well as dog training. During winter, on most estates, deer need to be fed. He must be equally at home on a tractor and a hill bike, in an all-terrain vehicle (ATV) or a Landrover. Having spent his season performing these energetic duties he will start off some time after 20 October, often in conditions below freezing, to cull the hinds. With the swollen deer population on the east side of the Highlands the number needing to be removed is often proving more than a lone man can handle. Each beast after shooting requires loading on to pony, hill-bike or ATV, unloading at the larder, preparing for the game dealer or, alternatively, preparing for sale to the private customer, with all the attendant work of skinning, hanging, and perhaps butchering into suitable cuts. There are many Highland keepers hauling home a hundred hinds in a winter. Furthermore the day is short, the weather inclined to be inclement, and the part of the season when the hinds are in good order for the venison market over by New Year.

My own experience of Highland keepers is that they are a collection of exceedingly resourceful, hard-working and capable men. The depth and strength of character required to do these jobs produces individuals who make a deep impression on the sporting people who travel to the Scottish hills in the summer. Many a sporting tenant routinely returns to the same estate on account not of the superior stags, more numerous grouse or bigger salmon, but the keeper, with whom a relationship may have been powerfully enjoined. These relationships are mutual, for the keeper himself has a hard and isolated working life, the tedium of which is relieved when the season opens by the arrival of familiar faces.

At the back of all this is the fact that in the enjoyment of most Highland sporting activities lies the chance for forging human friendships. The moment of shooting a stag is an exciting and emotional one; shortcomings are exposed, sometimes overcome. The credit in any case partially goes to the stalker who negotiated the approach and selected the beast. It is a shared pleasure and a miss is a shared disappointment. The same is true, in a different and independent sense, of relationships worked between the shooting gun and the keeper, and the fisherman and the ghillie. Much of the evening commiseration or satisfaction about the day on the hill or river revolves around the keepers and ghillies, their wry comments, telling anecdotes, impressive knowledge of the hill. Some of these characters, like the old elusive poachers of the nineteenth century, are known throughout the sporting fraternity and are permanently inscribed in the immemorial annals of sporting people.

This brings us, haphazardly, to 'the season', or that part of a Highland estate's activities which is most written about. Fishing aside, the Highland sporting season formally opens with grouse shooting on the Twelfth of August; an activity which officially halts on 10 December. The Twelfth is a day faced with some trepidation by the keeper. Although they will have a fair idea of what the ground is holding from their forays onto the moor after nesting, most keepers aver that only when shooting commences do birds show their true numbers. Although those numbers are often related too literally by shooting tenants to the keeper's skills, recent research into grouse populations shows that grouse can defy the best efforts to improve their habitat and environment, and conversely can appear suddenly in the worst-managed moors for no apparent reason.

It is often irksome to diligent keepers that ill-kept moors are still capable of providing good shooting, whilst their own efforts show little result on the day. Usually, these lucky moors are blessed with rich underlying geology supporting a naturally abundant fauna. Or sometimes high numbers on bad ground are the result of chance immigration after rough weather. The population dynamics of grouse are still imperfectly understood, and the widely-held assumption that grouse populations swell and fade according to some form of cycle related to the build-up of parasites and disease is being disproven by recent research from the Game Conservancy. Cold winters with prolonged snow-fall appear to be far more consistent regulators of grouse stocks, predation occurring when the birds are weakened. The habit of grouse forming into packs is reckoned partially to be a survival mechanism to bamboozle predators, helping individuals to hide in the pack.

There are, however, two recognised major diseases in grouse, both of which can seriously affect numbers — strongylosis and coccidiosis. The former is transmitted by a threadworm and more likely to result in the bird's death in wet, cold conditions when resistance is low, generally in April or May. Coccidiosis is a disease affecting many birds, caused by a tiny self-replicating parasite which occurs in the gut, especially of grouse chicks. Both diseases result in birds losing weight. Overcrowding on the moor is a contributing factor. It is these two diseases, sometimes affecting birds one after the other, in combination with general lowering of resistance from prolonged bad weather, that account for the extraordinary swings in populations of grouse which were noted as long ago as the eighteenth century. This fast-breeding bird, capable of hatching twelve eggs, is able to mount, in ideal conditions, a tremendously fast population build-up. Equally, the onset of disease followed by a bad winter, with snow freezing solid over the heather, high winds and blizzards blowing the birds downhill, coastwards, and even out to sea, can reduce a grouse population to very low numbers indeed. This explains the entries in the late 1880s in the Borrobol gamebook of successive grouse bags of around 1,000 and 1,500 brace, followed by a year of one-and-a-half. All grouse moors demonstrate this sort of downswing somewhere in their history, and indeed bonanza bags shot in the Angus glens in 1988 were followed by severely reduced numbers the following year. The build-up to respectable figures and full stocking is of course more gradual. Experiments with quartz grit medicated to kill the strongylosis worm have recently been tried and early results are promising. In the Game Conservancy trial, grouse population worm infestation was reduced by nearly half in a single year.

Whether a moor is driven, worked with dogs, or simply walked by a line of guns depends on its location and the density of birds. The driven moors which correspond to the popularly known image of grouse-shooting are principally in the East Grampians, Angus, Perthshire, Moray, Nairn, Banff and parts of Invernesshire. The concept of driving grouse, which emanated from Yorkshire, was at first the subject of controversy: 'It is in no sense SPORT to have the birds you are to shoot driven up by a zealous crowd of beaters to the very muzzle of your gun,' fumed J. G. Bertram in 1889. However, the suspense and tense anticipation in a line of butts waiting for the first stocky, dark, contour-hugging targets to come swinging into view is something to be experienced to be understood. Presumably the sheer excitement of driving, and the rapid realisation that shooting birds going this fast was far from easy, broke the mould of resistance.

There is nowadays probably nowhere else in the world that game birds are driven to produce such fast, testing shooting as grouse on British moors. This type of shooting demands the utmost of guns in smooth and rapid co-ordination of body and eye, and judgement of speed. Inadequacies of technique or lack of experience are immediately exposed on a good grouse drive. It is understandable that a day on a good driven moor should command the high price it does. Although the English moors have overtaken Scottish moors in the presentation of very large numbers of birds, it is worth noting that before the First World War moors such as Cawdor were capable of producing over 7,000 brace in a season, and could compare with bags in Yorkshire today. That achievement was before scientific moorland management had been developed into the specialised art it is now. Those moor owners depressed by declining bags, despite any amount of moorland management, may regard with chagrin the halcyon shooting years when grouse were so abundant that special measures for their destruction under Defence of the Realm regulations to protect crops were ordered, as happened in February 1917!

The head keeper on a driven moor has beaters and flankers to organise, birds to be picked after the drive, and a plan of operations to be worked out to make full use of the wind. He requires to know where birds will fly under different conditions when pushed by beaters from their territories. His butts should be placed to accommodate a variety of circumstances. There is a sound management reason for driving moors where possible, and that is the greater efficiency of driving in killing the old birds which tend to fly in front of the coveys towards the guns. The objective of the keeper is to preserve a young and fertile stock for the following season.

The ancient style of grouse shooting, portrayed in any number of eighteenth-century prints, is 'dogging'. A pointing, or bird-dog, usually setter or pointer, works with the wind to detect birds crouching in the heather. The dog moves forward 'on point' with tail raised and nose lowered, the guns on either side prepared to shoot when the birds rise. The practice is described by such authors as Osgood MacKenzie, Charles St John and John Colquhoun at a time when the Scottish Highlands were bursting with game of many varieties and the bag was delightfully eclectic. As presently done, the dog handler or keeper works closely with his dog, which is trained to quarter the ground methodically. Different dogs in a team perform in their own idiosyncratic way, and one dog at least must be accustomed to working with the wind at its back, picking up the scent downwind. At the 'point', keeper and dog and the two guns move forward slowly, often turning and following the birds which are trying to scurry further off before rising. The demands on the dog's game-sense and physique are unmatched in any other form of shooting. To those who prefer dogging, the pleasure is a comprehensive experience, embracing the harmonious combination of handler and dog, and the easy rhythm of walking and shooting and picking up. The finesse required to bring down driven grouse is exchanged for the unhurried satisfaction of covering the moor on your own feet, enjoying the changing scenery and making each shot count. Dogging moors survive in the north, in Rosshire, Sutherland and Caithness, and parts of Invernesshire, where the expanses of ground to be covered are formidable and the density of birds lower.

Much in dogging relies on the keeper's qualities as a handler, and considerable work attaches to this in the summer. Usually, at least one puppy in the kennel is being brought forward to replace an old-timer. Repeatedly finding birds for the dog to point, perfecting with it the practice of following the birds and the discipline of remaining still when they rise, combined with acclimatisation to the volley of shots, is a job requiring patience, perseverance and a keen understanding of individual dogs to get the best from them.

If the objective of the shooting party is walking as far as possible, and there are eight or so guns to do it, walking in line is as good a grouse shooting method as any. The disadvantage is that if birds are scarce they also come as a surprise, shots are late, off-balance and often off-target.

Some of the most sporting grouse shooting of all is to be had on the 'old cocks' days in late autumn. At any rate in Sutherland, these are undertaken by a line of guns, mostly composed of keepers. By November the birds are richly plumaged, very strong and alert, and the cocks are asserting their claims to territories prior to pairing in the new year. These belligerent old cocks are often unable to fertilise eggs and their removal opens up the ground for younger pairs. It is therefore a happy coincidence of these days that the bag is usually heavily weighted in favour of the old codgers, who strut about on the knolls stubbornly holding their ground. Apart from the benefits imparted by this end of season clearing-up operation, the shooting is extremely challenging. The majority of birds killed are shot on the rise, necessitating non-stop vigilance from the guns; by the time there is wind under the wing the birds are travelling so fast that the lead almost invariably fails to catch up. One cannot but respect this phenomenally hardy bird, by this time, with the exception of eagles and crows, the only resident left on the lonely moors.

These days of blustery fun are hugely enjoyed, despite the bracing ambience of sleety showers and high winds. The keepers get a chance to fraternise with neighbours after a hard season on home beats. Stories, anecdotes and jokes are swapped and conclude the season's activities prior to the hind shooting. Although some people disapprove of late season shooting I believe at worst it does no harm, and has potential to improve the stock. In times past, the keepers prowled the ground at this time knocking the old cocks off their perches by stalking them with a ·22.

Chapter Four
Stalking and the Stalker

For half of the estates in the Scottish Highlands, the grouse season has ceased to exist. Although in the nineteenth century grouse were found ubiquitously, even an estate in Lewis being capable of accumulating a bag of 1,000 brace, by the early nineteenth century the grouse range had begun to contract eastward. The present-day grouse populations, sufficiently dense to offer more than occasional sport, are in the eastern half of the Highlands. It is no coincidence that this is the half with much lower rainfall. In Sutherland and Rosshire the annual rainfall in the west exceeds 118 inches in several mountainous districts, whereas in the east, including much grouse moorland, the fall is under twenty-four inches. In the heavy rainfall districts, there were historically never as many grouse, but that invaluable almanac of rentable Highland sporting estates published in 1888, entitled *The Scottish Sportsman and Tourist*, advertises plenty of west coast properties with grouse bags that could not be envisaged today. The decline of the grouse range is a subject that belongs elsewhere, but it has bequeathed a situation today in which the only use of the hill in the west Highlands, apart from the sheep stock, is stalking. Where grouse bags have declined across the board over a hundred years, the number of stags shot has rocketed up. The turn of the century stag cull of 4,500 climbed to 10,000 in 1939 and has increased to around 14,500 today.

Red deer have existed in Scotland for the last 20,000 years. Even when roe deer, moose and reindeer browsed Scotland's ancient forest it was the red deer that Mesolithic men hunted for food. How the hunters of 7,000 years ago killed the deer is a mystery, but their success in doing so is evident in the red deer bones found in all their settlement remains. The Picts hunted red deer, according to depictions on Pictish stones, by lying in wait armed with short bows or crossbows; also by netting them. With the immigration of the Scots from Ireland came the practice of hunting deer with hounds — which became the classic form of medieval hunting and the prerogative over large areas, of the king alone. The common people extracted their toll on the deer with snares.

The red deer, one of nature's most adept survivors, reacted to man's encroachment on the ancient woodlands by retreating northwards, and when the Highland forests started to be substantially reduced in the seventeenth century, the deer sought the only untrammelled regions, the wastelands of the tree line and the windswept high ground above.

In the process, the weight of the animal, deprived of shelter and nutritive browsing, declined sharply, probably by nearly half. After 1760 the flockmasters arrived, clearing deer for sheep pasturing. It was only when Highland sport acquired reputation and status in the early nineteenth century that land-owners again moved to protect their deer, and parcel their huge properties into deer forests for letting. The red deer had been saved in the nick of time; already all other members of the deer family in Scotland, excepting the nifty roe, had died out. The fallow deer had just outlasted the reindeer, and disappeared around the ninth century. The Deer (Scotland) Act of 1959 established close seasons (stags, 21 October–30 June; hinds, 16 February–20 October) and put management of the population under the supervision of the Red Deer Commission (RDC).

Stalking the red deer is now an extremely valuable asset to whittled-down Highland communities. In the areas of poorest grazing and worst exposure to the elements it is often the only form of land use, and the only one possible to imagine. As the late Sir Frank Fraser Darling said of the deer on the deer forest, 'There is no animal, wild or domesticated, better adapted than the red deer to use it and to render a crop to humanity.' The red deer is a natural expansionist, and its population has to be controlled to protect farmland and forestry. Whilst stalking has lost the social cachet it had in Victorian times, it is of fundamental importance to the Highland economy. It creates employment, brings outside money to fragile rural economies in sporting rent, and provides a wholesome clean meat, low in fat and devoid of any of the artificial impurities found in intensively reared animals. The spin-off economic benefits of stalking accrue to a wide range of businesses including hotels, bed and breakfasts, garages, game dealerships, supply shops, the craft trade utilisation of by-products (skins, antlers, hooves, tusks), the motor-trade in the provision of four-wheel drive and all-terrain vehicles, gunshops and outfitters. The value of venison from the Highlands is £2–3 million a year. Deer forests fund local economies directly through sporting rates, a contribution that is particularly important because of the scarcity of other taxable subjects. In terms of the proportion of money generated in those remote areas which constitute the main deer forests it is obvious not only that deer stalking is a pivotal rural industry, but without it the life in many small communities would drain away.

It is inescapably the case, though a rarely-addressed subject, that wild deer also prop up a huge black or illegal economy. Salmon farming may have squeezed salmon prices so low that poaching is hardly worthwhile, at any rate on a small scale, but deer farming has not done this to venison. Venison prices may have marked time for ten years but a good stag carcase is still worth around £100 at 1990 prices and a hind £60. Only the poachers themselves know exactly what the total value of poached deer is, and then only in their area. It may well be the case that the equivalent of the legal cull is taken illegally. A radio programme on poaching featured a well-known poacher claiming, possibly in order to run a scare, possibly accurately, that £5,000 per week could be made from deer poaching. Certainly a stir was caused in complacent circles when two small farmers in Sutherland were allegedly given a tax bill by the scrupulously arithmetical Inland Revenue for £20,000. This was the tax owing on their clandestine activities over two years as calculated from the books of a game dealer whom the Revenue decided to investigate. The courts have always been notoriously reluctant to mete out to poachers punishments which fit the crime. Local sheriffs have frequently made plain where their sympathies lie in a curious neglect of duty which passes muster without comment. However, the Revenue is not hide-bound by these out-moded conventions, and the onus of disproving the justice of such a tax demand will be on the hapless poachers. As the difficulties of making a poaching case stick in local sheriff courts have always been famously problematical, the attentions of the Revenue to poached gains turns the tables neatly. Without more ado, it is fair to say that the benefits afforded by the red deer to the Highlands go a lot further than the economies of Highland estates only.

The argument of the old poachers was that a share of the deer, part of nature's bounty, belonged to them as a birthright; or put another way, wandering deer belonged to nobody. In the modern deer forest where management of the wild population is more precise, where deer are fed in winter, where ground is burnt and managed for deer and trees are planted to shelter them, the old anachronistic excuses do not justify, if they ever did, breaking the law. Today's stalker has a difficult enough job, and it is a pity that on many vulnerable estates so much time needs to be spent supervising the well-being of his deer and protecting them from marauders.

It is probably true to say that most Highland keepers are stalkers first and gamekeepers second. To the men who patrol the hills, stalking is a way of life, the shooting season an interlude. In life in the Highlands the offer of a day out stalking is generally more eagerly accepted than a shooting day. It is not only that stalking is open to anyone who can hold a rifle steady, whereas bird-shooting is an art requiring long practice; it is that stalking the red deer seems to touch the spirit of the hills. Stalking is, of course, a moving and deeply-involved experience, even for those used to it. I have noticed in the most experienced stalkers a quickening of excitement as you and he approach the firing-bank, an extra urgency in his whispered instructions. Thus it should be. Anyone who fails to feel the profound seriousness of deer stalking should restrict his or her activities to the shooting range. For this and other reasons most stalkers feel their responsibilities in a very personal sense, and often appear to outsiders to be especially at one with their environment.

Stalking rekindles in us an ancient craft. We have to revive the hunting instincts of primitive man, using the wind, the shallow cover in boggy undulations, or the shoulders of rocks and crags on the ridges; then we must wait, frequently cold and sodden-wet with the wind pinching our extremities, for the beast to rise to get a clear shot. The same resourcefulness filled the cave-larders of early man. Getting close to deer is no different than it ever was; only the methods of securing them have changed. Too many times I have seen complete newcomers to stalking, venturing forth on the hill largely out of interest's sake, returning at dusk filled with an elation which is unmistakable, to doubt that at some level the hunting instinct is intact, deep-down, in many of us. Given a mode of expression which satisfies all the reservations about big-game hunting natural to contemporary man, the instinct is best indulged and enjoyed for what it is. Stalking offers this balanced and challenging mode of expression. It is a constant source of sadness to stalking people that their sport has a small following in Britain, an anomaly made more strange beside the general interest and acceptability of large game shooting in North America and all over Europe. The contemporary stalker in Scotland is conscious that his is a minority vocation, his sport appreciated by only a few, and probably inexplicable and incomprehensible to many of the rest. This is the background to his job.

The stalker's job when out stalking is in essence an odd one, that almost of an intermediary, although in most big-game hunting worldwide a guide or professional hunter takes the guest hunter close in to the quarry in a similar way. The experienced stalker must match the objective to the rifleman. The test shots taken on the target, whilst theoretically to test the rifle's telescopic sights are more usefully to inform the stalker of his man's capabilities. How fast the shot is taken, the shooting position adopted, the closeness of the bullets' grouping, these are quietly observed and noted down. The rifleman who comes off the target with a cut over his eye from the telescope's recoil, whose shots have been a long time coming, and then accompanied by stertorous breathing must, the stalker knows, be taken in close to his quarry. In the end, the stalker hardly needs to look for the shots on the target to assess his man; he gets a shrewd idea from how he looks taking the shot.

Fitness is made much of in stalking talk. Certainly, a man is at a disadvantage if he needs a rest after every mile. But the level of fitness required for most deer forests today should not tax any young person in reasonable condition, nor most older ones. On the west coast and central Highland forests, where the first manoeuvre is to get high up on the ridges for spying down into the corries, the hardest of the walking is at the beginning. In the north-eastern Highlands where the hills tend to rise less precipitously, sticking to a steadily-held pace is the secret of covering large distances in open terrain. The stalker, to get the best out of his man, should not tax his walking powers unduly, and the older stalkers never do. Every experienced stalking man though, somewhere along the line, will have encountered the young stalker anxious to show his paces, who skips merrily up the hill and then waits with disapproving expression on the ridge as his poor charge toils painfully into view. The stalker's first duty is to get his man into position for the shot in the best possible shape: flattening his self-esteem is a poor preparation.

When considering which stag or hind to stalk, and what approach to make, there are many factors at play in the stalker's mind of which the rifleman knows nothing. Consequently, a stalker's decisions, lines of approach and general tactics often seem bewildering. One purpose of the stalker's thinking from the outset is to use the wind to work his marches.

Working the marches means avoiding driving deer onto neighbouring ground, and deliberately winding deer over the march in such a way that they move forward onto the stalker's ground. This is not unfair, it is simply optimising opportunities within accepted frameworks. A good stalker knows well enough where stags and hinds are likely to be at a particular time of year in a particular wind. I have known a stalker actually to summon stags, which are inclined to curiosity, by whistling them out of a concealed corrie. The stalking tenants who told me this story were nonplussed. One moment a sprawling empty landscape stretched away before them, the next a line of stags trotted out of nowhere, presenting themselves for selective shooting. They might have heard of, or seen, stalkers roaring to attract combative stags in the rut; whistling stags into line out of thin air they had neither seen nor ever expected to see. The other positive utilisation of wind is to ensure that deer within the marches which do catch human scent only move deeper into home territory. How far deer will move on their territory, and where they will settle, the stalker will fairly be able to reckon. He will be familiar with the hefts of the hinds, although not of all the stags during the rut. The most risky time to move stags is in summer and the early stalking season, when they are grazing in large parties and prone to run on impulse for several miles.

The stalker, then, is always considering, like a snooker player, the next move, whether for later the same day, for the next day, or even the next week. As the stag stalking season progresses he will have marked out all over the ground particular old, retarded or imperfect stags, hummels and switches (stags devoid of antlers and stags with unforked rapier points dangerous to other stags), which he will hope over the season to weed out. In a party of stags, if he intends to shoot more than one, he will be thinking of the probable reaction of the second stag after the first shot. The first stag to be shot, if the rifleman is capable, will be the further out. Above all, the stalker will be keyed-up for a follow-through in the event of the stag being wounded. Any stag likely to run he will despatch himself, taking the rifle decisively in his own hands.

The advent of telescopic sights on sporting rifles has given everyone a chance to kill clinically and cleanly. Far fewer stags are wounded than used to be with the rough approximations of the old open-sighted rifles. With enough practice, certainly, many people used to use open or 'iron' sights with extra-ordinary accuracy on the hill. With open sights came the obligation and thrill of getting in to close quarters with deer, plus the advantage of having within your field of view after the shot the whole situation rather than just one beast isolated down a telescope. However, from the humane point of view, telescopic sights have considerably reduced potential margins of error; wounded deer need never escape, and there is less chance of the wrong stag being shot.

In approaching deer, the stalker has not only his own advance to consider but the physical characteristics of his rifleman. These people come in many shapes and sizes. The ponyman, these days more frequently the ATV driver, knows full well the faraway spectacle of two figures approaching unsuspecting deer. It is one of the private pleasures of his job to watch them. One hugs the ground, insinuates himself smoothly through the vegetation, pushing the rifle in front steadily, and is camouflaged so as to be almost invisible, blending with his surroundings. Behind him a very different figure claims the observer's attention. Clambering uncomfortably about on the final crawl, he bears a resemblance to a shock victim floundering about after a gas attack. Back arched stiffly off the ground, his elbows and feet flap erratically as he attempts to negotiate local humps and hollows without getting wet or dirty. Sometimes the poor stalker has two of these armchair *habitués* to contend with. By the time the stalker reaches the firing-bank, the deer are all up and standing, gazing in disbelief at the advancing circus. The rifle never leaves its case, the deer prance smartly off, and the backward miscreants enquire innocently what happened to spoil the stalk. It is an old scenario, no less comic for its familiarity.

There is another stalking archetype, no less wearisome for a stalker to be saddled with for a week. This is the one who has done a certain amount of stalking in different places and quietly thinks most stalkers are missing a trick here and there. This one never falls behind; he is breathing down the stalker's neck all day. He spies ardently, swivelling his binoculars round to be first to spot the deer. Whichever approach the stalker favours he can think of another, better one. His talk is of past triumphs, better days, better forests, even possibly, better stalkers. In fact, although he will not say so directly, he has seen it all. Strange then, that he misses the shot. But whoever said stalking was easy? No, he has all the explanations — one elbow was too low and sliding down, a midge bit his eyelid, the beast turned as he fired. Or, he will claim unashamedly, the stalker moved and his target lifted its head out of the sure trajectory of his neck-shot. There is an expression used in the north to console those who miss. The stalker uses it now, with unfailing restraint and a little sardonically, 'Well, there's plenty of space around them.'

Much has been written about stalking. It has spawned a mass of anecdotal and nostalgic literature because these days on the hill have become engraved landmarks on the sportsman's memory. Stalking has a powerful effect on people. It is partly to do with the red deer itself, an animal which at last is being studied scientifically in a detailed way. The old stalkers always maintained that they continued learning more about deer every time they went to the hill, and recent research has given some idea of how much there is to know and how much still to discover. Frank Fraser Darling, in his prolonged solitary vigils in the hills of Wester Ross recorded in that classic of deductions by simple observation, *A Herd of Red Deer*, anticipated many of the findings of later scientifically-trained research teams, notably that of Tim Clutton-Brock and Steve Albon. Knowledge has moved a long way from the time a century ago when it was believed wild red deer lived twice as long as man, and the rut only lasted a week.

In their latest book *Red Deer in the Highlands*, Clutton-Brock and Albon chart several new areas of growing knowledge useful to landowners and stalkers. It is now proved that very few hinds travel far (more than five miles) from where they were born; stags tend to disperse more widely. There is evidence to suggest, perhaps not surprisingly, that old hinds are more successful upbringers of calves than middle-aged hinds and suckle their calves for longer. That hinds invested more heavily in their sons than their daughters before weaning, a situation reversed after weaning, they had already illustrated in a previous work. Yeld hinds (those without a following calf), contrary to traditional assumptions, are less successful mothers when they do produce a calf, than milk hinds calving regularly. This supports the case for shooting yeld hinds in the winter hind-cull. The poor condition of some old hinds is due to investment in their offspring, and does not devalue them as next season's breeders.

The authors advocate the aim for deer forest managers of maintaining a mosaic of different vegetation communities for deer. Stags favour a coarser, less digestible diet than hinds, filling their frames with greater quantities of roughage; and they occupy hefts of lower grazing calibre. It is shown how dramatically the fecundity of hinds and calf survival is affected by overpopulation and how rapidly their populations compensate by their breeding performance — a finding which has obvious implications for management. The survival of stags is strongly affected by rising hind populations — a key fact in the present debate about the proper level of hind culling. Fittingly for the largest mammal in Europe, the red deer is also now the most thoroughly researched.

Despite its diminished physique in the Highland environment, the red deer is in many respects to be seen at its best in this inspiring setting, and its scientific study has been easier than is possible in the woods.

No-one who has viewed the huge summer parties of up to a thousand stags can fail to be impressed by scenes more suggestive of the African plains or North American tundra. Perhaps the main reason the red deer has graven itself so forcibly on sportsmen's minds is its perfect grace in movement. Few African antelopes, despite the easier terrain, move so well as red deer. The red deer's flowing full gallop over broken, boggy country interrupted by peat bogs and deep gullies is the facility of an animal supremely adapted to its environment.

Devotees of the hind-cull probably find out more of the animal than the stag shooters, for behaviour in the rut is hormone-controlled and many of deer's finer instincts get subsumed. When hind shooting it is possible in the smaller parties to see in practical operation the sort of matriarchies that later researches confirmed, and Fraser Darling first described. The presence of the old knobber and young staggie is irrelevant by the time the rut has slowed down in November. The group leader is a dominant hind, usually an older female with a calf, and sometimes last year's stirk still following on behind. The party will be composed of her female kin, and when on the move another senior matriarch will bring up the rear, stopping in view if the others are crossing a burn, acting as a sentinel until the leading hinds are safely up the other side.

Hind shooting occasionally necessitates taking most of the animals in a small party — one of the reasons superior marksmanship is called for — and it is remarkable how severely such a social unit will be pressurised before the hierarchy breaks down and the remaining deer run off helter-skelter. This can work to the advantage of the stalker, who will have a good idea when the hinds turn and prepare to run off which animal will be in front.

The circumstances which make the hind season a good one for watching the deer also make it a difficult proposition to shoot them. The hind is shot not when distracted and worn out like the stag in the rut, but when she is at her peak, nourished by a summer's feeding, sexually content, with a calf becoming more vigorous and independent. By the hind shooting season, which is usually commenced in November, the weather will be turning harder, gales are common, and the hind is extremely alert. Conditions may cause unexpected problems. One windy day shooting on Ben Alder, our little party was obliged to stop on an exposed ridge. We took the opportunity to lunch — or attempted to. The girl among us opened her mouth, inserted her luncheon bap, but was too cold to chew it. The bap was withdrawn and we proceeded.

No casual stag shooter, thrusting his head over a knoll or round a boulder, will do any business approaching hinds in the same way. For the hind parties have look-outs on all sides; the hind is the great survivalist. When coming into view of hinds you do it inch by inch — usually to find yourself staring down the muzzle of a hind looking directly at you. If a hind sees you, or thinks she sees you, she plays safe and skedaddles. Or she drops her head then suddenly raises it, staring hard at you as you move. Good luck often attends the stag shooter in the rut — a shootable stag may be sleeping in a burn, or fighting stags may charge obliviously in your direction: with the hinds you have to work for every beast.

The hind also employs a sense that stags only engage erratically — the instinct of self-preservation. The occasions when you crawl into quietly feeding herds which for no ascertainable reason suddenly sprint off, are legion. I am sure they sense the danger instinctively. They do not look up and gaze in your direction; they just go, at high speed. I have seen proof of this in another way; the hinds which you do not intend to shoot seem to realise it. They allow you much closer than usual; sometimes they completely ignore you. I have seen this on a march bisecting an open hill-side. Following round the shoulder of the hill to stalk hinds on the other side, I have been watched by a small party of hinds below which never budged, even when I was walking parallel to them within shot. They were beyond the march. Either some racial memory told them that danger never came from that particular angle of approach or, more likely, they knew I was bent on other purposes. Stags, as is commonly attested by all stalkers, know full well when their season of peril is over. A few days after the stag season is finished they appear on the hill beside the road at Borrobol, by their winter feeding grounds. Within a few weeks there are seventy or so. Of course, stags which are vulnerable to out-of-season poaching will not be so daft. But the others have caused many a stalker a wry smile, as those crowd him near home, which only a week or so before he had assayed strenuously to bring into the larder. That these big animals know the purposes of man is one of many sobering realisations that come to you stalking in the hills.

Hind stalking, then, is not for beginners — or only under expert instruction. Emphatically it should only be conducted by, or with, a seasoned professional. For much of the difficulty lies in distinguishing which hinds to shoot. In the same way that a stalker can determine at long range the differences between hinds and stags, so at close range he can identify at a glance yeld hinds from milk hinds, and old ones from young ones. This takes practice, and when all the hallmark signs of age and yeld condition have been accounted for, ultimately at certain angles and in uncertain light, the stalker knows the hind from a firm, general impression difficult to describe precisely. Although the red deer research teams have cast doubt on traditional assumptions about shooting old hinds, pointing to their excellence as reliable and motherly breeders, their findings support that very old hinds (above thirteen years) should indeed be culled, and the desirability of removing yeld hinds is confirmed. Their conclusion that poor calves tend to emanate from poor mothers one after another reinforces the correctness of the usual practice of culling very poor-looking milk hinds, along with their calves also. Most responsible stalkers have anyway been operating hind culls on these lines for several generations: it will be gratifying to know that modern research underpins their assumptions. The reinforcement of the fact that the control of hind populations, which tend to monopolise the better feeding areas, is the key to improving the quality and number of revenue-producing stags, coincides conveniently with the RDC's insistence on a higher hind cull on the eastern side of the Highlands.

Estates which call themselves 'hind forests', meaning there are more hefted hinds on them than stags, have every incentive now to develop and utilise hind-shooting tenancies. Whilst hind-shooting does not offer quite the grandeur of stag shooting, nor the opportunities to watch the extraordinary behaviour of this magnificent animal in the rut — challenging his rivals, sometimes fighting them, indefatigably herding and chasing his restless harem — it is infinitely cheaper. Stags on a good forest command a rent of around £220; hind-shooting, usually let for the day with the opportunity of several shots, is under a third of this figure.

The old-fashioned view perceived the stag season as sport and the hind season as a cull. However, that was in the days when only the biggest stags were shot, those with superior antlers, a policy which became outdated when deer numbers started increasing after the war and it was reckoned the best stags should be left for breeding. Nowadays the stag season is conducted in the spirit of a cull, to weed out old and infirm beasts that may not last another winter, stunted beasts of any age, and stags likely to be of danger to other stags from their antler formation. Trophy stalking hardly exists in Scotland, and where it does there is generally a deer fence discreetly out of sight, to prevent the carefully-nurtured colossus from escaping. Trophy hunters go to Europe, where the best are reserved for the deepest wallets.

The awkwardness of the hind cull and the relatively short season militate against its suitability for renting *en bloc*. However, the central pre-Christmas period can be rewarding for both estate and tenant, and it leaves the last half of the season for the stalker to pick off the most debilitated animals. Such are the ones and twos found eking out a mean existence in the deep burns and known as 'burn-creeps'. This gives the stalker special pleasure because these old maids in the burns have often been the bane of his life in the stag season, jumping out of nowhere at the last minute and taking all the obedient stags with them.

The stalker's other mid-winter duties will involve deer feeding in most forests today. Although Clutton-Brock and Albon cannot verify that feeding stags in winter has any ascertainable benefit, it is because they have not tested its efficiency. Most stalkers think it provides a support in the worst phase of the year, and promote stags' general condition for good antler growth in the spring. A common use for winter feeding is to keep stags at home when they might otherwise wander off to crops on the lower ground and be shot as marauders.

A risk attaches to retaining stags in unnaturally exposed or debilitating winter quarters which most stalkers are very conscious of, and also of attracting too many stags to one area drawing them away from their traditional shelter. Feeding hinds in winter, always more difficult, provided the food is close to their hefts, can surely only benefit them. Stalkers have been caught out in the past with feeding programmes which have been too ambitious, and when bad weather has closed in, have found their feed supply running out or their feeding places becoming unreachable. Sometimes this has had tragic results. If there is this risk, they should either not be feeding, or have prepared caches of high-value, low-bulk concentrates in places they can invariably get to.

The interminably long, wet, sunless spring of 1989 had fatal results for west coast deer populations. A population which was probably top-heavy was hit by horizontal early spring rain which penetrated and waterlogged animals' coats. Conditions may have been exacerbated by a lack of snow. Total snow cover protects the soil from temperature loss; low soil temperatures delay spring growth. The worst casualties were found above forestry deer fences thoughtlessly staked out across hillsides, blocking the deers' access to shelter and low ground feeding. The public nowadays is more aware and sensitive about the suffering of wild animals, and whether or not weather conditions have historically controlled wild deer populations, and regardless of whether forestry fencing is primarily responsible, it is embarrassing for deer managers and stalkers that accusations of neglect come their way. More balanced planning, with consideration for all land uses, is called for.

The other winter activity for stalkers is poaching prevention, a task that can be arduous and thankless if the deer are in a vulnerable locality. The old-fashioned poacher skilfully extracting 'one for the pot' is not, nor ever was, the problem. Deer poaching is now a seasonal activity for organised gangs of criminals who prey at other times of the year on salmon, sheep, undefended property or anything else that comes to hand, in a calendar of busy untaxed profit-taking. No tears need be shed for this freebooter. The cruelty of night shooting, the injuries to deer which run away, the legacy of unmothered calves, and the sheer waste typical of much poaching (entire front ends of deer being thrown away to make space in the van for the concentrated meat in haunches), abolish sympathy for indiscriminate killing of this sort.

What makes the stalker's job more difficult is that, in some cases, deer numbers have undoubtedly been allowed to rise too high. Competition for feeding has pushed deer onto roadsides where they have never been seen before. Forestry fences to keep deer out, or perimeter fences to keep deer away from publicly vulnerable parts of estates, have forced them down the hill to winter in new places. Unintentionally, fencing has sometimes acted as a funnel, hundreds of deer pouring onto a small area which cannot support them. The stalker's problem is that such a scenario presents opportunities to ordinary citizens that are irresistible. Cases vary wildly, but in some circumstances where this sort of displacement has occurred, apportionment of blame falls on inaction or lack of foresight by the estates themselves. While poaching is clearly wrong, so is mismanagement of deer which gives rise to undue provocation to poach.

From the stalker's point of view, having deer spilling onto public roads, or neighbouring farms where they can be taken legally as marauders, is most unwelcome. Poaching gangs are mobilised, tough, and disinclined to let anyone come between them and their profit. The worst cases of poacher/keeper and poacher/water bailiff violence have taken place in England (one keeper was recently shot dead, in the back), and the more integrated nature of Highland society and remoteness from large cities has mercifully kept at bay, in large part, armed confrontations.

The token fines meted out for poaching offences in county courts, and the extreme difficulty in getting a poaching case to stick in the first place, show that the gravity of the problem is not widely understood. Keepers have a difficult enough job, and ostracism from the local community, which has occurred in some neighbourhoods, is a pressure they could do without. Increasingly, the role of the Highland gamekeeper, multifarious already, is taking on a public relations aspect.

The Highland keeper might fairly be said to be an overloaded man; he is certainly not an overpaid man. However, his job has compensations many people would give their eye-teeth for. He habitually works alone and is his own master. Most Highland keepers adhere to the principle that there is no point in employing a man if he is not left to get on with the job — and do not fail to say so if they feel crowded. On the bigger estates there may be an underkeeper or a seasonal ghillie to help with the donkey-work. On the major ones there is a team of keepers, each deployed on different beats. By and large the keeper is his own man, the caretaker of all he surveys, free to go as he pleases and do his work in his own time.

The sport which others pay their savings for is a perquisite of the job. On many estates the keepers enjoy free fishing, and even if they do not get the best water they are on hand to take advantage when fishing conditions are good. The dog and gun are his companions, his domain the open hill with its panoramic grandeur and heady breezes. In the summer sporting season he meets those from the big wide world who have fled for refreshment to the environment he takes for granted. While most of the year is a solitary vigil, the season is hectic, new tenant arriving on the heels of old tenant, in a stream of sportsmen revelling in being back on the hill and predisposed to enjoy themselves. What could be a happier combination, with the keeper predisposed to ensure they do?

Chapter Five
Hill Farming

A long way from the limelight, but no further from the hub of affairs on a Highland estate is the hill shepherd. He seldom sees the sporting tenants, indeed they may know nothing of his existence, but in many small ways his presence is instrumental in the smooth ticking-over of the estate community. He might, in fact, be seen as the centre of it.

Three-quarters of estates in the Highlands carry a sheep stock still. At the time of writing, the hill sheep economy is severely under threat, and rapidly contracting, but not many estates have closed down their farms entirely. Most have undertaken a damage limitation exercise and reduced their farm's size.

The modern form of sheep farming, in commercial-scale hirsels under the management of one stockman, had moved into the Highlands, as has been described, after 1760. Sheep flourished on the clean, rich pastures of the glens. Never before had the Highlands supported a domestic farm stock of anything like this size. In two autumn marts in 1827, 130,000 cattle and 200,000 sheep changed hands at Falkirk; this was stock moved by drovers down from the Highlands. Just as the southern markets became accessible to the Highland stock farmers, competition began to tell against the unimproved Highland animals. Loss of weight and condition in the weeks of travel from the faraway glens penalised them in the marketplace. A number of fortuitous events prolonged the tenure of the sheep farmers. Blackface wool supplied the carpet trade which extended its exports from 1850. The liver-fluke outbreak in 1860 and subsequent years left huge holes in English sheep flocks which Scottish stock could fill. Cotton imports stopped during the American Civil War in the 1860s, boosting the price of wool.

To make room for the expansion of sheep stocks the practice was started, still in use today, of wintering young stock in the lowland areas or along the coast on productive arable land. The wool price, squeezed by imports, went into irreversible decline from 1872. Irresponsible Highland flockmasters retained the same expanded sheep stocks at a time when wintering costs and labour costs were rising fast. These approximately doubled in the twenty years following 1853; by 1872 it generally required one-third of a hogget's value to winter it off the farm. This accumulation of problems peaked when fertility in the hills was suffering from a long-term decline. Intensive grazing over a long period without intermission, and without anything being put back into the ground had, in the opinion of graziers at the time, exhausted the pasturage. Into this parlous situation sailed the freezer ships with Australasian mutton.

The cattle trade closely mirrored the sheep predicament. The opening of the Perth to Inverness railway in 1863, and the Dingwall to Strome Ferry line in 1870, improved communications enormously at just the time the small Highland cattle were exposed to the competition of American beef. By 1890, thirty per cent of British beef consumption was imported. By the turn of the century, Ireland, Canada, America and Argentina were all putting competitive pressure on the quality of home-produced beef.

There was a corresponding transformation in land use. In his book *Deer Forests, Landlords and Crofters*, Willie Orr names around fifty deer forests created or extended between 1885 and 1900. The sheep farmers were on the run, and proprietors found it hard to let sheep farms despite falling rents. Sheep numbers over the whole of Scotland fell thirty per cent between 1880 and 1906. To those who would conclude this represented a woeful failure to compete with importers, it is worth considering that the period of true growth in the Highland summer is only six weeks; parts of New Zealand enjoy an eight-month growing season.

One thing militated in favour of sheep. Highland landlords could avoid paying rates on sport if the land could be entered in the rolls as grazing land. My Alltanduin hirsel at Borrobol in 1894 carried a stock of 1,500 ewes; but it was still considered by one contemporary commentator as primarily deer forest. As the stag cull in those times was about seven a year, it uncovers the hidden prejudice to argue that it was not first and foremost agricultural land. The overlap between what constituted deer forest and what were hill grazings was elastic then, as it is today. Although deer occur on around seven million acres of Scotland, only two-and-a-half million acres is presently termed deer forest. Equally, sheep and cattle in summer graze ground primarily used by deer. The old definition of deer forest, as land cleared of sheep for deer, in the present mix has no clear meaning.

During the 1980s the wobble in confidence in hill farming became a collapse. In 1988 and 1989 the ewe breeding stock in Sutherland, the major true Highland sheep county, dropped by 30,000 and the largest single flock-master closed down. A few years before, the Duke of Westminster's estate of Reay closed all the farms at a stroke. The north-west Highlands now supports very few commercial sheep stocks and there may be none before long. These same parishes of Reay and Eddrachilis maintained a cattle population of 6,000 beasts two centuries earlier.

The disappearance of the hill farms has extremely serious consequences for the Highlands, and for Highland estates. For the hill farm, which is typically one or two hirsels of sheep and a small herd of cattle, has a central role in Highland communities. Tourism aside, farming is Scotland's biggest industry. The hill farms supplying good quality, clean lambs to improve low-ground sheep stocks, and store wedders and calves for fattening on low-ground farms, form an essential link in a chain of interrelationship with the rest of the farming community. Hill ewes, exhausted after six crops of lambs, descend to milder climes and an easy retirement, bearing lambs for two or three more years. Hill farms put income in the pockets of low-ground farmers, who reserve turnips and grass for out-wintered hoggets. Pure-bred hill ewe-lambs refresh low-ground flocks and are tupped to produce the cross lambs the market favours. From other better-situated farmers the hill stockmen buy straw and hay, and in smaller quantities barley and oats. Essentially the hill farm sector operates in harness with low-ground farms; hardship for the hill farmer is felt all the way through the farming community.

The hill farm on a Highland estate is part and parcel of the world beyond the end of the glen in a way which the keeper and his ghillie are not. Hill shepherds belong to the wide world in a sense that is different. The range of suppliers and servicing industries with which they are in contact root them in the wider community in a way which, by comparison, makes the gamekeeper an isolated fellow. For the to and fro of a farm make it a busy place. Suppliers of fencing materials, feedstuffs, fertilisers and field dressings, sheep dips and medicines, farm machinery and tools, mix at the farm gate with drainage contractors, lime-spreaders, erectors of outbuildings, vets, and even the picaresque travelling salesmen who rove the countryside selling cut-price gates. In the autumn the farm road is busy with other farmers coming to hire hill-bred tups to cross with their low-ground ewes. Every now and then, in a distinctly smarter vehicle, appears the official from the Department of Agriculture and Fisheries for Scotland (DAFS), to check numbers of breeding stock, correlate capital works against claims for grant, or ensure health and safety regulations are being complied with. Sometimes, even more a fish out of water, the man from the insurance company arrives, whose first glance at the hill farmer's decrepit stock of machinery betrays his private wonderment that such vehicles are on a policy at all.

All of these people, grateful for a day-visit to the hills, stop for a talk on the farm gate. Rare are the shepherds who lack information on what is going on around. Rarer still the one who does not have a firm view on these developments!

Farm life is not as seasonal as sporting life, nor can any days be taken off. Domestic stock need daily attention. No sooner have the cattle started calving in early spring — the practice on most hill places — than the ewes are being brought to their best for the lambing in April. This is a wearisome and worrisome time of year, when exceedingly long hours are routine.

A few farmers on the west lamb, as their forefathers did, on the open hill, spying the ground for lying ewes, going to their help if they are lambing, noting down their whereabouts for their next circuit if they are preparing to lamb. The same discipline, but within hill-parks and fields, is observed by more modern hill shepherds, going their daily rounds from first light till last, and often on their feet for twenty hours a day. A few places, encouraged by the siren-voices of up-beat forecasters from the past, have the shedding to lamb their ewes indoors. Few will have seen a return on their investment in buildings. Some others, mostly blackface breeders in the west, at the opposite end of the spectrum, 'ranch' rather than farm sheep, a euphemism meaning lambing ewes are left to fend for themselves. At first gathering in early summer, the rancher/shepherd has no stiffer task than a head-count.

For hill farmers lambing is a time of both physical and emotional stress. Shepherds get wound up in the tribulations of multiple births and occasional deaths. Spring can be a cruel time in the hills, and hard weather stresses man and beast alike. When spring grass is slow to start, ewes wander far and wide to fill their bellies and their udders. Lambs get lost when they cannot keep up. Lost lambs have a habit of lying in the drains and bogs no good for them. Fit lambs tuck in behind the rushes, but weak lambs lie out in the teeth of the wind seeming to court disaster. Sometimes a shepherd suspects his fight to keep his stock alive is a struggle against nature itself; lambs will try every way to die and still he has to head them off. Disgruntled ewes which have lost their lambs, or not given birth, or are downright cusses, try and pinch the lambs off other ewes. Others will not stand to be suckled. If the weather turns really mean, blowing a gale and sleet, it makes ewes tense and they all start having lambs at once, typically in the middle of the night. In the worst scenario, the complications of an unattended lambing kill the ewe also. A majority of lost ewes are the inexperienced, younger, more valuable ones.

Over lambing-time shepherds get physically worn out. Their hands, which are frequently wetted, get chapped and cracked; they become footsore, sleep so little they cease to sleep at all, and risk getting deluged by the weight of work into losing the essential stabiliser of a steady rhythm. By the end of six weeks lambing a man is worn through, emotional, and tends to over-react to small setbacks. If it is fair to say that in the dead of winter hill shepherds often perform few duties, except feeding the stock, it is equally true that at lambing-time they work at a pitch which is exceptionally demanding. Animals which to us look all the same are identifiable individuals, some of which shepherds can remember as lambs themselves years earlier. Lambing your hirsel is a highly personal affair which, psychologically speaking, outsiders probably do not fully understand. The advent of hill motor bikes and three-wheelers may have taken some of the slog out of lambing, but the effort of concentration, and the intensity of the whole period, remain much as they were.

From lambing through to November, when the tups are put back with the ewes for the next fertilisation, a shepherd's life is busy. The Department requirements to dip sheep more and more often, necessitating gathering them off the hill, dipping, and letting them dry off before taking them back again, are taking more of men's time; and incidentally increasing the periods during which animals are under stress. Many of the old-timers in the sheep farming world believe today's methods are too lavish with chemicals and dips, particularly applied to a stock that is fit and parasite-free anyway. Liver-fluke, for which sheep have to be treated, in any case does not occur in Scotland, only in England. The more natural, old-fashioned methods involved less handling of stock, less medication and less stress, without loss of fitness and health.

The viability of the modern hill farm depends on the capacity to grow winter feed. The farms which need to buy in hay and other feedstuffs have probably squeezed their margins too far. For the restraints which decimated the hill sheep and cattle sector a hundred years ago are pertinent today —

quality is at a premium. Therefore, ewes have to be fed in winter to keep them in good heart for lambing. The old days of letting sheep fend for themselves are fast disappearing, and as the European Community attains self-sufficiency in sheep meat, they will go altogether. Some of the remoter, higher-up estates are selling off sheep and using what patches of arable ground they have to grow food for deer. The summer months on the farm are spent tending the stock and making winter-keep, normally hay or silage. Localised weather conditions and the constant threat in the hills of sudden rain, make this a touch-and-go business. When hay is safely garnered and the hayshed door closes on a sweet-smelling larder of winter-keep, only then do thoughts turn to sheepdog trials and the other variants of their work which shepherds look to for their relaxation. Some farms grow root-crops, requiring a complete soil cultivation, as an early winter booster.

Before the time of diversions there is the key period between the marking, when lambs are counted and the sale wedders speaned (castrated), and sales. This is traditionally when sheep take to the hill, working their way from the valley-bottoms where the first grasses are showing and move up the hillsides as the sun warms the ground and promotes growth higher up. Many lambs, meticulously nurtured through the lambing, suddenly take sick and die before shepherds can find them on the open hill. They fall in drains or burns, or merely succumb to the shock of new herbage to which life in the parks has not acclimatised them. But leave the parks they must, to let the grasses grow up for mowing.

Large hill parks, improved by lime and fertilisers and fenced from deer, have come into use to provide more concentrated feeding for sheep after lambing, in places where they can be watched. These serve simultaneously to leave free for deer and grouse the early feeding on the hill. One of the functions of a herd of hill cattle is to graze these parks intensively when they become rank and when rough grasses or bracken intrude. The cattle are more catholic eaters and their hooves cut up and break open the rough vegetation, allowing the sward beneath to come through. Cattle are good for the ground, when grazed sensibly, and their ability to refresh soil fertility is a key feature of the hill farm cycle. Frank Fraser Darling believed the ratio of cattle to sheep in the Highlands should never be less than 1:20 if rapid loss of soil fertility was to be avoided. The decline in cattle has been such that he would be disappointed now.

The middle of summer is the time of the clipping, once such a staple of the sheep farm economy, now a small fraction of annual income. The tradition of itinerant gangs of professional sheep-shearers, often Australians or New Zealanders, has started to fall away as the value of the wool-clip has declined. Frequently now farms handle their own clipping with what labour they can muster, phasing the operation over several weeks. Clipping is a laborious and back-breaking business made more awkward by sprightly gimmers (young ewes) and fleeces filled with sand and grit from rubbing under banks. The clippers get coated in lanolin from the fleeces and on a hot day in a stifling sheepshed the work is far from inviting. It is a sad reflection that since the value of British wool started to stagnate after the 1970s, the wool-clip, although necessary, barely justifies itself financially. Yet the wool trade was the economic motor behind the Clearances: we have indeed come full circle.

If a 'season' exists on the hill farm, it follows clipping and hay-making and is the period of summer sales, when shepherds come down from the hills to present the product of a whole year's work. The sales are major events, to the outsider a confusing jamboree of numberless sheep being handled through a maze of pens. The shepherd's shouts of greeting and muttered conversations in knotty groups, as they go about their affairs, mix with the energetic cries of white-coated auction-house stockmen, the sheeps' bleating, and the hiss of air-brakes from the huge sheep floats. The din in the cattle sales is louder still. The big auction rings have a bar and snack-room handy, and to represent the scenes in the former might stretch even the ability of Hogarth. It is not unknown for otherwise upright characters to leave the sale not upright, in the comfort of their stock trailers. At Lairg, the largest one-day sheep auction anywhere in Britain or Europe, over 30,000 lambs are sold in one day at the big August lamb sale. To those few tourists who annually are to be seen clinging warily to the stands, camera at the ready, the scene is utterly bewildering, made more so by the racing-commentator patter of the auctioneers, incomprehensible to all outsiders. The occasion is necessarily an exhausting one, for a year's work and the bulk of a year's income are decided in that minute or two in the ring. A nod here and a raised finger there can make the difference between a bad season and an acceptable one. In recent years, in the confusion of national and European agriculture policies, prices have bounced erratically about, adding to the nerve-wracking nature of the day. Lamb sales are followed in September by sales of cast (old) ewes, and breeding tups; calf sales start in October.

By the end of these the build-up of stock on the ground is relaxed. The sale stock is gone and the ewe lambs for replacing cast ewes are despatched to their wintering on low-ground farms around the coast. A thousand-ewe sheep farm supports a population of, say, two thousand head in mid-summer, which is trimmed back again for the austerities of winter. The same system applies to cattle. For the salient characteristic of the hill farm with extensive rough grazing is that the summer provides more than enough natural feeding and the winter lacks sufficient. The precious arable and 'in-bye' acres have to be carefully managed for maximum benefit, without punishment of pasture to the point of damaging it. In the pre-Clearance days of the runrig system, the good ground was parcelled out amongst the community in a distribution of random allotments. The system sacrificed productive efficiency for fair sharing. In the summer the small black cattle and the few sheep and goats would be moved off the pressurised low ground to summer shielings high up on the grassy hill tops, where they and their herdsmen would spend two or three months. The fallen stones of the shieling — houses they built to shelter in — can still be found on the slopes, often near the top of the highest hills. Runrig made sensible use in this way of high pastures, but the subdivision of the small arable patches or 'rigs' prohibited efficiency.

After sale-time the hill farmers settle down for winter, feeding stock and herding them whenever possible out on to the hill to eke out what nutrition they can from the fading herbage. In late autumn the ewes can be seen heads down, moving steadily uphill to the ridges and high-ground flows where they can chew the succulent cotton-grass stalks before frost takes the last life from them. This use of the sweet cotton-grass is called 'moss-cropping' — it applies equally to the deer — and is repeated in the early spring. Tup-time is from November to Christmas, and in the hill-parks the well-nourished tups tread their tireless rounds, fitted with harnesses with a chalk marking so that ewes they have covered are identifiable.

Mid-winter can be a time of open, clear, invigorating weather or it can as easily, and more likely, turn to the opposite — storms, gales and snow. Blocked roads, disrupted power supplies, and helicopter feed-drops are not uncommon in the Highlands. The high western hills are usually subjected to a prolonged thorough-going rinsing and the eastern Highlands get a blanket of snow. If snow fails to arrive, ground temperatures at high altitudes fall even lower and frost desiccation, when evaporation demands from the air exceed the amount of water being replaced at the roots, retards plant growth. Hill farmers prefer hard and clear weather in winter in favour of driving rain, which is most punishing on stock. Mild weather in early winter tends to unfold into a retarded spring, and much depends at lambing time on the first tremulous show of green growth.

Snow blizzards can cause scenes of nightmarish horror as sheep driven before the weather fall blindly into water courses, even into rivers and lochs. When they reach an obstruction, a bank or steep burn-side, there is a risk of snow drifting on top of them and then freezing. It has been known for sheep to pile into a corner which turns to a death trap as the animals climb on top of each other and become immobilised by the weight of wet snow in their fleeces. The shepherds then have to dig them out at the earliest opportunity, hoping they have avoided suffocation. It has been known for shepherds to face the heart-breaking sight of huge numbers of breeding stock literally immured in a drift of snow turned to ice, stacked vertically like so many bottles in a wine-rack. However, the survival ability of buried sheep is legendary. Sir Herbert Maxwell, in *Memories of the Months*, reports a case in which two blackface sheep were dug out fit and well after twelve days, when the shepherd noticed vapours coming from air-holes in a snow-drift. He goes on to record survivors of entombment for twenty-five days. Naturally, survival of sheep in drifts depends on the type of snow. Heavy, wet snow can crush the air out of a drift, and some of the driving storms in Sutherland in the 1970s resulted in losses of hundreds of lives on one farm alone. Such incidents make farmers, and their wives, who fully share the strains of farming, yearn for spring.

Although many ways exist now to streamline hill sheep operations, increase lambing percentages, and trim back the numbers lost between marking (early summer) and sale date (August/September), it is a notable fact that the numbers of ewes a man is considered able to handle has moved little.

Obviously, particular situations — topography, herbage types, climate — ultimately determine individual hirsel sizes. But in general terms, eight hundred ewes has for a long time been considered the maximum practical size for a hill hirsel, the number going up as one moves southwards into denser grazing swards. In the places where numbers have been pushed up to well over a thousand, there are perceptible losses of performance, lower quality lambs, and often the need for seasonal help. The question arises as to whether, over a certain figure, the quantity of ewes per man does not entail a loss of attention in husbandry, and results in unacceptable animal neglect. Hill farms at the end of their financial tether have been tempted in recent years to increase the hirsel-size and shed labour. Where there is understanding by management of the practical realities, and parks are improved and fenced to facilitate this, hirsel numbers can indeed be increased; but on an open hill hirsel this is often questionable. A factor too little taken into account is the grazing pressure on the same ground from deer.

The decision taken by the European Community agriculture ministers in 1989 to restrict hill subsidies on farms of over a thousand ewes, and upland subsidies on those of over five hundred ewes, suggests that the motives for expansion are going to be trimmed from now on. The larger, more profitable units are to be penalised. Either the hill hirsel will be made to pay in an increasingly free market in lamb prices, which will involve some market recognition that the hill product deserves a premium value for taste, or the hill farms will close. The time has come for this form of marginal agriculture, an innovative land use only two hundred years ago, to face squarely the bleak options available.

Chapter Six
Salmon

There are three species emblematic of nature's bounty in the Highlands, and the most talked of, the most universally admired, is the salmon. Though not unique to Scotland, the salmon benefits, as do the red grouse and the red deer, from the enhancement of a Highland setting. Scotland is the home of salmon fishing by virtue of having given the art its most stylish form. Speycasting with a double-handed rod, as practised by its most skilful performers, is an art which complements the grace and strength of the fish which is its object to secure. Fishermen worldwide come to Scotland not only to fish but to see fishing tradition. This may indeed have its drawbacks, inhibiting change in fishing methods, but it has established a body of thought and experience which gives pleasure to successive generations with the same magic.

Salmon fishing exerts a hold on the imagination which, I think, is not quite matched by shooting or stalking, and is perhaps not paralleled by anything. I have seen people so utterly in its grip they can scarcely see or think of anything else. In the course of a week on a river, if there are fish about, individuals can succumb to the daemon of the king of fish in an extraordinary way. Each day gets a firmer hold on them. The man that sauntered to the riverbank on the Monday, idly flicking line off his rod, by the Wednesday is an hour earlier out of his bed and hurrying to collect together his tackle in a distracted fashion. By the end of the week the early bird is wearing a fixed, intense expression; the picnic or 'piece' is forgotten in the car or in the kitchen; he bends over the pools mesmerised by the movement of the water, lulled by the tinkle of splashing cataracts into a benumbed reverie. The rhythm of the cast, the arc of the line as it curls out over the promising water, and the tranquillity around are powerful drugs. For such a fisherman it is a saving grace that fishing holidays are only once a year. In his *Days of Salmon Fishing*, published in 1842, William Scrope tells how he was woken at midnight in his hostel-room by the cries of his fishing companion. The man was fishing in his dreams, but yanking the bell-rope and shouting 'I have him.' I know present-day stories which mirror this one in all essentials.

I have mused often on the fascination of fly fishing. Partly it belongs to the fascination of rivers themselves, following their eternal courses in byways otherwise unfrequented by man. In the nature of a river the stream is every moment refreshed, kept alive by its ceaseless evacuation of water to the sea. Rivers have a repetitious motion which is never tedious. They are hidden places, often fringed by trees; in some way being by them restores the child in us all and stirs the imagination, for we know that somewhere we cannot see a river has a beginning and an end, and it is beyond our scope to know all of it at one time.

The second part of the fascination is in the salmon itself and, to a degree, in all fish. In plying the surface with our wares we acknowledge a large element of chance. For very often we have no idea if a fish is lying below or not. The fish is the mystery we are trying to tease into being: thus so many fishermen talk of the thrill of seeing a fish rise, like a ghostly presence, only partially on view, from the occluded depths. A fish which moves to the fly is not only a mystery unravelling, but it is an inscrutable creature that, whether we catch it or not, retains its dissimilarity to ourselves — cold-blooded, slimy to the touch, an involuntary emissary from an alien world.

The great Canadian fishing writer Roderick Haig-Brown, at the end of a life pondering on salmon and fishing, climbed into a wet suit and slid into the salmon pools better to observe the species that had dominated his imagination. Many fishermen feel like this about salmon, and as we plug away at an unresponsive pool our minds drift into speculations about the river bottom, whether a fish moved to the fly, or what eyes are down there disinterestedly watching it. Such reveries, periodically interrupted by volcanic action and the need for dextrous skills, cool the tired sensibilities of doctors, lawyers and scientists, ease the stress out of weary travellers, suiting man, woman and child alike. We think we catch the salmon; actually he has us hooked, and his is a mighty hold.

Like the red grouse tenaciously clinging to its deserted winter moorland, like the stag in its awesome antics during the rut, the salmon is a creature of beguiling habits. Its life cycle is a triumph of strength and adaptation, an extraordinary evolutionary example of an anadromous species capable of using vastly different habitats. The dark, fungus-covered, decaying skeletons in the burns far out in the hills in early December have at one time fattened themselves into streamlined, silver beauties off the shelf of Greenland. The same fish may have leapt high waterfalls, and surged through crashing white water, to scuttle into the creeks and streams it left as a diminutive fry. For the salmon goes through numerous metamorphoses. The November hen salmon flicking out a depression in the gravel with her tail, depositing her eggs, promptly covered with milt by the attendant cock salmon, is a spectacle any keen observer can witness. According to water temperature, the eggs take three to four months to hatch, providing frost has not killed them, nor floods washed out the redds. On emerging, the ugly 'alevins' push upstream, surviving on the attached yolk-sac. Little is known of parr, the first fish shape developed by young salmon, except that they shoal, and take up territories in the middle of rivers which they strongly defend. The productive capacity of a salmon river is closely linked to the area and quality of parr feeding territories.

The parr generally stays in the river for two more springs, growing in summer and hibernating listlessly in winter. In the smolting phase the fish prepares for the sea by becoming silvery in colour, developing a forked tail and enlarged fins. After swimming down the burns, into the rivers and out to sea, the smolts disappear and enter a phase of development we know nothing about. Certainly, at this stage they provide a tremendous repast for cormorants and mergansers. Our next meeting with the fish is as a grilse or a salmon, returning from its rich winter feeding grounds after a minimum of fifteen months (in the case of grilse) or two, three or even four winters in the case of salmon. It has been conclusively shown that older salmon return to the river earlier in the year. At the point the grilse or salmon enters the river it becomes of the greatest importance to a large number of individuals, many of whom are at odds with each other.

It has always been so. The salmon has been a prized fish since the earliest law-makers. The pre-eminent importance of the right to fish for salmon has created the situation in Scotland, strange to some, where the owner of a river-bank is not necessarily allowed to wield his rod from it. Salmon fishing is a separate right. Extremely complicated laws also apply to the fishing of salmon with net and coble (sweeping with a net from a small boat) and with so-called 'fixed engines', that is to say, forms of anchored contraptions. These include stake-nets (set in estuaries to catch salmon moving on the tide) and bag nets. Nets are regulated according to times of day, season and position in the water.

Despite these manifold restrictions, the salmon has long been pursued by local people on the pretext that to do so is a natural right. The nineteenth-century sportsman-writer Charles St John describes one such episode of 'burning the water' replete with all the drama that characterised these community recreations. The Highlanders carried torches to see into the water. Occasionally they would plunge their pronged spears or 'leisters' into the depths, on the end of which would appear a quivering salmon. The whole performance was entered into with a spirit of eagerness and excitement, and St John reports that once he showed his enthusiasm for the sport too he was happily included in the fun. In the middle of the nineteenth century it was thought that for every salmon caught legally another was poached. Such activities were obviously contrary to the interests of the rod anglers, a circumstantial detail which may have added to the challenge.

Rod angling is worth a huge amount to the Scottish economy. At various times different bodies have attempted to quantify the value of the salmon to the economy of Scotland and widely varying figures have emerged, depending on the criteria used. A 1983 report estimated the annual worth of the Scottish rod and line fishery at £140 million, and the number of real jobs at 30,000. A report presently being undertaken by the Marine Resources Unit at Portsmouth Polytechnic is briefed to evaluate the salmon fisheries of all Great Britain. A 1989 report commissioned by the Highlands and Islands Development Board and the Scottish Tourist Board seemed not to have successfully grappled with fishing realities and extrapolated too much from a low database. One of its few illuminating findings was that fishermen came to Scotland for more than the catch: expressing deep satisfaction, most respondents had caught only one fish every three days.

Capital values of fishing have been vaulting up all through the 1980s. These are based on the average annual catch with a premium for double bank fishing, water especially suited to the fly, and a variety of pools. Gossip is generally frothy in fishing circles, but it seems probable that the Arndilly beat on the Spey fetched over £10,000 per fish in 1989. Since then, extrapolating the price paid for salmon fishing in sales incorporating other assets, it appears the figure has risen, at the top end, to around £13,000 per fish. To hazard a guess at the value of the rod and line fishery in Scotland it might not be unreasonable to put an average value on a fish of £8,000. As the catch is around 100,000 fish a year, Scottish fishing is worth £800 million — at least. It is obviously an astonishingly bountiful resource which it would be madness to impair.

Unlike the grouse shooting season which is short, and the stalking season which is used for around three months, the salmon is available for the taking somewhere in Scotland in all months except December. Big rivers like the Tay actually have salmon entering them in every month of the year. Some smaller rivers enjoy runs of salmon which lure fishermen to the extremities of Britain when no other visitors are about. The season at home on the Helmsdale opens, as do various northern rivers, as early as 11 January. Although sometimes no fish are caught during January, the beats are fished assiduously, usually by local people, everybody hoping to land the first springer of the season. Some visiting fishermen are prepared to travel hundreds of miles to brave an icy February blast and then negotiate with their ice-encrusted tackle those few parts of the river not frozen up, or where the ghillie has hacked a stream clear in the ice. The path they beat northwards is a lonely one, and their rituals might seem to have a devotional air in these days of depleted spring catches.

Only, however, to those unaware of fishing traditions and the history of British salmon runs — a favourite subject with piscatorial writers trying to read into past records patterns which explain present riddles. Spring was originally the time for salmon fishing. The spring fish arrived big, fat, and silver-fresh from the sea, took the fly like a terrier, and raced with it in impressive spirit up and down the river. The same fish by mid-summer would be more reluctant to take, softer in the flesh, redder in the skin, and weigh less. It would have developed more sedentary habits in the depths of a holding pool in preparation for the last phase of migration into the spawning burns or lochs, or the main river redds further upstream. The spring fish then, or a late-run fresh fish, was the only prize worth taking.

Very early records are given by Scrope for the river Ness, then the earliest river in Scotland. Scrope reports that the Ness never froze. This enabled fishermen to concentrate on the January, February and March run of fish. In the eight-year period 1812–1819, in each of these months over 3,000 fish were caught; the most — 3,554 — being caught in January. One assumes most of these were netted; but the figures testify to a mighty influx. Apart from a showing of grilse in August, the rest of the season was poor. The Ness is still a productive river, but I can think of no more compelling argument for a salmon cycle moving in mysterious ways than a comparison with the 1988 and 1989 January catches, nought and one respectively.

Fishing records are an imperfect indicator of the level of fish stocks because the effort put into fishing goes unrecorded, fishing skills are not easily

Spying, Gobernuisgach Forest, Sutherland.

Top: Resident wintered deer at Gaick, Invernesshire, in February. The foreground rocks are where the old lodge was situated before it was covered, with its occupants, by a landslide.

Bottom: A herd of wintering stags at Borrobol waiting for feed-time. Ben Griam in background.

Top: The head stalker uses his walkie-talkie to call up ponies on a late-season stalking day on Reay Forest, Sutherland.

Bottom: A wet day coming off the hill at Ben Armine.

Overleaf: Dragging on Lochiel Forest in October on a very wet day.

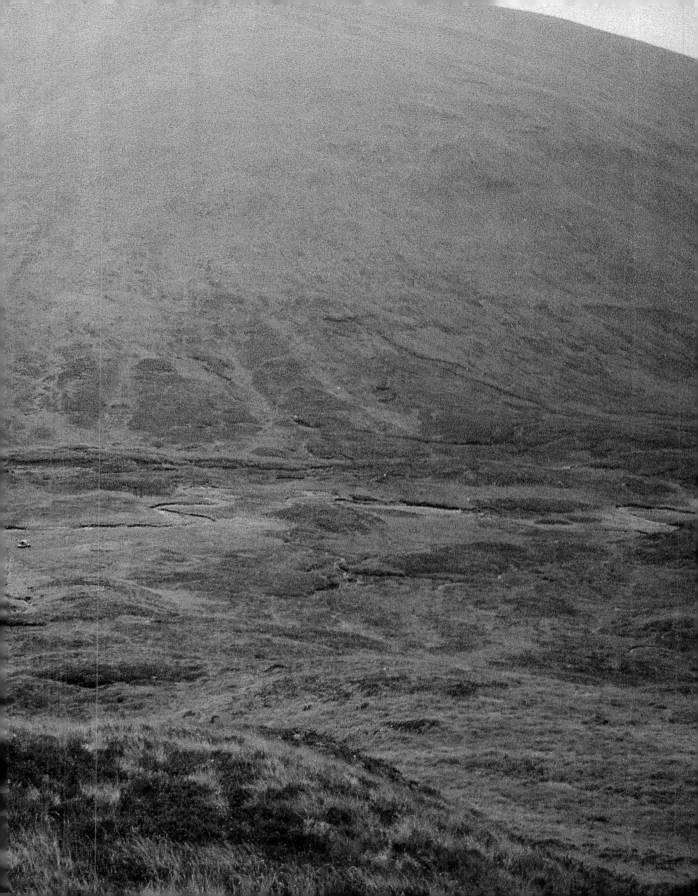

Top: Dragging a stag on Kintail, Rosshire. The National Trust for Scotland is the landlord, obliged like others to cull deer, but without sporting usage.

Bottom: Two ghillies and stalker coming home on Reay Forest. In front of the two garrons is a foal. Achfary is the village in the valley-bottom.

Top: North Country Cheviots and lambs being gathered in the Strath of Kildonan.

Bottom: Lairg sheep auction, the ewe ring in 1989. In the lamb sale 35,000 lambs are sold here in one day.

quantifiable, and many past catches are anyway unknown. It is only since 1951, when the Salmon and Freshwater Fisheries Act (Scotland) made it a statutory obligation for riparian owners and netsmen to submit data to the Department, that catch returns have been provided annually. The essential point evident from the early Ness records is that there was a substantial mid-winter run of fish which was met with considerable fishing effort. Later fish were not much bothered about, nor were the reddening fish which had been awhile in the river. This is confirmed in the Borrobol gamebooks later on in the 1880s. Two rods on the Helmsdale were recording daily catches of salmon of up to ten, occasionally over, in the months of February and March. Fewer fish were caught in spring, and by June fishing effort was sharply tailing off; by the grouse season, fishing had ceased altogether. To catch late summer or autumn fish was not thought worthwhile, in addition to which the programme on the hill was a busy one.

Comparatively recently, spring fishing has shown a decline and summer catches have begun to climb. The Department's records since 1951 show a steady decline in spring catches from both nets and rod and line, and an increase in summer catches by rod and line, with a diminishing net-catch. The graph for fishing catches by rod and line, net and coble, and fixed engines combined shows a peak in the latter half of the 1960s, with a falling off since. Total catches of over 350,000 tonnes in 1950 have fallen well below 300,000 tonnes today. The graph is very similar to that for sea-trout. However, those who sound the alarm over a short cycle of poor fishing seasons should take note of the past. As far back as 1864 fears were being expressed about the possible extinction of the salmon. Many fisheries, blighted by pollution, obstructions, improper regulation and the wholesale removal by poachers of spawning fish, had been languishing for some time. On the Tweed this had led to an alteration to fishing law by Parliamentary statute in 1857 and 1859. Entire netting stations were closed down to allow fish stocks to recover. It is amusing when reading accounts of the time to note the late nineteenth-century opinion that commerical netting on the estuary of the Tay would be worth considerably more than rod and line rents. As most fishing people will be aware, today the added value of a salmon caught by rod and line is estimated variously to be between eight and twenty times the value of a netted fish, a differential due partly to the suppression of the salmon price by farmed salmon. But then in the nineteenth century, despite having ardent advocates, salmon fishing had not assumed the position it has now as the most valuable field sport practised by the largest number of people. Although we have no figures for the number of active fishermen in Victorian times, it is interesting to note that in the lists of contemporary sporting agents the fishing possi-bilities were an added attraction, not a primary one. Gun and rifle counted more than rod and line. Although the assessments of valuations and costings a century ago are not detailed, J. G. Bertram in 1889 in *Outdoor Sports in Scotland* claims fishing rents in Scotland were worth about £110,000, and a fisherman spent an average of £2 in getting his fish. As it seems unlikely, extrapolating from this figure, that as many as 55,000 salmon and grilse were

Opposite: A lone fisherman on Loch Culag, with Suilven behind.

caught on rod and line, the figure of £2 is presumably a general expenditure item. At one and the same time the value of grouse shooting and stalking were thought, by the same author, to be worth £2.25 million and £500,000 respectively. As these last two took place over a smaller, more concentrated area, and there were fewer landlords, their figures are more likely to be realistic. Salmon fishing as a sport was very much the poor relation.

However, the fishery inspectors did record commercial salmon catches year by year. On these figures reasonably certain values can be placed. In the 1890s the English salmon fisheries were worth £140,000, the Scottish £300,000 and the Irish £500,000. The nettings were then major industries, particularly when it is remembered that over the course of the century catches had been falling due to the impacts of heedless irrigation, widespread poaching, irresponsible netting, and industrial pollution.

During this period in many big rivers in Europe and the east coast of America the Atlantic salmon was inadvertently exterminated. Nowadays a growing awareness of the importance of salmon has been marked by the formation in recent years of bodies such as the North Atlantic Salmon Conservation Organisation, to which all producer nations belong.

The place of salmon fishing in the Highland economy as a whole is highly important, and becoming more so. The days when on the Findhorn's best beat estate workers were deployed to catch salmon on rod and line, merely for their commercial value, seem a lost memory — but they were only a few years ago (the ghillies thus engaged compained of boredom!). Although historically the poor relation of grouse shooting and stalking, salmon fishing has now moved into an altogether different echelon as far as popularity and value are concerned. In the heady decade of the 1980s values of salmon rivers increased by probably six times. Millions of pounds, not thousands, are now required to buy substantial salmon water. Few estate agents dare hazard a guess at the ceiling price good fishing might realise, and the record sum paid for fishing on a per fish basis is routinely increased. The good fishing beats in Scotland could be rented five times over and, except in places where rents have escalated as fast as catches have dropped, for riparian owners it is a seller's market. The only sporting estates in the Highlands which have the potential to give a regular and respectable return on capital, special development and raw material extraction facilities aside, are those with good fishing water.

The reasons for the salmon bonanza are interesting. Salmon fishing is in vogue at a time when sociability in sport is at a premium. Although the sociable element in early spring fishing in the far north — lonely rodsmen getting obliterated from view in passing snow-showers — is questionable, as the weather grows warmer, the riverbanks in the Highlands fill up with people. Fishing is a sport at which anyone can have a go, and at which newcomers can be successful. Unlike the use of firearms, there is no intimidating bang for the uninitiated. The fact that a violent and energetic tussle can commence at any moment is not manifestly apparent. How many novice fishermen might be somewhat startled if they could see through the water, down into the stream where those patient, unblinking torpedoes lie waving in the current?

The riverbank being what it is, and possessing in itself much that is of interest, fishermen's companions find plenty to amuse themselves. The bird-life on Highland streams is much fêted. There are dippers bobbing on the stones to delight the eye, the pretty passage of nesting sandpipers and their dainty way of landing, smartly-dressed oystercatchers crying, and the mournful notes of the curlew. Summer brings the ducks fussing over their broods of vulnerable ducklings, every little one seemingly bent on drowning itself in the fast water, until they pop up at the outwash like fluffy corks.

Unlike a windy moor, the riverside invites relaxation — sprawling in the grass with closed eyes, listening to the rhythmic swish of the casting and the gurgle of water over stone. Reading, painting and story-swapping are encouraged by the soothing setting, and the prolonged lunches which have graced many fishing huts testify to the riverside's general appeal.

Few salmon fishers think or talk of fishing experiences without considering fishing ghillies. These men are a breed apart. To generalise about ghillies is rash, for they are a mixed bunch. But the Victorian sportsmen-writers established a form of stereotype when they encountered in the Highlands a taciturn, dour class of worldly-wise countrymen given to pithy witticisms and memorable rejoinders. Some of their heirs, today's ghillies, are famous names in fishing circles in their own right. In the localities they know well, their intimacy with the home river, knowledge of its salmon lies in different seasons and at different water-levels, take on an aura of almost clairvoyant perception. The best ghillies become part and parcel of the beat and an indivisible element of the enjoyment in its fishing.

Everyone has their stock of stories about fish and about ghillies. Most of the stories about ghillies go to show that although in certain conditions catching salmon is a matter of chance, or of simple perseverance, there are occasions when having the edge in skill and local knowledge makes a telling difference. This is how skilful fishermen over a long period amass far more fish than the lucky tyro. My ghillie story is intended only to suggest the tone of many others, stories which comfort the fisherman into believing if he improved sufficiently, he too would be able to defy the odds and catch testing fish.

The pool was a deep, round pot with a small overhanging cliff at the upstream corner. My fishing companion had fished it slowly and meticulously twice from the rock. Fish had been showing but not taking. As he and the ghillie crunched over the gravel at the tail of the pool, heading downstream, we all saw a fish gently break water under the cliff-wall and make a leisurely dive under the rockface again. The distance was too far for my fishing friend, so the ghillie took the rod and stripped out line, then faced into the wind. In a single cast his fly landed where the nose of the fish had shown, only to be immediately pulled below the surface by the same inquisitive customer. The pumping rod was handed to the amazed fisherman, who had been polishing up his casting technique for three days without so much as a nibble.

The good ghillie can read water and weather conditions and advise adjustments in fishing technique accordingly. The eyesight of some ghillies astounds many people, in their ability to distinguish in moving water the tell-tale movements denoting the presence of a fish. I have fished some water in which local knowledge, and this development of the art of deciphering water motions, regularly result in the fisherman with the ghillie hooking two or three times the number of fish managed by his unattended companion.

This is not entirely as surprising as one might first think. Knowledge of summer lies is clearly a great advantage in economic use of time, and the ghillies' ability to see much in the water that escapes the notice of the fisherman is often to do partly with his different angle of vision, as well as the hyper-developed visual acuity which comes from staring into water for protracted periods.

Not all rivers have ghillies in attendance and there are many places where a fisherman confronts unhelpful-looking water on his own. Just as there are fishermen gracing the river who would catch as much if they were asleep in the fishing hut, so too there are ghillies whose minds are on other things. One such man I was despatched with instructed me to start casting before we reached the water. I looked at him puzzled as he took up his position closely staring at the moving grass. Such had been his lunch-time assault on the hip-flask that he could not see where the water was. As he was an extremely nice man, I suggested I waded further in and advanced forward until we got to the water.

The argument exists that says the ghillie is an encumbrance because part of the fisherman's challenge is reading the water himself, selecting his own tackle, and generally facing up to things alone. With experienced fishers on familiar water this is probably true, although a second pair of eyes from a different angle of vision should increase the chance of seeing fish movement. However, for the huge rivers which require a boatman, and for waters such as the Grimersta in Lewis, where an extra boatman look-out is employed to scrutinise the water for signs of fish and net them when caught, salmon fishing is necessarily a team effort. The skills in holding the boat in a wind, to cross fishing water at a steady pace, are integral to success. The camaraderie this can build up in a boat on a day far away on one of those lunar-scaped lochs is half the fun. I remember a July day on one of the Grimersta lochs with the late Robert Biddulph when the centre-boat ghillie, perched on a raised plank, laughed so much at a joke embellished over the duration of the morning that he very nearly rocked himself out of the boat. And it was not one of those days there was nothing to do but laugh; we were catching fish too. On this river-system only one of the two rods in the boat fishes at a time, so just one of a team of four fishes: but the days still passed too fast.

The teamship aspect of fishing can be taken too far when a rotation of several bank fishers pass the rod from hand to hand at fixed intervals for every permissible hour of the day. Such is the pressure on productive water that this trend has crept in. For my taste it is a privilege turned into a fragmented pastime, for the pleasure in a fishing day lies too in the changes in light with the position of the changing sun, fluctuating wind, temperature and atmospheric pressure and, in short, the slow development of the day. One pool fished in the morning may be a different pool in the afternoon; fish may have moved in or out or started to break surface. Rotation fishing gives fishers the uneasy feeling that someone is at their elbow, and makes them hurry through water which should receive more careful attention. It comes into the same category as misuse of double-bank fishing when the fisher opposite throws his line far into the water beyond. It seems a pity. Regulations will no doubt develop to account for it, but it signifies the end of the days when a fisherman wandered his way peacefully down the bank looking for the right spot. If a fish rose and he tried it without success, he observed the maxims of the old writers — sit down and give the fish a rest, and try him in ten minutes. Gone are the days recalled by Osgood MacKenzie when a fisherman, Fraser of Culduthel, tired from catching fish in quick succession on the Ewe, tied a tuft of moss on his hook which a fish took straight away. He gave up in disgust, complaining about the lack of sport in it. (The same sickening from catching too many too-easyfish afflicts some British fishermen visiting Alaska today.) My father remembers bygone attitudes at the end of a spring month on the river Helmsdale when the river proprietor came down to the bank and enquired how his tenants had been doing. My father replied that he had not done well this year, whereupon the landlord airily suggested he waive the rent altogether next year — for the whole month.

Times have changed radically. Fishing is more commercial, but then many more people get a bite at the cherry. People react to the new opportunities in interesting ways. I fished as a guest on the Tay once, and arrived in the morning to a very busy scene where six fishermen were tackling up at great speed. At the appointed hour they ran to the water like famished men. The same party had fishing booked simultaneously on two other rivers. A telephone call in the evening confirmed fishing conditions, the day's catches, water levels, and so on. If it sounded encouraging they thought nothing of driving in the night to be on different water next morning, although both rivers were over two hundred miles away. Indeed, the rivers were deliberately far apart to get the maximum range of weather conditions. If they were not on the beat themselves, they had local contacts who manned the rods. As I said before, fishing can exert an unholy grip on a man.

In the recent scramble for fishing, some refinement has developed about what constitutes desirable water. This varies between individuals, being a shadow of personal character. The big-name rivers still command high rents, and for those uncertain of their path in the fishing world, fishing classic beats is a safe option — if it can be bought. Big-name rivers have big names because, by and large, they are simply the best. Outside the classic rivers and famous beats, the Highlands offer an astonishing choice of water. This is dictated by geology.

The north-south watershed of the Highlands does homage to the colossal pressures mounted on the Highland rocks by the ice ages; it meanders erratically about. In the northern Highlands the mountains are near the

Atlantic seaboard, therefore west-flowing rivers are short and fed by rain showers. On the east are the classic, slow-flowing peatland rivers, gliding down the silty straths, some of them perfectly constituted as elongated spawning beds, rivers which unhappily in recent times have been visibly disrupted by flash-flooding caused by afforestation and the absence of proper bank maintenance. Below the Great Glen the watershed bends to the east, leaving on the western side the large rivers of the western central Highlands, such as the Awe, and creating on the eastern slopes the headwaters of the long, steady, east-flowing rivers — Spey, Tay, Findhorn, Deveron, Don and Dee.

For every stretch of fishing water there is the fisherman who loves it above all others. It may have been the place he landed his first fish or where he lost his biggest fish. For one man the astonishingly dramatic beauty of the Dionard's upper waters, with perfectly natural fishing pools following one after the other, will mean more than the romantic rocky chasms of Findhorn's Darnaway beat when it is choked with springers. The magnificent hard-driving waters of the principal Spey beats offer a challenge in wading and casting, playing fish in difficult conditions, which the pastoral charms of the Thurso do not attempt to match. The diversity of these Highland waters is what makes Scotland's fishing famous.

That fishermen develop a liking for a particular beat, which rekindles happy memories in unproductive periods, is fortunate. For moving from beat to beat and river to river is a difficult thing, because of the tradition of last year's fishing tenants getting first refusal on the next year. To get on the tenancy list of a letting agent or proprietor is the first of many steps before the final one that brings you to the riverbank. The fishing fraternity, buzzing with gossip like any other, has ears constantly pricked for news of a new proprietor needing to fill his fishing weeks, or an old one getting a little shaky in his tracks. This has led to the somewhat peculiar advent of unsolicited speculative enquiries addressed to the owners of fishing by potential purchasers. Fishing rights have become, in some eyes, tradeable assets in line with stocks and shares. This has led to fishing timeshares and sometimes over-ardent efforts by proprietors to maximise their fishery's potential. When dealing with a species whose free passage in the river is a condition of its survival, this can go wrong.

A contemporary problem which also has an ancient lineage is poaching. The poaching for food of the nineteenth century was often consummated by the devouring of the fish on the spot, broiling it on the river bank. Poaching was frequently a communal act, cocking a playful snook at authority. Then, as now, the bailiffs were generally sidetracked in the night, and because poaching excursions involved large sections of the community, turning a blind eye was a common water-watcher's practice.

This type of poaching spurred by hunger was not averse to capturing red, spent and autumn fish, and probably substantially contributed to the decline in salmon numbers in the nineteenth century. Today's methods and objectives are different; commercial gain is the spur, and the fish must be in condition, if necessary taken at sea. The contemporary river poacher has no salmon-pocket sewn into the tail of his coat (William Scrope's poacher claimed the salmon had jumped in there when he was crossing the river). He operates by night in a gang, usually equipped with vehicles, walkie-talkies, and weighted nets. Pools are dragged and the fish rushed to conniving game dealers, hotels or the nearest fish market. Profits can be enormous. A Tweed poacher has recently been asked for £120,000 by the Inland Revenue in back tax owing on fish sales. A poaching mafia exists on rich salmon waters, which logs and exchanges information about salmon runs, states of different waters, bailiffs' names, addresses, car numbers, radio wave bands and so on. Sentimental attitudes about salmon poaching, which muddle contemporary poachers with empty-bellied old-timers are farcical. At the less sophisticated end of the poaching scale are the poachers who tip in poisons to de-oxygenate the water and bring groggy salmon to the surface. These operators have no regard for the river systems they exploit, the vegetation and small river life they inadvertently kill, the unwitting consumers of the fish, nor the future of the salmon. Usually, incidents involving the environmentally-destructive rat-killer Cymag are motivated by malice.

Despite strengthened legislation attempting to control the market in unrecorded salmon, there is profit in it enough to secure the intermediaries who are prepared to ask no questions about the origin of the fish they buy. Further attempts by government to introduce a salmon dealer licensing scheme have been abandoned because of the strength of objections from all those businesses, particularly salmon farmers, without whose co-operation there would have been too many loopholes to make it workable.

On some rivers poaching is such a menace that its impact on the fishery is accepted in a philosophical way by whatever fishermen can be induced to rent it, as part of the time-honoured problem of meeting the king of game fish. On the Ericht in Blairgowrie ten years ago, I saw salmon crashing round deep pots below the falls as young teenagers ripped them with big hooks on strings with all the naked bravado of their ancient predecessors. Every so often in the Highlands poaching gangs get the upper hand to such an extent it makes a scandal, and mention in the newspapers forces the police to take action (the police traditionally have given a wide berth to all poaching activities, unless directed to specific and blatant abuses). The rising value of salmon fisheries has pushed many riparian owners into protecting their hitherto unpoliced waters for long-term improvements. Poachers are loath to forego their untaxed gains, and if driven from one part of a river meet the salmon coming up in another part, or go to sea and trawl for them there. The notorious difficulties for fishery proprietors of getting successful poaching convictions are compounded when the traditional method of paying a poaching fine is to net more fish. The salmon's drop in real value, from competition by the farmed product, has taken the pressure off wild salmon from commercial poachers. This may have saved the salmon from extinction; although poaching, for a complex of reasons, is destined to persist.

One definite effect of the suppressed salmon price has been to render uneconomic traditional estuary netting stations, some of which have closed down, and many of which have been bought out (including those on the Conon, Beauly, Ness, Nairn and Findhorn) by the Atlantic Salmon Conservation Trust, a consortium which raises money by private donation to put nets out of operation. Estuary netting, for so long the cause of bitter arguments between upstream riparian owners and commercial netsmen at the river-mouth, is dying out on many rivers. On others, nets owned by riparian owners have been suspended to allow more fish for the rods. On the Spey, riparian owners recently engaged in the costly exercise of paying the nets not to operate. Some of the big commercial nets, most controversially on the Tay, are continuing, but the day is foreseeable when they too will face operating costs outweighing the value of the catch, and rod rents rising so high on well-stocked beats as to make netting illogical.

The salmon, in all its presence in the Highlands, has become an economic mainstay, conspicuously so in remote parts where sea, river and mountain stretch away in their pristine glory untouched by human endeavour. In the north-western Highlands salmon fishing is by far the largest employer (aside from salmon farming). Ghillies, hatchery employees and water bailiffs constitute the majority of people in employment in many small communities. The rod and line fisherman has become identified with the Highlands in a unique way, more strongly nowadays as the once-great rivers of England and Wales suffer a falling-off in sporting quality caused by water impurity and agricultural improvements affecting water levels. Over England's most famous river, the Wye, hangs the threat of a tidal barrage; whatever the proponents of the scheme argue, the natural run of fish will unavoidably be affected. On America's east coast, vast sums of money are being spent to reintroduce salmon driven away years ago by unwise developments, and it is baffling that in Britain we proceed gaily with projects similar to ones the Americans have regretted to their cost. Arriving in our fresh water with faithful regularity every year, providing us with sport and delicious eating, the salmon is one of the great gifts of nature that enriches the animal kingdom. The same applies to the sea trout, at present an undervalued and underused asset, particularly on rivers where its larger relation has ensnared all the fishermen's attention. To harvest a proportion of this crop we are required to provide nothing; we have only the obligation to protect the fish's environment. To fail in this would be unforgivable.

Chapter Seven
Trout

Salmon fishing may have the social cachet, it may pull in big money, but there is a breed of fishermen which scorns the opportunistic impulses of salmon fishermen, the way they flip their flies into the water and leave the stream to give them movement. They have none of the braggadocio of salmon fishers; the rough edges have been worn away by dour days on inscrutable dark lochs. These are the fishers of Scottish lochs, which are mostly in the Highlands.

The trout fisherman is a specialist of a different type, to outsiders a strange, incomprehensible figure hunched in his boat on the blackest of days, or moving along at the water's edge performing the same repetitive action, seemingly impervious to rain, squalls and the gathering chill. The truth is that he waits eagerly for poor weather, racing cloud and ruffled water, raindrops on the blank face of the water to give it movement and oxygen, fluctuating temperatures to remind trout of times to feed. The Highland trout fisherman is not after immigrating fish hunted on their helpless surge to breeding grounds; his prey is a wily resident. He cares not for gaudy salmon flies cast at fish which have ceased to feed, presented to annoy and aggravate; his flies are the delicate, often dingy, replicas of natural life, no use unless realistically and artfully presented to trick the redoubtable local on his own front doorstep. Not for the Highland trout fisher the motion of the river imparting life to the fly; rather a careful manual retrieve, not too fast, not too jerky, nor any motion that could not be natural, or reminiscent of an insect wetted by the water and trying to rise off it.

The Highland trout fisher has no ghillie as in the pre-war days; those masters of the loch environment have gone. The trout season, 15 March– 6 October, is too short; the grandiose appeal of salmon, and the richer pickings, have drawn them away. The art of wild hill loch fishing itself may be languishing. The volumes of literature left behind by pre-war Highland men testify to a concentration on this art that was impressive; some of the writers even upped sticks and moved to live on the waters that absorbed them. For trout fishing is a philosophical, very personal activity, likely to take men to places they would otherwise not go. Many of the Highland lochs are high up in hung valleys or high corries. Because it has been the pastime of less moneyed people, and the locals, there are not always roads to lochs; crossing the hill to get there is part of the anticipation; the water's promise is richer. The trout man would scorn a fishing-hut. Some of the west coast lochs are so remote that to catch the morning and evening rise you need to pack a tent to be there when those tell-tale rings appear on the water-surface. A row of fat fish on the bank, by a tent snuggled under a peat-hag, the uninterrupted mountain skyline against the crisp, bird's-egg colours of a boreal summer night, only the divers for company — the trout fisher has an experience the salmon fisher cannot know. Or perhaps, more accurately, a salmon fisher no longer knows, for pressure on space has peopled nearly all salmon waters, whereas many lochs never see a fly alight on them all season.

Trout fishing is a great leveller of men, which connects people from all walks of life who know the contentment after a day on the still waters. The arrival of the new season is heralded every year in the local press by a photograph of a small boy with a wide smile holding aloft with difficulty a leviathan of the deep, often caught in an unheard-of loch. For trout vary in size more than salmon, the species retaining the option to migrate to sea as sea-trout, and occasionally to grow to excessive size. Whilst normal fishing fare in Highland lochs is the half-pounder, the possibility exists on all but the shallowest of encountering a beast far bigger, something three feet long. Routinely, though rarely, such fish are caught, generally in April when they commence the season's feeding before spending the summer on the bottom consuming their fellows; or in September, when they range abroad once more to fill the stomach before winter. Some trout fishers attempt exclusively to catch big fish, and some of the deeper lochs, like Loch Awe, are famed for their elusive monsters, special deep-working tackle being devised to tempt them.

Trout fishing is a contemplative, thinking man's art. Knowledge of fish movements and behaviour is a prerequisite for being in the right place at the right time. The values of shoaling water on the edge of steeply shelving bottoms, shoreline coves and promontories for early-season fish, reedbeds and the middle of lochs for summer feeders — these must be understood. Identifying natural fly-life helps in selection of a fly, or the quick assembly of an imitative copy; some other fly patterns are not imitative but configured to elicit a trout's traditional fighting instinct, and a pugnacious response. Concentration cannot be allowed to flag; whereas salmon hook themselves, trout need the hook struck home an instant after they turn to dive.

Trout fishers tend to divide into boat and bank fishers. The majority use boats which take the slog out of negotiating new water on foot, and impart a natural swing to the fly as it arcs back in line with the stern. In still conditions sometimes only boat fishing is worthwhile; and boats offer the option of presenting different fly-action by trolling. Boat fishers cover more water, utilise the middle of lochs, allow fishermen to pursue awkward hooked fish from an advantageous position above, and offer those on board the invigoration of regular rowing sorties into the wind. The bank fisher, on the other hand, can cover the water more precisely, has a greater challenge playing the fish, and contents himself with the knowledge that most trout cruise near the water's edge. I have in my mind's eye a favourite picture of wading for loch trout in a book by one of the great old-time specialists. It is a grainy black and white photograph of a broad-backed man standing deep in a hauntingly bleak loch, with a steady drizzle falling from an uninflected sky. The caption reads, 'The Loch Mind'.

The big-basket trout days are mostly a memory, unless you seek out a loch which is a half a day's walk away. Most of the fish are warier now and have observed the presentation of innumerable gawky-looking flies with aroused suspicions. In my grandfather's gamebook he casually recalls several hundred-plus days on Sutherland lochs. The same lochs would not offer so many fish now, although they might be larger. Present day trout fishers who score well are not the lucky lads of yesteryear who struck a free-taking loch on a good day; they generally know their water well and have winkled these fish out against the odds. The disparity in success between one fisher and another on the same loch is marked. My loch at Borrobol is let, along with two holiday cottages, and the tenants record their weeks in the fishing book. It must be a matter of chagrin and puzzlement to the newcomers failing to catch fish to read of the carefully detailed lists of fish caught the week before their arrival. Reluctantly they acknowledge that conditions have not measurably changed. I know of one ardent trout man, not a day under sixty-five years old, who will regularly catch thirty to forty trout in April when the next chap along will swear nothing has started to move and there are no fish taking. Yet both will be using the fly.

On the cream of Scottish trout lochs, the limestone lochs of the north-west, the gap between good and less good fishermen is crucial. On this eerily pellucid water a false cast, too heavy nylon or fly, the boat turning to throw a shadow from the sun behind it, these will be fatal misdemeanours. The abundance of food produced by the rich bedrock means fish can afford to be choosy. In the clear water you can watch the trout watching the fly, assessing its credentials before, with a doubtful glance, turning meditatively away. Lochs in this class do not need to be big to have big trout; little Loch Lawlish is the size of an athletics ground.

Considering the universal appeal of the trout lochs, it is surprising that not more use is made of them. Most are on sporting estates; those attached to fishing hotels, generally in the north-west and northern Highlands, are run with care. The usual level of management, however, is the act of putting a boat on the loch. Populations are not monitored, vermin are not controlled (it is thought that seagulls' droppings have a chain-role to play in some trout diseases), the water quality and weed growth are not monitored nor improved when necessary (done by careful lime applications). Trout lochs with innumerable tiny trout have merely suffered from an endless subdivision of the available food supply. Management exercises such as netting, which has the advantage that you can abstract the exact quantity required from the exact place necessary, are rare. Treatment of lochs is too often lazy and exploitative. Where restocking has occurred, it has frequently caused long-term problems because instead of developing home-bred stock, thoughtless managers have bought discounted surplus trout farm stock, effectively messing about with an evolutionary process dating from the last Ice Age. Unlike with the artificial introduction of young salmon there is no rigorous, long-haul migration to force out, by natural selection, poor types. A loch is a sensitive organism and every alteration affecting its catchment or its main body of water should be carefully considered. Many lochs have indeed benefited from being stocked by our keen sporting forebears, but we lack a record of their condition before, and changes in our atmospheric climate and the spread of forestry have heightened the threshold of critical response in the fragile freshwater ecosystems. Precipitate actions should be avoided.

In an age when peace and leisure are at a premium, it might seem strange that in many parts so little attention has been paid to this fecund recreational resource. The primary reason for neglect is legal. It is a sad anomaly that trout fishing is not a property right in Scotland. Technically, anyone may fish as they please for trout during the open season; not long ago there was not even a close season. Naturally, there is a disincentive to improve a fishing loch if anyone may show up and use it. The spirit of the law, and tradition, are at variance with the legal position. In practice, a natural right entitles the loch owner to charge a rent and to substantiate this he usually provides a boat. It is rare for visiting fishermen to disregard this tradition. Trouble has only occurred when coachloads from the cities have materialised on the water's edge and, equipped with otter-boards, baits and nets, have hauled out fish in commercially useful quantities and left the loch bereft. Lochs near main roads have suffered from this treatment and it has never been legally resisted. Trout fishing's absence of proper status has meant that their preservation has never been a matter of consideration when land uses which damage them, such as forestry, are discussed.

The 1976 Freshwater Fisheries Act provided a sort of legal protection in the form of Protection Orders. These are granted on a case by case basis by the Secretary of State for Scotland, but only to entire catchment areas, not individual lochs (unless one loch monopolises a catchment). The process of acquiring Protection Orders can be laborious, agreement needing to be sought from many individuals. Furthermore, financing the fisheries' protection remains in the hands of the proprietors themselves, and the small revenues raised from loch rents seldom warrant policing. The time will surely come when fishing rights for trout will be recognised as they are in England and Wales. The purpose of the original exemption of trout from fishing law was to provide local people with access to the resident fish. In the days of mass tourism and full-scale violation of lochs, this is outmoded. The trout fishery is a national asset requiring automatic protection and regulation, and deserving of thorough research to facilitate sensible management. The salmon has monopolised public attention to the detriment of its freshwater relation.

A fish that has barely impacted at all on anyone's attention is the interesting Ice Age relic, the char. Originally a sea-running or anadromous fish, the British char is now only found in fresh water. The char is more common than is realised, and it is known to occur in 170 lochs in northern Scotland and the Western Isles alone. Although characteristically living deep down at the bottom of lochs, char are to be found in surprisingly shallow lochs also. They surface to feed by night at certain times of the year, being otherwise adapted for dark, deep waters. Char vary markedly in body proportions and colour, a characteristic observed long ago, which has led to speculation about the number of char types. Scientists at the Freshwater Fisheries Laboratory in Pitlochry have now proved that in Loch Rannoch two distinct types co-exist and intermingle. The scientists' speculation that almost certainly physical and chemical influences in Scottish lochs will have already depleted individual strains of char and reduced diversity is disquieting; char have disappeared from some Scottish lochs within recent time (e.g. Loch Leven).

Few char are caught by fishermen and usually only by accident. The serious char-man does exist, though perhaps his arcane practices might be looked on with bafflement by trout fishers. He sits in a boat on a deep loch winding out baited tackle from a huge drum of line. If he locates successfully the level where the char are pursuing their mysterious purposes, a jigging motion might result in the arrival in the boat of a strangely beautiful crimson-striped fish with large, light-gathering eyeballs. The char fisherman's reward is most toothsome.

The closer the inspection of a trout loch, the more the interesting and varied fauna is revealed. Eels are almost ubiquitous in trout lochs, except those located at altitude. It is a sobering thought that in one loch might co-exist for a short time a salmon travelled from Greenland's seas and eels born in the tropical Saragossa. For those who believe Scottish loch waters to be acid and sterile, it is worth recording this: Loch Lomond contains thirteen species of freshwater fish, including its unique freshwater herring, the powan, and eight brackish water fish, in addition to migratory salmon and sea trout. For those inclined to fishing specialisations there is ample choice, and the local Loch Lomond angling club has over 800 members.

At a time when, in England, leisure fishermen circle a small put-and-take pond converted from a disused gravel-pit, and pay handsomely for the privilege of yanking out a guileless hatchery-bred nurse-fed fish, and when more accessible lochs, like Loch Leven, have been squared off into beats and fished in short rotas, it seems amazing that so much Highland water goes unutilised. The wild trout multiply undisturbed, and unappreciated, feeding the water with their decaying remains, or nourishing the occasional diver or osprey. It can be looked on as a wasted resource — or as a comforting thought — that even in our crowded islands, man's impact is far from universal. It depends on your point of view.

Chapter Eight
Other Activities

The moors and hills possess what contemporary European man needs above all other things — space. The impression given by England and Wales is of a congested, bulging island covered, if not smothered, by higgledy-piggledy developments and a physical expansion which is pushing at the limits of the coast-line. The few remaining open spaces like Dartmoor, Snowdonia and the Lake District, are so over-utilised that consideration is being given in the national parks to limiting access by numbers. Already ramblers' pathways and hill-climbing routes have been trodden so relentlessly that peat moorland has been pulverised to a mush on the Pennines and erosion of the actual rockface is causing problems on Snowdon. South of the Scottish border, the British have acclimatised themselves to taking their country air in multitudes, in a landscape criss-crossed by insect-like trains of gaudy anoraks. It is interesting to note that novel outdoor sports develop ways of using the places where open space can still be found — the air above us and offshore. Nobody in Britain is too distant from the coast. Microlighting, hang-gliding, sail-boarding and surfboarding all utilise parts of our spatial environment which are relatively uncluttered.

In the context of overcrowding, the Scottish hills have much to offer. Scotland's population is small by European standards and almost entirely urban. Excepting the belt, now zoned for amenity forestry, between Edinburgh and Glasgow, there is little of Scotland which qualifies for the term applicable to most of England — suburban. The capital of the Highlands is Inverness which, despite its very rapid growth, would still rank in the south as a small town. The Highland area otherwise is remarkable in modern European terms for its extremely low population, nowhere nearby being so sparsely populated until you reach Scandinavia. The emptiness of the Scottish hills and the smallness of their few communities is one of the reasons that the big conservation battles of the 1980s were focused here. Contests between developers and conservationists are already scheduled over several projects in the 1990s. This spaciousness has been a determinant factor in Highland land use since the agrarian changes which started in the eighteenth century, and is the key ingredient in some of the lesser-known activities going on in the Highlands. One of these curiosities is falconry.

If hunting deer has an old royal lineage, falconry has a much older one. In the east, falconry was flourishing in many cultures before the Christian era, and it was practised in Britain by the Saxons and reinvigorated by the arrival of the Norman nobles. King Robert the Bruce had a falcon-house at Cardross in Dunbartonshire, and James III of Scotland made the protection of hawks general in 1474, and the capture of wild hawks a severely punished crime. By the reign of King James I of England (James VI of Scotland), falconry was the principal diversion of monarchs on both sides of the Channel, for Louis XIII was an enthusiast too. Hawks were worth astounding sums of money, up to £1,000. A statute of 1621 increased the fine for stealing a hawk from £10 up to £100, an indicator of the pre-eminent position of the sport. Gentlemen only were allowed to practise it; and the species of hawk carried by the falconer was indicative of the rank of the owner.

The Civil Wars put an end to the general popularity of falconry which had such close associations with the monarchy. The advent of the gun ended falconry's monopoly of game bird hunting, but the late nineteenth century, with its spirit of refreshed vigour and out-of-door stimulations, stirred a revival which carries through to today. Gone are the exotic days of heron and crane hawking (imagine the outcry if they were revived!), and present-day falconers find as testing a quarry as any in the red grouse on the moors.

The ideal terrain for falconry is, as it happens, also the place where it can be incorporated without undue trouble into other uses of the hill. The modern falconer, anxious as ever about the loss of his valuable birds, wants undulating moorland with good open vistas so that he can mark a bird that flies far off or decides to fly away completely. The upland moors of Sutherland and Caithness, with their smooth curving slopes and gentle gullies, answer perfectly to this description.

Large numbers of grouse are not required, and on populous grouse moors shooting rents will outdo those of falconers. The hawk only takes one bird at a time and the procedure of getting a hawk into the air above grouse, flushing the birds, and retrieving the falcon takes time. The spatial requirements of falconers depend on the quality of the hunting birds. Young, inexperienced birds behave unexpectedly and may fly off. Falconers then need a free passage over the hills to trace them, by their electronic bleepers, to where they have landed. The falconers I have encountered have always expressed themselves happy to operate on a corner of a grouse-moor, perhaps on an area of no more than 4,000 acres. They usually set up camp in a nearby house for one or two months, getting their birds fit and strong, and used to the conditions, while the grouse too wax stronger over August and September. An outbuilding can easily be adapted for the birds, which spend the night sitting on their perches wearing hoods.

The appeal of falconry is easy to understand. It is the development of the point of interaction between man and bird taken to its ultimate refinement. The use of pointing dogs to flush grouse adds extra satisfaction to this exhilarating relationship between wild instinct and civilised control. First of all the falconers patrol the moor with their dogs to detect sitting grouse and get a point. The dog has to hold the point patiently while the bird is unhooded, 'thrown off', and encouraged by the falconer to gain height. The hawk rises in circles, mounting the air, while the falconer holds its attention by swirling a falconer's leather gauntlet. When the bird is high enough, the dog is commanded to rush in on the point, flushing the birds from cover.

Without a good following wind the grouse can outfly the peregrine, with the result that only two to four grouse are killed in a good day. The object of hawking is a good swoop, followed by a breakneck chase and good clean kill. Despite the peregrine's ability to swoop at speeds estimated at over 150 mph, the grouse is quite able to jink and outmanoeuvre its opponent; and once the velocity of the swoop is spent the grouse is the quicker flier. The instant of excitement in falconry is sudden and thrilling, as bird follows the tail of bird, linked for a second like two zapping space invaders, until the peregrine strikes or the grouse streaks away.

The ideal time for falconry on a grouse-shooting moor is after the first two or three weeks of intensive shooting, using the hawks in a mopping-up operation to pick off weak or erratic birds. Falconry obviously runs counter to the old keepering principles; introducing predators deliberately to the moors is something few keepers will automatically sympathise with. The falconers' argument is that hawks tend to take the odd bird out in a covey, the last to get up, or the one that breaks sideways. This is frequently a weak or injured bird. Therefore, falconers contend that hawking benefits the moor by removing surplus stock. Certainly, when I rented part of the ground to falconers at Borrobol, the moor was adequately stocked at season's end and the stock in good condition the following year. The worries that I had had, and many keepers and lairds still have, that hawks will clear the ground, scare birds, and decimate breeding stocks, proved false. The peregrine, unlike the eagle or harrier, will not shift populations of grouse in a way detrimental to the shooting. Shooting, however, remains the basic control of numbers on grouse moors and no falconer would suggest that hawks take off adequate birds on moderately-stocked moors.

In this way, and on odd corners of the moors, falconry can provide an excellent diversification, and a source of revenue from grouse in late autumn at no real cost to the stock. Using experienced birds, competent handlers should cause no inconvenience to stalking parties on other parts of the hill. In the unlikely event of a bird flying off and bisecting a stalking operation at a critical moment, falconers tend to make a bee-line for their bleeping signal and invaluable bird quite regardless — a temporary annoyance generally out of proportion to their usefulness. A little compromise and understanding can go a long way on the open hill; relations between falconers and shooting or stalking parties run more smoothly with familiarity. The falconers who visit or live in Scotland tend to be a close fraternity from mixed backgrounds, including a smattering of Europeans. Prominent newspaper stories of peregrine chick thefts and huge values of stolen or smuggled hawks, sometimes blackening the name of falconers by association, are mostly inaccurate baloney. In the real world of dedicated falconers birds tend to be given away, not bought.

Of course there are many human uses for the amenities offered by the Highlands. Field sports, fishing and falconry are only one type of activity, a form that involves men and women in the remorseless wheel of nature, one species living off the dynamic of another. In the Highlands ecosystem, only the red deer has no non-human predator, excepting the occasional capture of calves by eagles and foxes, and man, in this ecosystem of his own making, has to trim excess numbers. The sporting man is sometimes perceived as a rapacious and intensive predator — a false view. Sportsmen study the objects of their pursuit and grow familiar with their ways. To do so successfully requires careful observation, immersion in their environment, and an imaginative understanding of how they live and thrive in aspects which simple observations cannot illumine. Sporting man regains his evolutionary roots as a predator, a different thing from reverting to barbarism, because the ethic of sport is that in the chances of escape or evasion the odds must lie with the quarry. If the aim was to kill wildlife, the use of modern technology would make meeting it simple — but unsatisfying. The sportsman observes unwritten or agreed rules of engagement, ensuring that success is worth winning, and that the quarry, a core-population of which must survive, will go off and multiply. (When hunting has been for sport this has always been the case. Since the Middle Ages strict laws circumscribing hunting methods ensured the contest was fair and protected the habitat of the hunted.) The need for a healthy population balance enlists the sportsman as a front-line conservationist. If his quarry is threatened, so is his sport, and the special relationship with the quarry. If sport did not exist, our understanding of game birds and mammals, and the ecological pyramid, would be infinitely poorer; and red deer and salmon would have almost certainly died out, along with the other redundant species that have already gone.

It is a well-rehearsed point in England that game management has effectively determined much of the woodland-dotted landscape of today. This is the case in Scotland also, though less manifestly. Without grouse shooting, heather moorland would have diminished severely or disappeared. The dictates of sheep farming, or rather the needs of sheep farming as then understood, led to widespread and repeated heather burning in the western Highlands which over two hundred years has virtually obliterated heather altogether. The hills are green and the grouse have gone. The values of heather as a universal winter food, and snowstorm shelter, were unappreciated then, and grouse shooting never dictated moorland management as it did in the eastern Highlands. This habitat loss is irreversible.

Without salmon in the rivers there would have been no brake on the proliferation of hydroschemes, industries pumping out untreated effluents, irrigation schemes washing silt into rivers, or afforestation of river banks and spawning catchments. Without protection from poachers, salmon would have been rapidly wiped out, and the need to understand water tables, hydrology and natural springs, and the ecology of rivers would not have arisen in time to put in place today's more environmentally sensitive restrictions. Sportsmen's interest in the fish led to its economic importance, which decided measures for its conservation. In the meantime, we have discovered that the conservation of salmon and also deer, trout and grouse has a beneficial effect over an entire environment. The contribution of sporting interests to the preservation of the Highlands should not be overlooked. The removal of sport could lead to a single purpose forestry land-use, not in the best interests of the general environment.

To project the Highlands as a sportsman's preserve would be ridiculous. Of course, the majority of summer visitors are not sport-orientated; only a proportion of them. The Highlands is an area renowned primarily for its scenery, and most visitors come mainly or partially for quiet contemplation of beautiful countryside. Though most of us would agree about what constitutes beauty in scenery, few would wish to quantify its value. Enjoyment of the view contributes to nobody's local taxes and creates no employment. But the Highlands and their power to please have a meaning and value which are cherished long after the view has faded from sight. As a holidaymaker put it: 'In the south it gives us a good feeling just to know the Highlands is there.' The importance of this renowned scenic area reaches not only those who visit it, but also those who are comforted to know they can do, and it will still be the same. For the English landscape has changed in many places beyond recognition and the Highlands, on the whole, has not. The psychological need of many people to anchor childhood experiences in a country setting has focused often on the Scottish hills. The power of the hills to place us once more back in our humble evolutionary niche is subtly recognised. The sense of freedom is more pronounced there.

Chapter Nine
Forestry

A sense of freedom is not something to be found in conifer plantations. Conifer plantations provide a differing habitat for humans at different stages of growth. No-one is immune to the cathedral-like serenity of very large fir trees, and the peaceful and restful magic afforded to those strolling along the mossy cushion of their forest floors. As the sun filters through the airy crowns and slants between the tremendous boles, the forest provides a beautiful quiet unlike any other.

However, British conifer growing policy does not provide this type of woodland, least of all in the Highlands. Evergreens are being grown on shorter and shorter rotations, now sometimes truncated to thirty-five years. Forestry plantations in Scotland have generated a bad press and stirred public hostility, partly because they have been planted in enormous unrelieved blocks, girdling the hills in dark aprons. Walking in them is often found to have a depressing, rather than stimulating, effect. Forestry bodies are prone to boast of their numbers of visitors. The truth is that some people walk in forests just because roads, signposts and picnic areas are provided. If these were on the open hill, they would more happily walk there. The greater popularity of the mountain routes shows this.

The main land use issue for the Highlands is the spread of forestry, and where the balance of a sufficient planted area lies. Disputes about hydroschemes, mountain railways and ski runs are local issues; afforestation affects the whole area, north-south and east-west. Also it is a long-term issue. The conifers, once planted, remain *in situ* for thirty-five to sixty-five years, assuming they are not blown over. After that, the ground is seldom suitable for anything but replanting. Recreating heather moorland or flow ground from the jumbled landscape of tree-stumps and wagon tracks is out of the question. A policy to plant up the Highlands with conifers is effectively a once-and-for-all decision. Afforestation is a long-term option which also carries long-term obligations, a rarely raised point. When today's young plantations reach felling stage, a huge mileage of small Highland roads will need upgrading in order to take extraction vehicles. The cost will be mind-boggling and has never been calculated.

The modern history of afforestation in Scotland begins with the formation of the Forestry Commission (FC) in 1919. Its remit was to make good losses of timber in the First World War. However, the wartime toll of timber, amounting to around half a million acres, was substantially of deciduous or 'broadleaf' trees, the type of tree with which most people are in sympathy. The FC replacement crop fell far below its stated proportion of broadleaves and concentrated on faster-growing softwoods or conifers. The argument that Britain needed a strategic reserve of trees was abandoned in 1957 after the report of the Zuckerman Committee pointed out the new terms of warfare. The new rationale for forestry was to boost employment in rural areas and mitigate the cost of wood-product imports. To these two justifications in recent years has been added the concept that forestry must be planted to satisfy the needs of newly-established wood-processing plants. Forestry bodies have even spoken of forestry being a form of conservation, which is duplicitous.

Britain presently has forest cover of over three and a half million acres, the broadleaf proportion of which, a seventh, is almost all in England. Two-thirds of this whole afforested area lies in Scotland. A very large area of the Scottish Lowlands has been planted up, and there are large parts of Argyll, Caithness, the Inner Hebrides and Perthshire which will be permanently under trees from now on. In some recent years, over ninety per cent of new planting has taken place in Scotland. Forestry is very much a Scottish matter, in recognition of which the FC's headquarters have been moved to Edinburgh. Government statements made in 1988 revealed that forestry was going to become more a Scottish matter than ever with the announcement of restricted planting aims in the English uplands, and the restatement of Scotland as the targeted forestry zone for the future. Environmental, scenic, agricultural, wildlife and rambler objections, backed up by the national parks system (absent in Scotland), had made planting more of England a political hot potato. Scotland, despite the heat generated by the flow country debate, was seen as a far easier pitch on which to satisfy the demands of the national planting programme. Most suitable land in the Lowlands already being under trees, the focus narrowed again and it became clear then that the area zoned for planting was the Highlands. The Highlands as a target area has the advantage that there is a very small local population, environmental pressure groups can be stigmatized as outsiders denying local people jobs, and land users in the Highlands suffer from lack of a concerted purpose, caused by the area's bitter history.

The argument about the rights and wrongs of forestry is complex and easily polarised into inadequate simplifications. Forestry in itself is neither a good nor a bad thing; it is a matter of where trees are planted, at what cost to other land uses, what species of tree is planted, how the plantation is configured, what short-term purposes the forest will serve, what possible processing industries might eventually be supplied, and who is going to plant the trees. The history of twentieth-century planting in the Highlands has so often been a sad one. Whilst establishing perfectly good plantations in parts of Argyll and in the Great Glen, the FC in the early days also made some horrendous mistakes, mistakes which people today are obliged to live with. Monocultures of trees were planted in enormous unrelieved blocks, without any regard to landscaping, the natural relief of the hills, deer management within or on the fringe of the woodlands, or timber extraction in the future. Deliberate ringing and killing of native oak woods, now a cherished environment, sometimes paved the way for conifers. Some locations certainly, such as the degenerated stock pastures in Argyll, were best suited to tree cover; others were not and have been problematical ever since.

One of the FC's problems was that the new conifer species had never been grown in Britain through a full rotation and established satisfactorily second time round. The fast-growing tree species favoured were of foreign, usually west Canadian, provenance. Growing them in Britain was a gamble, a gamble which the private sector too was encouraged to undertake. Unlike Scotland's native conifer, the Scots pine, sitka spruce (now Scotland's commonest tree) and lodgepole pine are both vulnerable to dangerous pests. Most of Wales has on and off been subjected to restrictions on the movement of spruce affected by spruce bark beetle; future effects could become very serious. Pine beauty moth caterpillars strip the needles of lodgepoles and have wiped out large tracts of trees close to home at Rimsdale in Sutherland. The effect is extraordinary — ghostly white rows of dead trees criss-crossing the rest of the plantation and marking the stands of defunct lodgepole. Pine beauty moth is still spreading and threatens all lodgepoles. The insect is present at low levels on every lodgepole site, and emerges in suitable conditions in March and April to multiply. The tree is vulnerable at all early stages of growth and a lodgepole plantation owner lives in constant dread of losing his entire investment in a few months. Plantations near outbreak areas are uninsurable, making lodgepole plantation owners guinea-pigs in the ultimate sense. Chemical spraying by air is an option, but it is very expensive, does not guarantee the pest's elimination, employs a chemical with unknown side-effects, and might require repeating a few years later. In addition to all these horrors, lodgepoles grow crookedly, are prone to windthrow and produce low-grade timber worth less than other softwoods. All in all, the lodgepole grower is not a man to be envied.

On top of these problems, twenty more years of silvicultural studies have unearthed evidence that the poorer peatlands on which lodgepoles were predominantly planted might well, in retrospect, have supported a mix, including the more valuable spruce. Future research may indicate that other mixtures would have been preferable; attention is now turning to birch. Twenty years after my plantation at Borrobol was established, I discovered much of it features the wrong tree. Wrong advice will cost me dearly, although at the time it mirrored conventional forestry wisdom. Softwood plantations of the type described are a pioneer crop in Britain. It is seldom pointed out that the burden of risk falls on private individuals.

Another of the risks in conifer-growing in the Highlands is from gales, resulting in what foresters call windthrow. This came up as a conspicuously weak link in the forestry companies' argument during the flow country debate in the mid 1980s. In the flow country, trees are usually planted on the tops of turned-over peaty furrows; they therefore have a higher wind profile than ground level plants. The north of Scotland is, in any case, one of the windiest places in Europe, and historically big gales have flattened the trees with monotonous regularity. The Scots pines behind the lodge at Borrobol have been blown over three times since it was built in 1900. This is at three hundred feet above sea-level. The forestry company responsible for planting in the flows is inserting its little bobbing saplings at nine hundred feet and over. Such is the heedless rush to get acres under plantation that trees are being planted even in the areas of worst windthrow hazard as zoned by the FC. No local people I have talked to believe these trees will ever require felling. Gales like that of January 1968, in which 20,000 acres of trees were knocked down in one small corner of Scotland, will see to that. Evidently, other forestry companies share this pessimistic view, for only one out of the four main investment companies buys land in the flow country, the others concentrating on higher-quality sheltered sites in other parts.

The windthrow hazard classification has a further implication for management. It becomes dangerous to thin out trees. If they are to stand at all, the best way is propping each other up. The days of first, second, even third thinnings before final clearfelling, in the tradition of classical silviculture, are long gone in the Scottish uplands. The FC itself has adopted a no-thin policy in windthrow sensitive areas. Once the wind is allowed in through the thicket of needles it wreaks havoc with trees that have stretched upward fast on shallow rootings. Dates of clearfelling have been brought forward to thirty-five year rotations. Efforts to produce high-grade mature stands of timber have been foregone. It has correctly been pointed out that much conifer growing is becoming similar in type to any other agricultural crop. The ground is prepared and ploughed, fenced and fertilised, vermin is killed out, and the crop of cellulose is harvested all at once, where possible by enormous tree harvesting combines. This form of forestry is more accurately described as tree-farming.

There is nothing inherently wrong in regarding conifers as a crop of giant vegetables. But it would surely be unwise to sacrifice the remainder of the Scottish uplands to a single-purpose use unless there were compelling reasons to do so, reasons sufficiently compelling to outweigh the benefits already described from a mix of sporting use and farming; and the benefits for bird-watchers, archaeologists, hillwalkers, botanists, campers, mountain climbers and scenery lovers. Exactly what is this pressing need to substitute for these mixed land uses a single one?

The original object of conifer planting, to replace the strategic reserve consumed in wartime, is obviously gone. Timber substitutes such as plastic have gone a long way to reduce wood product needs. The forestry bodies point to our timber imports, at nearly nine-tenths of requirements. It is a spurious argument. Britain is presently a large user of timber and will remain an importer of timber regardless of how much is planted. The optimum planting ambitions of forestry companies would result in reducing our dependence on imports by a few percentage points and only at the end of the crop several generations hence. Even in the Scandinavian economies, where tree-growing and processing is the cornerstone industry, second rotation tree establishment has been problematical, and entire processing plants have been constructed for recycling wood products.

Then there are the dark prophetic warnings about future timber shortages, a world in which suddenly wood product values rocket as supply runs out. These have proved consistently exaggerated. In 1969 the FC predicted timber consumption in Britain rising to sixty million cubic metres by 1980: the actual figure was about half that. A 1977 FC timber consumption forward estimate was thirty per cent too high after only eight years.

Predictions about forward markets have been frequently askew. There is an obvious difficulty in anticipating a market as far off as sixty years hence, and the more changes in the timber market in the last half-century are contemplated, the more awesome the difficulty becomes. Substitutes can be invented, the products served by timber can disappear, and timber waste can be reduced. Woodland owners in England who were advised and grant-aided by the FC to grow poplars for matchsticks twenty years ago have recently found this to their cost. At the end of the rotation no market at all exists. The timber is bad for burning and most poplar growers are lucky to get the wood cleared at no cost. The financial loss, compounding interest and inflation, is grotesque.

A favourite forestry argument has been to compare the small woodland area as a percentage of Britain with that of France and Germany. Why our woodland area, in a much smaller country, should equate to theirs is unexplained. We have less suitable land available, and more prime agricultural soil. In any case, a third of the plantable uplands in Scotland already carries trees, a percentage on a par with the most densely wooded countries on the Continent. In a sensible world, target planting levels would be guided by the agreed aims of a land use policy for the hills, and trimmed at the point of disrupting or destroying other land uses. At present the government periodically announces target planting levels without reference to how they are to be met. The 1987 target of 81,000 acres, like its predecessors, was not reached. Forestry investors, despite the huge planting grant incentives, remain obdurately sceptical.

The forestry companies have made much noise about mixed land use, certainly a fine objective. Mixed land uses are generally attractive and in the Highlands, with their limited fertility, particularly applicable for the preservation of a delicate environment. The problem with forestry is that it takes land absolutely for itself. If planted in large blocks there is no mix; this fact cannot be sidestepped. Yet the 1988 budget made it perfectly clear, by raising the grant levels far more generously for the largest blocks (over twenty-five acres), that blanket afforestation is to be encouraged. This is quite incompatible with a mixed land use. Carefully sited forestry provides shelter and can enhance other land uses on occasions, although normally tree growers demand the land best suited for farming, shooting or deer wintering. The requirements of good soil and shelter suit trees and mammals equally.

The contradictions between utterances about mixed land uses and the practice of monopolising the good land areas might appear strange until, studying the smaller print of FC pronouncements, it becomes apparent that the word 'sport' is often missing from its short list of other land uses. The use of the uplands for grouse shooting, deer stalking, and fishing rivers and lochs, is apparently not recognised. The only competing land uses which are recognised are hill farming and conservation, which is not a land use in itself but an enlightened broad approach with which to regulate specific land uses. Farming, then, is the only obstacle perceived by forestry bodies lying between them and their planting plans for the remainder of the uplands.

The non-mention of sport is significant. For as the NCC and the RSPB realised during the flow country debate, sporting use provides the best possible argument against more afforestation. Sheep farming, subsidised, moving towards the status of a surplus producer within Europe, with failing financial returns, guilty over the years of chronically reducing much hill herbage by overgrazing, and in any case shifting from the hills onto grass fields vacated by dairy herds, is a feeble barrier against the tree growers. Sporting use, on the other hand, from the conservationists' viewpoint, had a great deal in its favour. It provided employment, recreation, a discipline of moorland management, considerable cash injections from outside the community, and abstracted from the countryside a sustainable yield without damage to the scenery. No wonder FC officials make no mention of accommodating sporting land use. Furthermore, large scale plantations are a threat to the survival of sporting use.

Firstly, the ground that is planted is, characteristically, the slopes below 1500 feet which the deer use in winter. Forestry plantations stretching in an apron round the foothills not only physically steal from deer their wintering areas and winter feeding, they also not infrequently block off access to alternative feeding and shelter lower down in valley bottoms. Indeed the present crisis-size of many east Highlands deer populations is due to their being fenced out of traditional wintering areas. In search of winter sustenance they have pushed outwards into unfamiliar parts. Forestry is certainly incompatible with an unchanged open hill deer population.

It is even more incompatible with grouse shooting use. Upland forestry is generally suited to the ground used for grouse shooting, the heather-covered belt below the high tops and above regenerated grazing pasture and hill parks. In addition to supplanting grouse habitat, forestry has an effect outwith its perimeter fence, and a punishing one. The trees act as a sanctuary for the species which prey on grouse — foxes and crows. It is difficult to find foxes in thickets of young conifers, or crows' nests. Foxes and crows then use the open hillside as an adjacent larder for their hunting. The Game Conservancy has reckoned forestry sterilises for game management an area two-thirds its size all around it. The presence of the trees also means heather-burning nearby is difficult, if not impossible. The presence of a forestry-block means in practice the abandonment of moorland management and moorland use for grouse shooting in the area surrounding it. I have found this to be true at Borrobol, where numerous fox droppings testify to fox densities amongst the trees. On a hill which traditionally supported more grouse than any other on the estate, the half that is not afforested has barely any resident birds. This is despite an effort, involving considerable risk, of getting it properly burnt. Whether grouse stocks near forestry are decimated by predators, or whether the grouse simply move elsewhere is unsure. However, ornithologists have shown that other species such as moorland waders instinctively shy away from the edges of afforestation, presumably for sound security reasons. The sterilisation effect of forestry has the further impact of making areas which gradually get surrounded by trees unfit for any use except planting. In this way forestry plantations have a domino effect on other land uses.

If the effects of afforestation on Highland fisheries are not literally exclusive, as they are for grouse and red deer, they are certainly insidious and serious. As regards salmon fisheries, afforestation may have thoroughly damaging effects on water catchments, hydrology, water purity and water tables. For the value of peat moorland as a water-retentive sponge which slowly releases water down through the watershed has great significance for fish. A regulated flow with an even water level suits fish best. On the Grimersta river system in Lewis, which has been called the best Atlantic salmon fishery in the world, the water-table is almost flat, spreading far away on each side to a low horizon, and fed at the top end by the huge loch waters of Langavat, which is beneath a high rain-catching mountain. Levels in the Grimersta river and its lochs move almost imperceptibly, the peaty unirrigated plains providing the steady drip of an even water supply. The very reverse is evident in short, west Highland spate rivers, water coursing down the rockfaces and converting a sluggish stream into a raging torrent in a few hours. Salmon run these spate rivers when they feel the rising water and drop out to sea again if the rivers dry up.

Afforestation of watersheds increases the tendency of a river to spate, and makes conditions for fish unstable. In the bad old days, forestry ploughs excavated their furrows straight up and down hillsides. Rain poured down the furrows in a torrent, not only rapidly raising river levels below but playing havoc with mineral and sediment outwashes. These swilled down the mountainsides, crashed into the rivers, and spread out in the riverbed, obliterating clean, gravelly spawning beds and filling in fish-lies. Heavier spates pushed this siltation further down water-courses, extending the damaged area. The FC's acknowledgement of the damage early hill plough- ing did to Scottish rivers is implicit in its new advisory codes on environ- mental afforestation with regard to water. Scarifying (breaking the ground) is recommended instead of ploughing, where possible. Furrows and drains, as shallow as possible, are to stop short of water-courses and debris is to be trapped by sumps. Rivers are not to be overshadowed by trees nor disturbed by forestry roads running too close. Trees are not to be felled into them and banks are to be maintained with vegetation. There is an overall emphasis on protecting the stream from damage. Other organisations have developed their ideas for mitigating the worst impacts of afforestation, including the generally-accepted recommendation that a band of deciduous trees should be planted at the bottom-side of forestry blocks, providing a cleansing sieve between acid leaching from forestry and water-courses (alders are excepted from these bands, being acidic boosters).

It is when the insidious effects of afforestation are considered that the intractible problems arise. The Department of Agriculture and Fisheries for Scotland (DAFS) and the Freshwater Fisheries Laboratory at Pitlochry have researched these effects and come up with indications that are disturbing in the extreme. They confirm that afforested watersheds are inimical to fisheries, a suspicion harboured for a long time by country people who had witnessed the gradual depletion of fish populations beneath afforested catchments. The river Borgie in Sutherland, crowded in by thickets of trees on both sides, is one example of a severely depleted fishery; the Highlands is not short of others. The quantity of water taken up by mature trees which otherwise would sustain the river below is thought to amount to twenty per cent of the total flow. Because of forestry drainage, soil dries out, becomes prone to wash away, and bogs turn to hard ground. The consequences of a heavy planting programme for the Highlands could be extremely damaging, and any environmental assessment of specific planting proposals should take on board the potential deterioration of fisheries. These fisheries at present provide an irreplaceable income for the Highlands, dependent only on the reappearance of migrating fish and the health of resident fish. To impair this resource for lack of proper consideration of the scientific warnings would be irresponsible in the extreme.

The scientific picture is only now being formulated. Not enough is known, and more research is vital. However, a 1986 DAFS report observed a close similarity between heavily afforested areas and those with declining salmon catches. The report's authors refer to the damage caused by outwashes from ditching, draining, ploughing and road building to nursery stream beds; the potential harmfulness of forestry pesticides; the higher evapo-transpiration losses of forestry compared to moorland; the alteration by forestry to stream flows, especially in summer, and the consequent exposure to migrating fish of drying-up waterfalls. Loss of light on the water from overshadowing trees affects the fauna and flora of the stream, and fallen trees can block swimming channels of migrating fish. All these effects are not felt by watercourses to the same degree all the time. At forestry establishment and clearfelling, the traumas of watercourses are exaggerated. Whatever preventative measures are built in at the outset, the effect on watercourses of clearfelling on a steep hillside are inevitably severe.

The problems mentioned above are, by and large, capable of solution, or partial solution, by sensitive landscaping and work practices on forestry sites. More awkward altogether are the problems of acidification in streams and lochs, when atmospheric pollution combines with forestry to increase acidic inputs. 'Acidification in Scotland' was the title of a symposium in late 1988 which pooled the results of contemporary research on this complex subject, and attempted to prescribe a way forward for the future. An understanding of forestry's role in acidification cannot be acquired without reference to air pollution.

Air pollution started to acidify Scottish lochs at least as long ago as 1800, and became apparent from the disappearance of lichens on urban buildings in the industrial English Midlands in the 1850s. There has always been difficulty in separating effects of air pollution (falling sulphur and nitrogen compounds) and natural acidification. Scotland's bedrocks are generally nutrient deficient, and in combination with high rainfall there is an overall tendency towards progressive acidification of the soil naturally. However, man-made atmospheric pollution is established as being the larger partner of overall acidification of Scotland's soil. Wind-driven fog and cloud play a part in carrying high-altitude atmospheric pollution which has fallen as rain on the Cairngorms, profoundly affecting the Alpine-type flora there and the lochs situated at high altitude. Certain types of rock, including granite which is a common bedrock in the Highlands, with poor topsoils are less able to buffer atmospheric pollution by filtering out and neutralising acid effects before the water is leached into watercourses.

Forestry enters the picture not as a primary acidifier but as a collecting net for dry pollutant particles in the atmosphere, which adhere to the fresh foliage and are then washed off by rain. Although acidification of Scottish freshwaters definitely predated afforestation (demonstrated by loch-bed core samples), on acid-sensitive sites with low buffering capacities afforestation can exacerbate acidification, particularly in places which suffer high sulphur pollution from the air. Forestry provides the medium by which airborne sulphur pollutants get into soils and streams. Several papers at the symposium made this point. In addition to filtering man-made air pollution, conifers catch and concentrate marine airborne salts. The effects of both together are additive and can result in considerably acidified water in the catchment. The result of acidification is water with a low calcium content. Calcium carbonate is a major component of mollusc and crustacean shells. Acid water disturbs the salt balance within the body tissues of fish and inhibits phosphorus needed for plant growth. The fish most sensitive to acidified water is the salmon, particularly at the egg stage; the least sensitive its enemy, the eel.

The symposium, in conclusion, expressed a clear warning. Most speakers stressed the inadequacy of present data and urged further research. The only positive signal was that the critical sulphur content in atmospheric pollution is decreasing as British fossil-fuel power stations are forced to sophisticate their filtering processes. However, the reversal in the acidification trend in most sensitive open-ground catchments is, ominously, not visible in forested catchments. Forestry, it is now clear, is no innocent bystander in the acidification story, but a passive collaborator.

It may appear surprising, given forestry's negative effect on other land uses and the innate riskiness of much forestry siting in the Highlands, that so much has taken place without more concentrated and effectual adverse comment. This is due to a combination of factors, some of which go to the heart of the paradoxes about land use in the Highlands.

First of all, there is a certain amount of planting in the Highlands which benefits the general environment, has little or no deleterious effect on fisheries, being outwith fish-populated freshwater catchments, and is capable of growing commercial timber. In the western Highlands, especially in areas which had reverted to bracken and had ceased to be usable, where high rainfall encourages fast growth, and the steeper country affords shelter to an assortment of fertile tree-growing sites, many plantations fit into a productive land use mix without threatening the survival of commercial sheep farms or deer forests. Effects on fisheries are insidious and are only in the process of being understood. There are many sites in the Highlands where conifers have been imaginatively landscaped into broken country and have the appearance of a natural landscape feature. Plantations sited carefully can provide shelter benefits for sheep and deer and improve pastures by their protection. Trees do not always act as an acidifying agent in the environment; they interact with soil minerals, drawing some up into their trunks, releasing others, and providing living matter as falling vegetation which is broken down in a complex symbiotic relationship. The FC has gone too far in its attempt to justify further planting as a riposte to tropical rainforest depredation, and as a corrective to global warming; but local benefits do exist which should not be underrated.

In the ding-dong argument for and against the flow country plantings, much was made by each side of the great environmental benefits afforded by their favoured land use. The RSPB objected to the shrinking range of greenshanks, dunlins, curlews, divers, golden plovers and eagles, provoking a response from the forestry bodies deprecating flow country wasteland and singing the praises of bird life suited to conifers, and the delights of goldcrests, titmice and sparrowhawks. On balance the open moorland birds were rarer and more interesting (four species of recognised international importance) which led the forestry propagandists, racking their brains, into eulogies of badgers, pine martens and black-game. The ornithologists never mentioned the menace to the one arena in which birds are defensible from their commercial value — grouse shooting; and the tree planters never thought to defend forestry on the grounds of interesting new deer habitat in which to stalk roes and reds. Instead the forestry bodies stressed the values of trees as agents of conservation — a nonsense — and made out that forestry plantations would provide great recreational opportunities (actually open moorland walking and rambling is more popular). The ornithologists joined a throng of opponents to forestry who chose to focus their attack on the fiscal advantages enjoyed by forestry investors.

This was a mistake. To project forestry investors as cellulose millionaires was to tackle afforestation in the least advantageous quarter. But failure to analyse rigorously the cost benefits of tree-owning, and simple-minded credence of the figures put out by the forestry companies themselves in their quest for new investors, led the defenders of the flows up a blind alley. Despite their wrong aim, however, it was almost certainly the *brouhaha* about absentee pop star, snooker player, and television personality plantation owners that panicked Chancellor Lawson in his 1988 Budget into suddenly removing forestry planting from the tax brackets altogether. There had been no consultation with the forestry bodies, and for the first time since the war, in an awakened public consciousness of the values of the environment, the politically powerful forestry lobby saw its hallowed preserve under attack and one of the main engines of afforestation growth snatched away.

The government, aside from the political sensitiveness of high-profile absentee investors seen to be desecrating the valuable flows, also began to understand what the state forestry investment had amounted to over seventy years. This is where forestry opponents should have been looking for their arguments all the time, not at greenshanks but at balance books.

A 1972 Treasury review of forestry had surprised observers with its criticisms of economic performance. The National Audit Office (NAO) 1986 independent report went further. It stated that the state forestry sector, the FC, had produced a pitiful return on investment, even accepting the modest target return of three per cent, traditionally suppressed to compensate for the slow growth of the crop. British forestry did not pay. If the scrutiny had extended to the private sector they might have found that, adding on annual management costs levied by forestry companies, and writing in interest charges at market rates, private investors in conifers were getting an extremely raw deal. There are several reasons why this is not immediately apparent to private investors unfamiliar with tree crops, reasons which explain the success and steady growth of forestry companies.

The obvious one is that the value of a forestry investment depends on the worth of the end crop. Working out the market value of oak in over a hundred years is clearly so speculative as to be pointless, the value of softwoods in forty years only slightly less so. Compounding interest and inflation rates, an investment which yields no dividend, maturing in thirty to sixty years, has to perform astonishingly well to justify itself. Forestry opponents seized on the fiscal reliefs for forestry investors, who before 1988 could set off bare land planting costs against taxable income, and received annual management grants, and accused them of reaping ill-gotten profits from the despoliation of semi-natural moorland. They should have been alerted by the NAO report on the sad performance of state forestry.

Whilst the forestry market was buoyant, and before forestry's 'big-bang' in 1988, those who traded in commercial plantations could indeed make large profits. So did speculators in agricultural land. The difference is that the end value of a tree-crop remains a hypothetical figure for a very long time; the return on agricultural land can be calculated annually on concrete figures. The underlying value of planting land, which is the secondary capital investment for private sector investors, increased, moving forestry companies on to poorer and more exposed land to initiate their planting programmes. What was not explained to forestry investors was that forestry land prices depended on durable ground-rules for forestry; the switchback of legislative change, and the lack of all-party agreement on a long-term plan for British forestry ultimately put the plantation owner in a very risky position. Forestry, with its long lead time demanding bedrock legislation more than any industry, is in fact one of the most speculative investments. Broadleaf woodland owners in England have suddenly found this to their cost; the removal of management grants in 1986 has meant that in many cases management has been too costly to continue with; woodlands are going wild and gale-felled trees are being left to rot. Opponents of afforestation should have looked at the individual experiences of investors at the end of the cycle, trying to realise their long-held asset in cash.

My experiences at Borrobol in the early 1980s may not be exactly typical, but it bears some relation to other tree growers' experiences. I decided to sell a mature plantation of Scots pine, around sixty years old, planted in the manner of the time for amenity woodland, without drainage or ground preparation. A third of the thirty-acre wood was windblown, but the remainder consisted of reasonable timber and around 13,000 trees were reckoned harvestable, amounting to 2,000 cubic metres. So an investment which had lain up for sixty years, containing a good species of softwood, with reasonable extraction access, was put out to tender for offers. For a year no contractor quoted for the standing timber. Finally agreement was reached with a contractor who had recently installed a modern processing plant and wanted to quicken his throughput. He offered around £6,000, not a princely sum, all things considered. For lack of alternative bids I concluded a deal. Dogged by very wet autumns and the transformation of the site into a peaty quagmire, the contractor took three times as long as reckoned to complete the clearfell. He told me privately he himself had lost money on the operation.

It might be supposed from my viewpoint a small profit was better than none. However, to clearfell the woodland I had secured a felling licence from the FC. A requirement of the licence is that the same area as that felled, though not necessarily in the same place, is replanted. I was therefore bound into a circle of obligations which ended in a compulsory planting with a gross cost of around £10,000. After a planting grant, paid over eight years, I had performed the whole operation at a net loss. One area of almost worthless woodland had been replaced by another, the end-value of which is impossible to guess at. Money that had lain out for six decades had borne no fruit. This is a situation which fails altogether to square with that of the forestry profiteer ripping off the public exchequer.

Then there is the matter of my commercial young conifer plantation planted in stages about twenty years ago, principally of lodgepoles. Establishment costs over 350 acres of rough hillside, of which I have no record, must have been considerable. Non-costed keepering-time eliminating the rabbits amounted to hundreds of hours. The old management grants paid annually to help with running costs failed to meet costs, most of which comprised charges from a management firm and insurance premiums. Under the new system, with no management grants, the plantation is an unrelieved financial burden. Insurance protection is unavailable against windthrow or pine beauty moth, the only realistic menaces. The rest of the cover I have been obliged to reduce to save annual charges. I have suspended professional management for the same reason and now make do with one advisor to monitor pest build-ups. If pine beauty moth did build up to critical levels, aerial spraying costs would run into thousands of pounds, which could not be justified by any reasonable expectation of the crop's end-value. In the meantime, I have probably benefited inadvertently from my neighbours' spraying operations which resulted in birds flying over the strath transporting the prophylactic virus along with them into my trees.

Much has been made in the forestry debate about the employment value of forestry. The forestry bodies claim they employ more people than rival land users; the conservationists dispute these figures hotly and say forestry destroys jobs not vice-versa. The sporting bodies have been slow to point out peripheral part-time employment generated by sport within the estate framework, for example, housekeeping duties performed by keepers' wives. Certainly at Borrobol, since establishment operations ceased in 1970, the commercial forestry plantation has generated no employment barring one fire-line ploughing job and a spraying operation. Routine pest-control checks have been the only other tree-orientated activities. It is noteworthy that annual costs mentioned earlier were principally desk-work operations and insurance charges. The growth of the plantation, if it is not to be thinned, will generate almost no employment until clearfelling. This may surprise private forestry investors paying forestry companies an annual management fee.

Independent assessments come up with an employment profile for Scottish forestry in which over ninety per cent of work with a conifer crop is in the last years of the rotation, the remainder mostly being at establishment. The cyclical nature of forestry work, building up at the harvesting end of the crop, results in a transient and migratory workforce. In social terms this compares unfavourably with hill farmers, shepherds and gamekeepers who are residents on their patch. The forestry bodies have got themselves in a logistical tangle in arguing the case for more planting. If, as they claim, a cessation of planting would entail such appalling job losses, the employment regime must indeed depend on an extension of planted woodland to infinity. High employment in forestry must be inherently unsustainable.

Despite the steady increase of forest cover in Britain in the five-year period 1985–89, the FC staff numbers fell by one-sixth. Even if the FC's own forestry holding shrank minimally in this period, the Commission still oversees all British forestry for the nation as a whole. Mechanisation in the woodlands has reduced the need for manpower. The report commissioned by the NAO made the point about employment in forestry in this way: '. . . on any reasonable assumptions, forestry represents a highly expensive mechanism for job creation. Agriculture and other forms of development are significantly less costly and provide employment in the near rather than the distant future.'

The employment argument of forestry companies is further weakened by a comparison of levels of subsidisation. This shows an astonishing disparity. At the time of writing the planting grant for conifers is £615 per hectare for areas over ten hectares. A plantation of a thousand hectares would therefore cost the British public purse £615,000. The same area of ground might support, say, a flock of three hundred breeding hill ewes, the annual subsidy for which is presently worth about £13 per head (part paid by the EC). Assuming both subsidies and planting grants remained stable for the duration of the crop, say forty years, the sheep farm would have collected subsidies to the value of £156,000, just over a quarter of the conifer crop. In addition, interest charges for the one-off outlay on the plantation over forty years, as against the steady annual payments for the sheep farm, would make the conifer crop a non-competitor. If compared to sport, which is unsubsidised and, unlike farming and forestry, liable to annual contributions to local government costs through sporting rates, the forestry alternative does indeed look, as the NAO report states, 'a highly expensive mechanism for job creation'.

I have not exhausted the arguments against blanket afforestation of the uplands, by any means. There are arguments for the preservation of moorland as a valuable semi-natural habitat and a rich ecosystem of diverse life-forms from frogs to wild orchids. These have been assembled in detail by the Nature Conservancy Council when it mounted its attack on flow country planting. There are organisations devoted to widening awareness about the charms of peatland and the flow country, the unusual plant life, and the rare sense of unrestricted expanse offered there.

Birdwatchers, botanists, ramblers, stalkers, shooters, farmers, even the humble scenery lover (whoever heard of visitors to Scandinavia going to look at the trees?) — those people and many more would prefer the Scottish uplands to stay substantially as they are. As tree-growing in these areas is a heavy charge on the public purse, and on the private purse of those who own conifer plantations, how has it come about that, with a third of the Scottish uplands planted, the Highland Regional Council, the HIDB, and forestry bodies have persuaded the Scottish Office that more planting, without even an end-target in view, is justified? This is a difficult question to answer, and one that touches on much historical sensitivity in the Highlands, involving a prejudice against hearing the case for sporting use.

One simple reason is that the case for sporting use is never put. The body which might be expected to put it, the Scottish Landowners Federation, has inevitably got a growing number of members, and members on its regional committees, who are forestry owners, and disinclined to believe that their trees will ultimately yield a small return and represent a poor investment. For those who have already discovered this, there is the comfort that the original outlay was probably a generation or two back, and taxation schedules will have made the clear-fell profit tax-free. Scottish landowners were buoyed up in the 1980s by the sharply rising rate of planting land (now reversed by the effects of the 1988 Budget), and comforted to know that capital values of their land holdings rising ahead of inflation could provide cash if called on. To have argued against afforestation would have been to devalue their own capital asset. In the meantime, the big forestry estates often found their traditional saw-milling operations unprofitable and closed them down. Other Scottish landowners found forestry was damaging their adjacent grouse moors, harbouring their deer in winter (fencing being notoriously permeable), acidifying fresh waters, and generally reducing the quality of sporting assets. However, they failed to prevail on the Federation's overview of forestry, and the official position mirrored those of the other land-using organisations: a

Opposite: North Harris Estate, leaving the loch with the usual heavy load.

Top left: The late George Michael, well-known ghillie on the Ballindalloch beat on the Spey.

Top right: Johnnie Hardy, a familiar name on the Helmsdale.

Bottom: Michael Wigan, the author, in April on the Helmsdale with ghillie Billy Hardy at the net.

Catching up hen salmon for stripping on Helmsdale in October. From the cage they are moved to oxygenated tanks on a trailer. Head water bailiff Gordon Ogilvie in background.

Top: Loch Vosmid, North Harris Estate, in July. Flyfishing for sea trout with head keeper, Kenny Morrison, rowing. In loch fishing the boatmanship is all-important.

Bottom: Dapping on north Harris to entice fish to the surface.

Top: The gunroom at Invercauld, Aberdeenshire. Keepers and loaders cleaning guns for the next day.

Bottom: Grouse larder at Invercauld. Old and young birds in separate racks.

Overleaf: Spying on Loch Quoich. Knoydart is in the distance.

Top: A day just before Christmas on Kingie, western Invernesshire. Five hinds being transported the only way possible, across frozen Loch Quoich. Ice had to be broken to get the boat through. Farquar Boyd and his father Alex Boyd are in the boat.

Bottom: Again at Kingie with Farquar Boyd. His father had already shot hinds round the hill to the right. Loch Quoich below.

Opposite: A smokehouse at Rothesay, Bute. Traditionally smoked salmon off the rack with a fire of smouldering oak-chips.

Top: Preparation of 'pieces' (hill lunches), replete with whisky flasks, in Lochmore kitchen.

Bottom: 1985 get-together in September at Lochmore, past and present staff and children. In the centre is Anne, Duchess of Westminster, who still actively enjoys all the estate has to offer.

Top: The house-keeper in the dining room at Lochmore Lodge, polishing racing trophies. The background painting on the left is Handa Island, and on the right is a golden eagle by the German artist, Wolf. These paintings along with two others were specially commissioned and fitted into the walls.

Bottom: Teatime in Ben Armine's drawing-room after stalking. On the walls, carved and burnt, is the game-book, featuring many illustrious names from the past.

The old and the new. Top: Strathtulchan, Morayshire, was commissioned by Mark Birkbeck and completed in 1990. It is an elegant recreation of the Scottish Baronial style and an architectural asset to the area.

Bottom: Amhuinnsuidhe Castle on north Harris. Salmon run up foreground falls out of the sea.

Top: Angus Ross with his dogs at Achentoul, Sutherland. Removing fox from snare along forestry fence on a February afternoon.

Bottom: Angus Ross is also a proficient mole catcher.

Top: On Morvich, Sutherland, investigation of fox-den, eager terriers in background.

Bottom: Heather-burning in east Sutherland in March. Note the old birch-twig besoms (brooms).

Top: Feeding red deer at Cluanie, Invernesshire, with opportunist blackface sheep following.

Bottom: Beating in the central Highlands. The flagmen are using fertiliser bags tied to poles. Strip-burnt backdrop.

Top: Early morning gathering of keepers and beaters at Invercauld, the largest sporting estate in the Highlands.

Bottom: Salmon netting at Berriedale. In the background is a kittiwake colony and the mouth of Berriedale river.

mixed land use was the stated aim. Nobody broached the important question of the proportions the mix should be in. Therefore nobody attempted a quantification of the relative cost-benefits to the nation of the subsidised non-rateable uses — forestry and farming — against the unsubsidised rate-paying land use for sport, which would have been a first step in making this judgement.

The HRC and the HIDB broadly accepted the picture as put to them by forestry companies. The only other point of view they were required to consider was that of the conservation bodies, principally the NCC and the RSPB. These two had made a *cause célèbre* of the flows; they fought other local proposals on a case-by-case basis. Also the Council and the Board were aware that the NCC in particular had made itself locally unpopular in the Highlands with its cavalier use of the Site of Special Scientific Interest (SSSI) designation, and a habit of appearing to locals as an alien band of arrivistes, acting like overmighty government busy-bodies. The NCC was a controversial organisation in many Highland districts, and was especially disliked by farmers who were suddenly informed that traditional activities carried on by the farm were damaging an SSSI and must be stopped. The farmers' response, naturally, was that if the site was specially worth preserving, the traditional use of the land could not have been doing any harm. From the point of view of the Council and the Board, the NCC's case was fatally flawed in that their restrictions endangered jobs. The NCC counter-claim that they themselves were large local employers was met with bitterly ironic retorts. The upshot of these frictions was that in 1989 the NCC had its right to involvement in tree planting schemes on a consultation basis withdrawn, except where existing or potential SSSIs were involved. It is now proposed that the NCC in Scotland and the Countryside Commission for Scotland should merge, a move seen by NCC parties as an attempt to blunt their cutting edge in a merger with a more pro-establishment body. The RSPB, despite articulating a groundswell of environmental thinking nationwide, lacked the all-important credentials of being a local employer in a productive industry. Neither organisation was helped in its cause by the adherence to both of fringe environmental groups expressing extreme and polarised positions.

This left the Department of Agriculture and Fisheries for Scotland, a body that until 1988 had to be consulted before tree-growing use could be granted by the FC on any ground previously farmed with sheep. Despite the fact that DAFS habitually cleared eighty per cent of applications without demur, and a further ten per cent after agreed modifications, the forestry companies consistently assailed the Department's right to be involved at all. After 1986, DAFS' right of a veto on afforestation on blocks of less than 100 acres was removed. General presumptions in favour of afforestation have recently been clearly stated by the Secretary of State for Scotland, Malcolm Rifkind. The first reaction to the climax of opposition to planting the flow country, which was to freeze all planting applications, was withdrawn by the Scottish Secretary in January 1989 when he stated the aim of planting a further 96,000 acres, constituting nearly half of the whole flow country. In common with his response to the Countryside Commission for Scotland's report, 'Forestry in Scotland', no reference was made in Mr Rifkind's policy review statement to sporting use. It was as if all that lay between scenic conservation and blanket coverings of the uplands was a dwindling handful of sheep.

DAFS' involvement and the strength of the hill farming case are under particular stress. Although the contribution by hill farmers to surpluses is too small to be material, the forestry companies have used food surpluses as a component in their picture of hill farming as a redundant activity. Reductions by the EC in 1989 of the ewe subsidies for hill flockmasters with over 1,000 head indicate a definite shift in sympathy away from the big producer; these reductions may presage a further withdrawal of support from hill farming incomes. As many Highland estates have two or three sheep hirsels, of six hundred ewes and more, the impact on them, and on the economics of the uplands, is likely to be severe. The hill cattle sector has been reduced already to almost insignificant proportions. The meaning of this was not lost on forestry companies, which reported it with glee in the forestry press. Added to a catastrophic resultant fall in cast ewe prices, poor lamb prices in 1989 and 1990, long-term stagnation of the wool price, and ever-escalating costs, the widespread collapse of hill and upland farming is already far advanced. As soon as the price of planting land begins to rise the forestry companies will not lack for ground to plant.

The case for sporting use of land suffers not from lack of strong arguments, but from strong sentiments. For a variety of reasons it has become almost inconceivable for any figure in the public domain to come out in support of sporting use. Even those who personally enjoy sport in the Highlands are loath to attach their colours to this particular mast. When game shooting, stalking and fishing rank collectively as the most widely enjoyed leisure activity in Britain, this seems at first amazing.

One of the most intractable drawbacks faced by anyone trying to promote sport as a sensible Highland use is the shadow cast over it by the past. Although the nineteenth-century glens were cleared for Scottish sheep farmers, present-day demagogues have found it more convenient to shift the blame onto owners of deer forests, often outsiders who were English. Deer stalking use was a later development, but it fits better into the popular demonology of the landowner as a selfish pleasure-seeker. The Clearances were brought about for social and economic reasons, not to usher in country pursuits. The turn of the century spread of the deer forests was indeed economically motivated, but there was no social motivation, and by this time the population in the outlying Highlands was substantially lower than a century earlier.

Sporting use suffers from the hangover of association with a social elite. It goes against the grain of public opinion in Scotland to sympathise openly with Highland sports, not because of what they entail, but because of who is identified with them. The rifle, gun and rod in these egalitarian days still carry the connotations they had in Victorian times. They remain, in defiance of reality, the stigmata of a social class. This point of view, it need hardly be said, is an urban perception, not a rural one.

The fact that sporting estates are nearly all run by their proprietors as businesses, and that these properties ceased to be the pleasure-grounds of their friends and families long ago, is known widely as a fact; but sentiments about landowners themselves have remained obstinately unchanged. The truth today is that Highland estates are enjoyed by a stream of seasonal visitors. The fact that estates are often the focal points for multifarious outdoor activities, and have diversified into small, productive, on-site industries such as tweed mills, fish farms and smokeries, and weaving, and have, amongst other things, built power plants, golf courses and chalet villages — these developments have failed somehow to dent the preferred image of the laird as an outmoded, but privileged, irrelevance.

It may be easier for planners, sheriffs, civil servants, councillors and politicians to fall back on old-fashioned stereotypes with which they feel comfortable. Anti-landlordism is a current that runs strongly through Highland society and provides a failsafe nerve that can be tweaked with the guarantee of approval in most Highland congregations. It stems from the time of the Clearances and is the ongoing debt that will never be considered paid off by a people who felt their birthright was seized and traded cheaply. Many of the old folk can remember grandparents' laments about the lost up-country homeland, and the Clearances have become fixed in ancestral folk-memory. One way or another, they have become for Highland people a lost part of the common past, and have determined an orientation towards landlords which is unbudgeable. Just as during the Clearances there were many landlords who did all within their power to relieve the oppression of a starving and over-burdened population, so today individual lairds, for varying particular reasons, escape from the straitjacket legacy of historical censure. But anti-landlordism remains a deep feeling and it has meant that those in public office in the Highlands — although privately they may know differently — are obliged to sustain a tone of opposition to lairds when making public pronouncements. This has put sporting use of land beyond the pale of reasonable and balanced discussion, and threatens now, with the gathering gloom of forestry, to have tragic and irreversible results.

The class connotations of land ownership prevent landlords making the natural alliances in defence of sport in other areas. The RSPB realises full well that the balance of bird life in the Highlands hangs on the survival of sporting estates. RSPB officials realise that if sporting use was abolished tomorrow the uplands would be ploughed and planted from side to side; moorland birds and the habitat for many important rare breeding species would disappear, and British bird life would be reduced on a scale that has never been experienced before.

However, unlike bird-watchers elsewhere, it appears that British bird-watchers are unprepared to take on board the concept of game-shooting as an intrinsically conservationist form of management. Again, it is partly a problem of Victorian legacies. The days when predator bags were bigger than game bags are a sore memory. Re-introductions, for example, of the sea eagle to the western Highlands, are still taking place in a slow process of wildlife restoration that started a hundred and fifty years ago and has often been conducted on private estates. The process by which all bird life is getting statutory protection, except for a dwindling number of predator and game species, has not yet been completed. There are many bird-watchers in Britain who are also game shooters; but there are also many who would prefer to see the keeper himself pass into history and shooting abolished, a view which they find hard to reconcile with the sporting estate's role as a preserver of habitat and the locus of excellent bird life.

Senior people in the RSPB know and acknowledge this paradox. They acknowledge too that their church is one of many faiths. Moreover, it is a charity. The prospect of raising money to save endangered birds, whilst at the same time espousing the cause of grouse moors as a land use, sends a chill up the spine of the fund-raiser. The reason is that bird-knowledge in Britain has too much been garnered through experience of caged birds as pets instead of through a practical understanding of the interplay and interreliance, often macabre, of one bird species and another. British bird-watchers can err on the side of sentimentality. The net result of these problems is that whereas those RSPB officers in the field who have gained an understanding of sporting estates accept that, on balance, game shooting management is a vital linchpin in the Highland ecology, it is felt many RSPB members might not agree. The forestry bodies must look on these log-jams of understanding with great contentment.

They do indeed have much to feel happy about. The landowners' other natural allies are similarly at right angles to them. The NCC's SSSI designation policy has imposed management restrictions on parts of ground where traditional activities have to be curtailed, and new projects abandoned. Perspectives of the NCC have very often appeared too purist and impractical to curry favour with lairds trying to turn a penny. Hillwalkers, mountaineers and ramblers, or certain members of these groups, have for a long time conducted an informal war of attrition with landowners on to whose ground they tend to demand access throughout the year, even when it interferes with stalking.

These people, and many other occasional users of the Highlands, take the existing shape and face of the landscape for granted. Whilst certainly not wanting to see it changed to silvicultural use any more than it has been, they do not necessarily see the laird as a reliable buffer against change (they may instead see him as a buffer of another sort!). There is a powerful strain of sympathy in the hillwalking fraternity for a national park system to be introduced in Scotland. Their interest is focused on the physical space, rather than the detailed ecology. The particular consequences of national park systems in terms of employment, shrinking away of estate communities, and the lower density of fauna and flora are not always understood. Finally, a matter that need not concern armchair idealogues, but which is certainly of interest to governments: the cost of conserving Highland scenery would then become a drain on the public, instead of the private, purse.

Chapter Ten
Politics, Sporting Use and Access

There are no votes in the Highlands. The impasse of today, when self-appointed guardians of the wilds sprung from every conceivable environmental niche all argue their right to head or neutralise proposed developments, has come about at a time of large government majorities. There is no need to consider the Highland voter. The former chairman of the Crofters Commission, Dr James Shaw Grant, has commented caustically on the history of state intervention in the Highlands, instancing the First Crofters Act (1886), the Highlands and Islands Development Act (1965), and the Crofting Reform Act (1976) as times when reforming governments clinging precariously to power sought to snare the Highland votes. There is no natural political majority in the Highlands, unless it is Liberal. Of the Highland seats, Labour and Conservative combined presently hold fewer than minor parties; the majority of regional councillors in the Highlands are Independents. In the Highlands the view is that central government neither understands nor cares, so the natural vote is for an individual who will, firstly, play a strong part locally and, secondly, will represent the locality's interests down in London. Thus the MP in my constituency, Robert Maclennan, has changed party three times and has on each occasion been returned with an improved majority. His is a personal vote for a good constituency performer.

This attitude to national politics may seem quaintly idiosyncratic but it has serious consequences for land use. It means that there is no voice speaking from a democratic position of strength informing the Scottish Office of the reality on the ground north of the Highland line; nor is there any prospect of a voice while Highland voters side-step the main political parties. Scotland, like every country in which a majority urban population is concentrated in very few conurbations in a sea of open space, is schizophrenically divided between country viewpoints and town ones. It is partly the horror of rural policies emanating from the smoky fiefdoms of urban idealogues in Edinburgh and Glasgow that has deprived Scottish Nationalists of majority support for devolution in Highland constituencies that have strong isolationist tendencies.

The effect of this is that the Highlands is a political wilderness. There is no overall government policy for the Highlands, and the only strategy that has emerged — to plant it with trees — has been arrived at by default. The Scottish Secretary Malcolm Rifkind has been at pains to stress in his forestry plan that although he will look favourably on planting programmes in general, they will only proceed as and when the land becomes available — which means when an owner wishes to sell. In other words, development in the

Highlands will be guided by market forces, in tune with Conservative Party policy for the economy as a whole.

Apart from the fact that the Highlands is now perceived within the European Community framework as having exceptional 'heritage value', and should therefore be protected from the impacts of short-term free market exploitation, market forces are not the ones which are determining the direction of government-led development. Very far from it. Selective subsidies determine it.

State aid for forestry hugely overshadows any other subsidy, both in the form of planting grants and also financial support for the establishment of new wood processing plant. Positive aids for forestry are enhanced by the relaxation of tax penalties. Forestry is non-rateable, and legatees can delay capital transfer tax penalties until the trees are actually cut down. Hill farming is subsidised also, but at a total cost to the Exchequer which is negligible. Farms qualify for business reliefs on the owner's death, but the capital value of hill farms has fallen so low that these figures, too, are negligible. By contrast, sporting use is unsubsidised, fully subject to rates (except, since 1989, fishing, when governed by a properly-constituted river board), despite receiving no special local authority services; and sporting assets are fully taxable at death. Recently VAT has been applied to the sale of sporting rights, depressing capital values and penalising the sporting economy further. Like is certainly not being compared with like when official statements refer to the free market in land.

It is worth considering the political aspect of this. For a long time the Highlands have been a target for socialists because so much land is concentrated in so few hands. Superficially, the charge has substance. Highland estates are big; some individuals even own more than one estate. However, when political nationalists and the Labour Party have addressed this problem in detail and looked for solutions they have run into trouble. For despite their size, Highland estates have an extremely low level of productivity. Thousands of acres of rocky Wester Ross will produce a cash crop in venison carcases smaller than that of a raspberry grower in the Perthshire foothills. This is inescapable. If Highland estates are judged on the value of their output, including rents, it is plain that huge numbers of arable farmers in Scotland, on infinitely smaller areas, would be fitter targets for sequestration.

Politicians on the socialist fringe have for many generations played around with the fairytale idea of returning the Highlands to the people, a piece of nostalgic whimsy which takes no account of economics. If large estates are making no money from running their patches commercially, indeed often losing money, how much more dire would be the position of an agricultural smallholder? The concept of subsidising communalised shareholdings has financial implications which do not bear thinking about. In any case, the population which would return to occupy the glens, at present presumably living on the coast, tends to regard the hill-dwellers with amused tolerance and surprise that anyone today is prepared to lead such a cut-off and secluded life, deprived of the social amenities of the town. There is no evidence to suggest that agricultural skills survive in sufficient degree to make such a re-colonisation practically feasible, or that there exists sufficiently serious commitment to it. The declining number of crofters is hardly encouraging.

What to do about land ownership in the Highlands remains an intractable problem for political parties on the left. As they get pushed further towards an environmentally sensitive stance, the problem will increase, because it is the low level of interference with the environment on which sporting use thrives, precisely the management level environmentalists advocate. Sporting use, stripped of its outmoded class connotations, fits neatly into the philosophy of land use favoured by left of centre parties and to which even the Conservative Party is finding the electorate's sympathies leaning.

This leaves the problem of size and scale. Ownership of large areas is unpalatable to socialists purely on grounds of scale. But the reason the areas are large is historical and a sound one. When the nineteenth-century landowners parcelled up their hereditary lands into sporting blocks, the blocks were designed to constitute one sporting area, an area suited to management and utilisation by one entity. It was realised then that a deer forest needed to be of a certain size for practical management. In today's world of sporting lets continuing through an entire season it is vital that the deer forest has enough space for continuous use. This means there must be a part of the ground that has deer on it and can be worked, whatever the wind direction. Invariably, particular winds suit particular areas of ground, but it should be possible to stalk deer somewhere on any day after the season starts, which is usually by September. An estate which cannot guarantee this amount of usable space is in a difficult position for letting to action-hungry tenants, which in turn makes the employment of a resident keeper less cost-effective. Unless there is reliable sport sufficient to justify a full-time keeper the estate degenerates, loses value, fish, bird and beast and becomes barren ground. It may be hard to reconcile with the doctrines of socialism, but large areas under single management are vital if present land use practices are able to pay.

Unfortunately, the necessity for a degree of self-containment in deer forests is not widely understood. During the 1980s some developments took place on formerly integral Highland estates over which, in the long term, tears will be shed and resentments arise. To doctrinaire asset strippers occurred the idea that a Highland estate could be marketed like mixed lots at an odd-ends auction. Typically, a large area of land was purchased, previously under single management as a deer forest, and divided into lots. Naturally, most of the lots had no house, but to the southern buyer, dazzled by a glossy brochure of luscious scenic photographs, that appeared a minor setback. Why not, as enticed, own your own deer forest, and an area of land that sounded expansive, nay enormous? The estate was duly subdivided and sold in lots, the original proprietor often getting back his investment, and retaining the main house and an area of land for his own use, at no net cost.

It sounds a good idea, opening up a beautiful tract of country into multiple ownership, spreading the benefits amongst a wider society. The problem is that each new owner has a fillet of a deer forest. Deer ranging over the whole area will cross his personal patch erratically. If perchance his area contains sheltered ground with good grazing and he has hefted deer on it, extraction of a few carcasses a year will need to be very carefully undertaken, or the deer will move on to his neighbour. If his neighbour, also waiting expectantly on the march for his pound of flesh, shoots too hard the deer will move again. Perpetual disturbance will interfere with calving rates, gradually reduce the physical condition of the animals, and in time they will disappear — if the multiple mini-estate owners do not abruptly reduce them by overshooting before they are thinned down from the pressure of constant aggravation. Of course, the answer to the problem is an overall management policy agreed and enforced by the new owners as a group; in short, the treatment of the estate as one entity again but with a number of shareholders. The chances of this actually working with a group of owners who live far and wide, each one of whom wants his sport in the same holiday season, each one of whom will have a different perception of the value of his own plot as a holding-ground for deer, are at first glance remote. The same sorts of problems apply to fishing time-shares, which are far more widespread. Multiple ownership of sporting assets is a growing reality in the Highlands. Whether it will be in the best interests of the ecology and the game species themselves remains to be seen.

To the Conservatives, who tolerate sporting use rather than encourage it, the Highland estate has always been something of an embarrassment. Scottish Conservative MPs have found their party stigmatised by the sporting laird image long after such people ceased to be parliamentarians. Large land-ownership, with sporting recreation as a land use, was not something they could be seen to approve of, and yet to have deliberately urged dismantling it would have infringed personal liberty and imperilled private capital. Forestry as a land use has provided the contemporary Scottish Conservative with the perfect way out.

Through the Forestry Commission, the state owns about a tenth of Scotland. All of this land has, over the course of seventy years, passed from private landowners into the hands of the state. Nearly the same amount of afforested land is owned by the private sector; not, however, by the traditional Highland landlords and estate owners. The majority is owned by investors in forestry companies. These investors are an assortment of private individuals who came into the limelight of a sort different to that to which they were accustomed during the flow country debate, when it transpired that the owners of the hated conifer blankets included snooker players, television personalities and rich London councillors — in other words, people who had no personal connection with the planted area at all, nor wanted any. Forestry for them was a method of tucking away money. From the political point of view it was merely unfortunate that forestry investors had amongst them such high-profile absentee landlords; the main point about the clients of forestry companies owning blocks of trees was that more people were getting a slice of the cake. In the case of pension funds, whole armies of workers were, probably unwittingly, putting their faith in timber. The average holding of the private landlord in the Highlands is getting markedly smaller.

The private Highland landowner is being replaced by corporate lairds of many different stripes. For example, the Nature Conservancy Council owns four estates, Ben Eighe, Cairngorms, Inverpolly and Rhum, all over ten thousand acres. In the late 1980s the historical central Highlands stalking estate of Abernethy, cleared of sheep in 1869, was bought by the RSPB. Proprietorship in these cases has moved from a mixed land use to a specific-purpose land use. The proprietorship of a single-land use has complex repercussions, on the estate itself and on neighbours. The RSPB has made a primary objective of allowing old Caledonian pine forest to rejuvenate, bringing with it associated birds such as crossbills. The options to achieve this were to fence deer out or cull them hard enough to eliminate most of the pressure on struggling young saplings. The Society has chosen the second course, and is engaged in a systematic reduction of the estate's deer population. Neighbouring landowners may find in due course that their own deer populations suffer, pulled into Abernethy by the much less pressurised grazing. Possibly this will not happen; possibly it would not matter if it did. Certainly, though, one policy decision on Abernethy in the midst of open moorland will have results which ripple outwards. On the other hand, Kenneth Whitehead reports as long ago as 1960 that Abernethy had been 'virtually finished' as a stalking estate because of the numbers of hillwalkers on the Cairngorms.

It seems appropriate that estates which fall out of sporting use to make way for specialised conservation perspectives should be those on which sporting use had anyway ceased to be sustainable. The greater market availability of sporting estates which have declined and therefore lost their sporting value automatically makes this transference more likely to occur on the sites where least sport is lost. The absolute shrinking of the sporting capital of the Highlands appears an inevitable consequence. But if a wider range of interests are to be incorporated in the Highland scene, and specialist recreations catered for, the advantages, given the drift of public sentiment towards a mix of land users as well as land uses, outweigh the drawbacks. Estate owners on unenclosed land accept, up to a point, that interactions with neighbours are outwith their direct control. Moreover, there are ways in which institutional estate ownership, and nature reserve management, can benefit sporting land use.

In the same way that the RSPB operates its bird reserves on a 'honeypot' principle, concentrating public interest on one golden sight designed to cater for large numbers of visitors and thereby releasing pressure on the others (the case with Loch Garten's ospreys), so nationally-owned reserves draw in hillwalkers who would otherwise disperse over stalking ground. On reserves such as Beinn Eighe, considerable pressure on neighbouring deer forests is syphoned off by the reserve's ability to act as a honeypot. Neighbouring deer are left undisturbed, hillwalkers have the benefit of marked paths, clear nationally-recognised objectives, and the comfort of knowing other walkers are about if they suffer an injury. From the viewpoint of neighbours, it is reassuring that ownership by a quasi-public body means more leverage in the event of a dispute, because of the necessity for public bodies to maintain a clean landlord image.

The possible disadvantages — for example of walkers carrying on through the reserve and interrupting culling programmes — taken as a whole, weigh lightly in most cases. To stalkers having to explain to a party of hikers that such and such a route through a forest will spoil his day, it is a great advantage to be able to recommend nearby walking in a reserve as an alternative. Publicly-owned reserves, with their much heavier throughput of visitors, benefit considerably a full range of servicing operators, from hotels and pubs to grocers and clothes outfitters. Enjoyment of the hills and the different seasons attract enthusiasts over the whole year. Where the family party frolics on the odoriferous springy slopes in summer, the ice-climber with gritted teeth inches his laborious path in winter.

Institutional and quasi-public ownership has done something to take the heat out of the debate about public access in recent years. It will be some time, if ever, before there are enough reserves to neutralise the issue altogether. In the meantime it looks set to become an increasingly public issue with especial significance for Highland estates, some of which occupy a middle position by virtue of having small reserves on them.

The law is not fitted for everyday use of land in the Highlands. Traditionally, there has been freedom to roam on estate land for those who acknowledged that this entailed responsibilities. Walkers were fewer in number in the past, often developed good relationships with shepherds, keepers and landowners, and made a point of never impeding them in their business. This relationship corresponded well with the murky state of the law on trespass in Scotland (different to that in England). As everyone knows, the law of trespass is so framed that merely being on private property is, for practical purposes, no offence. The Trespass (Scotland) Act of 1865, apparently aimed at gypsies and tinkers, makes camping and lighting fires without permission illegal. Trespass is also an offence if property is damaged. The more polarised positions of today expose the opacity of the old law.

Freedom to roam, a cherished concept of hillwalkers, is obviously at loggerheads with stalking, which requires undisturbed ground and which theoretically could imperil the lives of walkers with straying bullets. The viewpoint that hillwalkers should have priority, and deer stalking should fit itself in to hillwalking habits as best it can, cannot accommodate the fact that deer stalking is a cull, and the cull is ultimately under statutory control by the government body, the Red Deer Commission. The Red Deer Commission is in a position to recommend culling at a certain level, and undertake the job itself if the recommendation is ignored. Therefore, the stalking party is not entirely engaged in recreation, as the hillwalker is. On these grounds, because deer culling is a duty, the stalker must, it can be argued, have the superior right. The stalker is conducting his business at the behest of the owner of the land, who is probably under contract to the sporting tenant. The landowner is paying a tax (sporting rates) on the right to go about his business. The hillwalker is a free-wheeling guest. The law fails to make distinctions between these two land uses, or cope with their interrelationship. In the days of long crocodiles of brightly-clad hikers, the old tolerant attitudes are coming under strain.

The law and conditions of access become more complex with the recent spread of Sites of Special Scientific Interest, as designated by the Nature Conservancy Council. Although these are often no more capable of being physically protected than tracts of deer forest, tougher localised rules may theoretically apply to them. For example, an area listed as containing rare breeding birds should not be disturbed in the nesting season. The area might be huge; divers in the flow country may desert the nest on first sighting of an intruder a mile distant. Yet the SSSI area is probably open, indistinguishable from surrounding areas, often unmarked on maps, and quite likely to have been listed without the cognizance even of the landowner. Practical control of access is out of the question. Why, ask the critics of such SSSIs, designate areas which by their nature are outwith any form of control, and from which only a handful of specialists may be able to benefit? The question is complicated by the principle, hesitatingly embarked on, and now fortified by payments for such things as agricultural 'set-aside', of compensating land-owners for preserving SSSIs. This commonly means leaving them be. Apart from the impossibility of funding such a concept in the long term, there is the considerable drawback that such payments are popularly perceived as hand-outs for nothing. The designation of environmentally sensitive areas (ESAs), in which farmers and landowners are paid to perform environmentally-friendly tasks such as maintaining stone dykes, seems to be a more promising and acceptable way forward.

Following the legal thread, the landowner or his employee has the right to ask particular individuals to leave the property; if they decline, his ultimate sanction is a court interdict, obviously unworkable at the foot of the glen when stalking party and hiking party meet each other setting off in the same direction. The general practice is for the stalker to try and dissuade hikers from inconvenient routes; he may meet with varying degrees of success, or complete failure. If they have decided to file on through the glen, some hikers will not be dissuaded. The stalker will make shift as he can, not easy if the wind and topography are against him, or turn round with his shooting guest and go home.

Such situations make it hard to manage a deer forest. For some owners, unfortunate enough to straddle high ground and peaks over three thousand feet (Munros), the deer stalking, as happened on Abernethy, has been so reduced it is inoperable. Although deer do partially acclimatise to hikers, they suffer loss of condition from constantly changing ground to get out of the way, and never being able to rest. At calving in June walkers are particularly disruptive, although no stalking is taking place. For the hind in parturition looks for a peaceful spot, generally a little distance from the heft, in which to calf. Directly after calving she wanders off to feed, often leaving the dappled new arrival for up to twenty-four hours. The calf, tucked up and still, will get up and totter about if disturbed, following the first moving object in view, even a hillwalker. Levels of knowledge about deer are not high in Britain, and what is mistaken for enchanting and delightful innocence is only mistaken biological imprinting. Calves do get mismothered when disturbed, and the response of deer populations to heavy disturbance from walkers is generally to migrate or suffer a population reduction. The parts of the Highlands devoid of deer altogether are mostly the favourite walking routes.

The matter of compensation for deer forest owners who gradually find themselves the masters of a barren empty wasteland, and possessors of a vanished capital asset, has never been addressed. But then the whole issue of conflict in land use as applicable to the open hill has never been seriously addressed, although times are changing and this has become a keenly debated subject in 1990. The recent advent of mountain bike riders, churning up soft ground and rattling over the ridges, unacceptable to hikers and stalkers alike, shows the complexity of the situation, as well as the speed of change. So far, we have muddled through using old laws to defend newly-hatched traditions, bumping squarely into conflicts without the guidance of statutory clarity.

It is not an easily resoluble situation. The tradition of informal access to open country in Scotland has worked well in the main and is the envy of other countries which have evolved more detailed legal codes. It is a pity, though perhaps inevitable, that increased pressure on access threatens to see the old liberal traditions bend under the strain. The point of view of the country visitor is readily understandable. The wild open terrain before him is the very definition of freedom. No fences or conspicuous human impact are visible. To walk on such ground, feel the heather beneath the feet, smell its bloom in the air, would seem a natural right that cannot and should not be removed. Of course it cannot, and should not be. There is no question of that. The Highland landowner is, or should be, aware that his role is a temporary one of stewardship, of infinitely short duration in the perspective of the evolution of the hills; he has no absolute possession. But that stewardship, apart from the requirement to be financed, also carries obligations. He is the manager of the deer population on his ground; also populations of farmed stock and wild birds, animals and fish. Many of these (badgers, otter, eagles, rare plants) are protected. Others (trout, salmon, grouse) are the objects of statutory control in law. Ideally, public use of the ground should be in sympathy with this aim of management. That entails being informed about the hill ecology, deer and deer management, the cycle of the salmon, and so on. The moral onus is on hillwalkers to know something of the country they traverse. The right of access brings with it, just as the right of use for the landowner, definite responsibilities.

One of the commonest complaints from stalkers is that other users of the hill seem frequently to go about their Munro-conquering in a dream, so fixated on their objective that the effect of their own presence on the hill goes unnoticed. Stalkers mildly enquiring about the whereabouts of deer as walkers descend from the ridges are often met with the response: 'We didn't see any.' They know full well that these unwitting ramblers have been shifting deer without knowing it since daybreak. Much interference with stalking is inadvertent, hillwalkers with heads bent to the ground for the step ahead (in contrast to the stalker, who never looks at the ground), literally unaware of the hundreds of pairs of brown eyes following them from across the corrie. The difficulties of seeing deer in foreign country are extreme, and even experienced stalking people going to new ground will fail to pick up deer in their binoculars at the speed of the native stalker, familiar with every bump, curve and hollow of his territory, and the likely hefts of deer.

There are problems for hikers spotting deer, quite often pushed for time to get round their ordained route in daylight hours and unaccustomed to looking for them. There are further problems when they do see them, for the hikers' path will generally follow a fixed course up the shoulders of hills and along ridges, or into the faces of hills up gullies: to circle round deer ahead may require difficult detours. There is the added hitch that in doing so they depart from the customarily-used paths on which the deer have become acclimatised to seeing people, and in trying to avoid one party of deer shift with their wind another party hitherto unnoticed. From all points of view the hiker makes the job for stalkers easier, and life for the deer less stressed, if he holds to the usual paths. During the period September to Christmas, use of deer forests by walkers is very hard to reconcile. Ideally this should be a time, like calving in June, to use the nature reserves and places devoid of deer.

This too has its difficulties. For in many instances the wildlife the public wants to see, deer apart, has vacated the reserve because of pressure from public access. Nature wardens world-wide face this problem of balancing means with objectives. The grander and more illustrious species disdain to share their environment; they are often notoriously shy. Eagles, badgers, merlins, wildcats, greenshanks, amongst many others, cannot tolerate too much disturbance. The reserves into which the public has been channelled suffer depleted wildlife variety. This deflates the public's wildlife expectations, lessens the chance of wildlife understanding, and encourages casual characterisation of the Highlands as wilderness.

It would be a preferable objective if the rush to conserve parts of an area were accompanied by educational programmes about the value and purpose of reserves and the habits of their occupants. Education about wildlife should be an integral part of the programme, reinforced by wildlife guides. For reasons simply of space, the great national park systems of America, formed in the last century before private landownership had become an embedded tradition, could never be replicated in Scotland. The American national parks are so large that wildlife unfamiliar with man is common; self-taught appreciation, out camping on the range, is the ideal way to experience and understand animals and birds, but it is impractical in the Scottish context.

Much future debate about the Highlands will revolve around public access. The situation is routinely inflamed by agitators in the wings of politics, some of whom take on the guise of conservationists. In the mêlée of opinion, some bodies want access limited further, to preserve habitat for shy species, and others want it opened up more, regardless of the wildlife impact. The spread of landownership in the Highlands to embrace a variety of single-use land management policies will increase public knowledge, widen public access, and hopefully help break down polarised attitudes on the fringe. But, it is important, in my view, that the Highlands should not develop too far as a mosaic of single-interest landowners with competing or antipathetic purposes. The Highlands must remain both a working environment for indigenous people, and an entity which works harmoniously as a whole in an integrated way. Compartmentalisation would be artificial and lead to the impoverishment of this tremendous land mass.

Already, apart from sporting proprietors, the owners of Highland property include the Woodland Trust, the National Trust for Scotland, the NCC, the RSPB, the Ministry of Defence, and the Forestry Commission. The Forestry Commission has made the provision of public access such a priority that, some believe, it has superseded the purpose of commercial timber-growing. The estates, too, have not all been backward in efforts to broaden the visitor-base. Holiday cottage businesses, on-farm visits, bird-watching parties, visitor centres, adventure schools, and wildlife parks all contribute to the modern throughput on Highland estates. The proper resolution of the built-in hillwalking/stalking conflict will be reached when general awareness of the purposes and needs of both is increased. Ultimately, remote areas are often fragile ecosystems, and non-destructive utilisation calls for restraint. Restraint will be agreed amicably only after cases have been put in the wider forum of publicised discussion and after the dissemination of information. Estate owners and factors, with their fund of experience covering a mix of land uses, are in a good position to play a leading role in this.

Chapter Eleven
The Dun Tenants of the Waste

Any appraisal of the future of the Highlands could usefully take as its starting point the future of the deer. About them misunderstandings and misapprehensions abound. The 1989/1990 winter gave the newspapers an opportunity once again to demonstrate their ignorance about an animal which in terms of its numbers and huge uninterrupted range has no equal in Europe. The death of large numbers of deer in the western Highlands was immediately blamed on landowners who were failing to cull enough hinds. A natural catastrophe, aggravated by the maze of forestry blocks through which deer now have to find their way downhill, became a scandal with which to belabour the Scottish public's favourite whipping-boy, the estate landlord.

The true situation was that deer numbers had indeed risen, as the Red Deer Commission had been saying for some time. But the rise had been predominantly in the eastern and central Highlands, not in the west. In the east Sutherland deer management group, of which I am a member, a comparison in the deer count after ten years showed that the ground on the east side of the high mountains had seen a great territorial and numerical expansion, and numbers had risen by as much as eighty per cent in one area; but in the north-western part of the group's area, coinciding with the higher mountainous country, no significant population increase had occurred. In the parts of the Highlands where deer numbers had markedly increased deer had not perished in the 1989/1990 winter, but had colonised grouse moors and ground left vacant by diminishing sheep stocks, and moved down in larger numbers than usual on to low ground and coastal areas. This expansion of territory had been going on for some time. Peripheral Highland areas such as Tayside, Deeside, Cowal and Kintyre in Argyll, now have resident red deer where they never had them before. This is despite increased winter feeding programmes on many hill places.

The RDC placed the primary blame for winter mortalities on extremely poor weather conditions in a season of record rainfall which lasted right on into the spring. They calculated that most deaths had occurred in animals over ten years old and in yearlings, the two categories always most likely to succumb to bad weather. Additionally, the deer were in bad condition, which had led to greater than usual parasite trouble, particularly from nasal bot-fly. The RDC notes that indeed some populations were high, in their estimation too high, but the mortality was definitely worst in the places which get the worst soaking. The eastern Highlands, which enjoyed a mild winter, were unaffected.

Deer numbers are presently at a record high. The RDC says the total population is over 300,000 and getting bigger. However, the idea that over its whole range numbers are denser, is fallacious. Population increases, within the east-west generalisation, are localised. Some west coast deer forests have actually ceased to practise stalking for lack of deer. One of the great old deer grounds, Blackmount, has been obliged to reduce its stag cull from one hundred to thirty-five; there are plenty of similar examples. Forests which have been obliged to give up stalking are unlikely ever to resume it; deer management simply ceases to exist. This constitutes an open invitation, understandably in my view, for local people to come in and mop up the survivors at their leisure.

This, it might be thought, does not matter and is of no concern. But it contravenes the law; and it puts an area out of productive use, in sport terms and in terms of game-meat production. Once the deer are gone, and there are no hinds on their hefts to beget the next hefted generation, deer will not return. The huge area of the Cape Wrath peninsular is an example of this, denuded of deer where formerly there were plenty, devoid of human residents or visitors, loosely grazed by wandering sheep, badly burned or not burned at all, supporting a grazing population way below its capacity.

Meanwhile, in another situation, deer numbers have multiplied rapidly — but also frequently without benefit to man. Deer numbers in forestry blocks are not part of the RDC's deer count and yet woodland populations are known to be prodigious. The Forestry Commission in Argyll, venturing rough guesses, using pellet counts and early morning and dusk watches from high seats, reckons deer populations in commercial timber sometimes exceed fifty individuals per square mile, a figure higher than much open hill. More average stocking rates are thought to be thirteen to thirty-nine deer per square mile. Scotland has a large acreage under trees and the hidden population of red deer alone is reckoned by one RDC employee to be as high as 50,000: this is probably an extreme underestimate.

No thought was given to 'the dun tenants of the waste' in the early days of planting in the Highlands. They were simply fenced out or, in the bigger areas, accidentally fenced in. The Forestry Commission, which had failed to take note of productive deer management within woodland on the Continent, learnt its lesson the hard way. For several years chainsaw gangs have been laboriously hacking out rides in the impenetrable unthinned thickets and opening out sight-lines, clearing open glades, even planting special trees and shrubs along burn-sides for the deer to browse. This will hopefully distract them from bark-stripping and bring them into the open where they can be culled. Current policies, chastened by this expensive experience, incorporate deer management into woodlands at the planning stage. The Norway spruce, which draws minerals from the ground favoured by deer, is deliberately used to attract truculent tree-thrashers. The naive original assumption that deer could be fenced out, quickly embarrassed when they ran over the fences after drifting snow, and wriggled through slack wires and under water-gates, has been cast aside. More enlightened policies accept that a deer population in forestry is a potential asset.

Woodland stalking for red deer has no tradition in Scotland. The woodland craft is typically practised by the roe stalker. The roe stalker is more of a sleuth than the hill stalker, his universe one of subtle shifts in the breeze, taut concentration for the sound of light footfalls, hearing and sight stretched to the utmost. To the open-hill stalker of red deer, drawing strength and satisfaction from the panorama of open moorland, the woodland stalker's is a poorly, hedged-in art. However, to Continental sportsmen, woodland stalking has always been the ultimate craft. A few of them, alerted to the negligent attitudes to woodland stalking here, shoot stags in forestry at a fraction of the cost of open-hill stalking, and delight in our underuse of the resource.

To those who have never tried it, red deer woodland stalking has interesting lessons to teach the open-hill stalker and also the roe deer stalker. Whilst it is generally true that the challenge and difficulty of stalking in Britain is often determined by how much any particular population of deer is conditioned to being shot, all things being equal I believe stalking the reds in woodland is considerably more difficult than roe stalking. The red deer in woodland is preternaturally alert and prone only to emerge into the rides as the last light lingers in the sky, or as the first gleams of dawn shaft through the trees. Just like its big relations in North America, moose and elk, the red deer has an astonishing ability to move through dense trees soundlessly. Reds in trees are back in their primeval habitat.

In woodland, red deer's hearing, reprieved from the continual blast of wind on the open hill, regains extra sensitivity. Their powerful hearing repeatedly astonishes me. One acquaintance of mine, exaggerating only a trifle, told me that if you can hear yourself, your own body movement, then reds in woodland can hear you at a hundred yards. I think also they regain that mysterious instinct for danger, sensing your presence in an unaccountable way. I have stalked red deer in woodland often, but it is very seldom, unless I simply sit and wait for them to come out, or adopt the ignominious high-seat, that I see them before they see me. They may not always know what I am, and there is a split-second moment for action, but generally their eyes spot my movement before mine spot theirs. Anthony Buxton has described his post-war experiences, stalking big stags in tall pines on the vertiginous slopes of the Caucasus, giving a wonderful account of the perseverance and slog which suddenly climaxes in a single moment calling for decisive and accurate action. Shooting is more difficult with woodland reds because of the usual requirement of a neck-shot to stop a beast charging downhill or getting lost in thicket; often the shot has to be taken free-standing or in an impromptu position. Unlike on the open hill, almost every plantation deer killed is proof of considerable skill. Scottish woodlands have much red stalking to offer, and as today's new plantations designed for stalking use grow up, the possibilities will increase.

Red deer not only alter their habits in forestry; they change physically, and their social structure adjusts to a new environment. They graduate to new areas in a plantation depending where the ideal cover is. Very young trees are too small to conceal them, and high trees with a closed canopy and thicket-like interior starve the plant life on the ground of sunlight. In large plantations planted in stages, red deer will concentrate on the intermediary woodland with open spaces between trees tall enough to hide them. Not only do they move about the woodlands as the habitat changes, but at different stages of growth, I believe, their behaviour also alters, and habits are adopted which ensure their maximum protection consistent with adequate feeding.

The physique of deer changes in forestry. In common with other animals improving their habitat in which males are bigger than females, the stags benefit more from woodland life; whereas hinds may weigh a third more than their open-hill counterparts, stags weigh two-thirds more. The antlers may not improve, tending over a period of adaptation to get flatter, heavier and shorter, but their bodies show the benefits of shelter by regaining much of their size from centuries ago, before they were forced northwards onto open hill. This is an indicator of how stressful the open hill habitat is; the small stags of Lewis are surely clinging precariously to the very edge of their habitable range.

The birth rates of hinds leap up when in woodland. In plantations of low deer densities, hinds can reach a hundred per cent calving rate, rare even on deer farms. Twinning has been known. In forestry, stags tend to occupy higher altitude areas and to frequent any open areas of enclosed hill at dawn and dusk. In the rut, stags pace the high-up fences looking for a way out, and the abnormally large, muddy wallows I have found on my top forestry fence seem to suggest frustrated stags working themselves up before somehow breaking forth. The rut is one time forestry stags become easier to shoot, assuming the forest is enclosed, for they appear on the fence-line, but they still tend to emerge from the trees only in twilight. Hinds move about less in forestry than on the hill, no longer needing to shift from the wind, and small family parties colonise a given area and remain there.

Little so far is known about the interaction between roe and reds in forestry, other than what can be gleaned from amateur observation. Reds do not appear to use the system of trails and sharply-defined territories that roe deer do, and certainly to some degree the two species can cohabit in one area. As both animals feed on similar herbage, competition for food is inevitable as numbers rise. Where the forestry fence is breached (normally the case when deer are in), or if the plantation is unenclosed, reds tend to wander much further on to the open hill than roe to search for fresh pasture. Exceptionally, on the south-eastern edge of the Grampians, roe have colonised quite open hill, presumably emanating originally from nearby forestry which could no longer support them. There are trees on the fringe of the plantation at Borrobol which have been rubbed and browsed low-down by roe and then thrashed by reds higher up. As populations build up, it seems inevitable that before long we shall discover which species predominate in a closed area; culling programmes will in future need to take account of this predominance in distinct, targeted policies.

The spread of sika deer in Scotland in the short time since 1972 is startling, and these animals of the forest-edge have shown a tendency to hybridise readily with reds. In the Wicklows of Ireland and the southern Lake District there are now populations entirely of hybrids, which bodes ominously for Highland reds. In the nature of woodland stalking, culling is a rough and ready activity, determined more by opportunity than fixed plan. Sika are probably more difficult to shoot. Clutton-Brock has already mentioned the possibility that pure red deer may eventually only preserve undiluted genetics on the islands. It would be a sad fate for the red deer if the introduction of a small Japanese alien resulted in miscegenation with our own glorious and persistent survivor, pushing it further towards the extinction it has so far circumvented. Sika spread out only where there are trees. It is conceivable that if the most ambitious planting targets of the tree growers were ever realised, and a further four million acres of the Highlands vanished under the conifer quilt, what red deer survived on exposed high ground would have too restricted a range to resist interbreeding with sika and hybrids would rapidly take over. This would be tragic.

Already the spread of forestry has brought with it an ever-rising population of roe; this has presented Scotland with a sporting opportunity it has been slow to take up. The roe is an interesting animal, reliant for survival more on hearing than sight, very highly-strung and hard to domesticate, and the same size today as it was when it dwelt in Scotland after the Ice Ages. The most significant attribute of the roe for silvicultural and sporting purposes is that it is a pairing not a herd animal. As young calves are driven from their parents' territory they seek out new ground for themselves: every generation of the roe is naturally expansionist.

The extent of the spread of roe, and densities of local populations, has never been studied, although something under 200,000 is a reasonable knockabout figure for the Scottish roe population. As with red deer in woodland, when localised population assessments have been attempted, numbers of roe are invariably higher than expected. It is a safe bet to assume that wherever there are new plantings, fenced or unfenced, by the time trees are a few feet high roe will be in there, hiding up discreetly by day and feeding on grasses and herbs at dawn and dusk.

Roe are often resident in trees for a long time without their presence being suspected. After a short while their trotting paths will be discernible to the sharp eye; they always cross open space in the same place, emerging with extreme wariness. The stems of saplings will be bark-stripped in spring by bucks marking off their territories with the scent gland on the inside of their antlers.

The roe rut is between June and August, and the doe has a delayed pregnancy, dropping her calf, or calves, in late May or early June. The calving success for roe in woodland approximates more to woodland red deer; two out of three is an approximate rate of survival and twinning is not uncommon. Roe have a shorter life-span than red deer, very few surviving beyond the age of eight.

The roe is an animal of great charm and delicacy. Many people who happily stalk red deer express reservations about turning their rifles on its nimble, shy and graceful smaller relation. Again, this is in sharp contradiction to Continental stalkers, for whom roe stalking is an art for the connoisseurs, and not to be rivalled by anything. The Continentals have a detailed methodology for classing roe antlers and are willing to pay large sums to shoot heads which combine in characteristics to qualify as good medals. Tardily, deer and woodland managers in England have realised what prizes the English woodlands are harbouring, and nowadays the top roe trophies internationally are to be found not in Eastern Europe or Germany, but in the Home Counties.

It has yet to dawn on many FC conservancies, private landowners and woodland companies in Scotland that they too are letting go to waste a lot of venison, and generations of good heads and possible trophies. It has astonished Continentals trekking as far north as Sutherland to see the heads I have blithely extracted from my plantation without an idea they might rank against roe trophies from further south. Body weights are excellent also. Yet much roe stalking is quite unutilised in the Highlands. Roe come to physical and sporting maturity faster than reds, and the buck season opens in May when the shooting and stalking calendar is otherwise empty. Roe venison is considerably more valuable to the butcher than red venison, a reflection of its sweeter and less gamey flavour. In a time of diversification in land uses, roe stalking, which is additionally beneficial to forestry, is an obvious resource for development.

It is inexcusable, given the FC's vaunted services to recreation, that some conservancies still do not welcome roe stalking tenants. Roe stalkers do conservancy rangers' work for them by culling deer inimical to young plantations. They tend, in any case, to take out 'rogue' bucks — those looking for territories and liable to do most damage to trees — and provide rents and venison for the state exchequer. No country in Europe is so prodigal with its roe deer asset. In the conservancies where roe stalking is run as a complementary business, considerable satisfaction is afforded sportsmen, employment is created for stalkers, and revenues are annually realised in an industry notorious for the infrequency of income.

The FC culls about 12,000 roe a year from all of its British forests. On a landholding of three million acres this averages one roe for every 250 acres, which fails dramatically to qualify as a serious culling rate. The FC presumably believes that sufficient roe are shot to satisfy their primary function of protecting trees, the sporting significance of roe being traditionally regarded as secondary. Some private roe deer plantation owners, however, trying deliberately to optimise culls without reducing the core breeding population, have managed to sustain a yield of around one roe to every six acres, and this is in north-east Scotland. Particular situations will obviously differ with quality of habitat, width of rides and numbers of clearings, pasture enrichment, presence of feeding licks, possible feeding competition from red deer, calf susceptibility to predation by foxes, and the stage of growth of the trees. But the FC culling rate compared to any moderately energetic manage-ment programme seems astonishingly slack. With shortages of rangers, and a shrinking work force, guided roe stalking may be hard to organise. To unaccompanied stalking there is no such objection. The loss to the nation when all is taken into account is indefensible and unnecessary. Private sector forestry companies are no less to blame. The proportion of the roe cull shot for sport is small and rents are low. Unlike the FC, there is no pressure on forestry companies to provide any recreational facilities at all.

It must now be clear that deer stalking in Scotland is under-utilised generally. Hind populations are mounting, but with no corresponding effort to market and sell hind shooting. Sika deer are stalked here and there, generally as part of a stalking package completed by other deer species, or as part of a mixed stalking-shooting bag; no policy exists to stop the spread of sika. Roe are proliferating abundantly while roe buck letting remains haphazard; doe shooting, which often involves taking a dependent calf as well, and is even more testing, largely goes ignored. Defenders of the status quo will say that the real meat of Highland stalking is open hill stag shooting and that, at least, is comprehensively used.

This comforting assumption does not stand up to examination. When compared to hunting abroad for stags, bull moose, elk, caribou, chamois or even roe bucks, British stalking is let for a trifling amount. Stalking rents are not only low, but rent levels are erratic, and the higher levels are no guarantee of quality. Rents are assessed on a per stag basis, and on many of the mainstream deer forests during the season at least one stag will be shot each day. Towards the end of the season, or whenever most stags are present on the ground, the number expected per week will peak. Stalking rents in 1990 will probably range between £150 and £250 per stag, which means that a week of, say, six stags will cost between £900 and £1,500. This is about the rate that North American outfitters (sporting agents) will charge for a single caribou or elk; a moose is considerably more. The hunt may be over after the first day.

There are some German hunting clubs where each member has a chance at a roe buck or red stag only once every three years. Such clubs are run extremely professionally with carefully managed beats on which each animal is known and regularly monitored, winter feeding is provided, and sight-lines are planned in forestry or on the forest-edge specifically for deer shooting. Applicants for membership to German hunting clubs must pass comprehensive proficiency tests proving an all-round stalking knowledge and capability, and may wait several years before the actual hunting commences. When eventually an animal is killed, the occasion is celebrated with elaborate rituals dignifying the lost soul of the hunted and attaching it in some spiritual sense to the soul of the hunter, a general demonstration of the seriousness of the act of taking life. Not surprisingly, when hunters with such a miserly quota at home, and with such reverence for a real kill, peer over a Highland peat bank and see a hundred stags strolling past, they are prone to the sort of excitement none of us would want to be in the grip of. Part of their thrill is that, even compensating for greater German affluence, the visitor is getting his sport cheaply.

There are an assortment of reasons for these anomalies, to do with the aim of British stalking managers, and the aims of foreign stalking clients. The key difference between the British approach and perspectives elsewhere is that since the rise in red deer populations the stalking season here is regarded as a cull. Stags surplus to requirements are sought. The stags with best antler conformation and body-type are deliberately left with the aim of long-term improvement of the breeding stock. Whether this is scientifically sound, precisely which stags successfully fertilise hinds and at what stage in the rut, is a separate matter about which not much is known. The fact remains that Scottish stalking is based on the premise that the grandest stags are inviolate. In maintaining this policy we go against the assumptions which prevail, and have always prevailed, elsewhere.

The stalking client is therefore performing two functions, one as the hunter, which is pleasurable, the other as the agent of the cull, which is a duty. There is an inherent contradiction in his role on the hill which many Continentals find exasperating. The British client, sensitive to the image of the game hunter as exploiter, and usually not trophy-orientated, finds the underlying culling principle positively attractive, because it enables him to cloak his enjoyment in the guise of humanitarian duty. Stalking is not pure self-indulgence. The Scottish stalking style, involving immersion in icy burns, exposure on windswept ridges, and general discomfort, reinforces this perception. British stalking people who want trophies go abroad, where trophies are sedulously cultivated for killing at the height of their maturation. Making the shot involves no discomfiture. The two hunting traditions have, I believe, a different psychological base.

Then there is the inverse effect of sheer numbers. The red deer on the hill may actually be no more populous in their habitat than roe deer in Continental woodland but, moving over undulating country in large parties, they conjure up scenes of antedeluvian wildness and abundance. The very number of them dilutes the value of the individual. It is hard to maintain the hunting worth of an animal which appears so numerous. Also, of course, Scottish deer forests need to cull large numbers in their short season; the impression of cervine abundance is reinforced. The foreign hunter drives home with his roofrack bristling with antlers, but he is wondering to himself why he did not shoot even more.

Stalking for the Victorians was a fashion leader. Increasingly in recent times it has lagged behind grouse shooting and fishing in popularity; there are far higher numbers of shooters and fishermen in Britain than stalkers. Nor are British stalkers drawn from any social elite: the smart set by and large have no desire to squirm through a peat bog being pelted with hailstones. Stalking is therefore not underpinned by a substantial home-based clientele. The numerical majority of British stalkers, furthermore, are roe stalkers operating in England. This has held back the rents open hill Highland stalking could command. The foreign stalkers, who comprise about a third of the clientele, come to Britain because it is cheap, unregulated, and there are plenty of stags. Unlike English roe stalking, the Highland red stag is a low-calibre sporting target.

The physical rigour of Scottish stalking, which to aficionados is an invaluable part of the sporting experience, has dubious appeal for Europeans. This is part and parcel of the same sporting ethic which inclines many British roe stalkers to frown on high-seat shooting as epicene and unfair (roe do not habitually look upwards), in comparison to Europeans, for whom the high-seat is the correct vantage-point. The British orientation is that you must work for your sport, whereas on the Continent emphasis of a spiritual kind is placed on the kill itself. For international hunters one of the joys of travel is to see regional idiosyncracies, but undoubtedly these differing standpoints have hindered widespread acceptance of Highland stalking virtues. Because it has lost social cachet, too many deer forest proprietors have accepted fashion's dictates and the unimportance of stalking, and sold it ridiculously cheaply. By so doing they corroborate Highland stalking's decline, and make it more difficult for those trying to raise stalking's image and realise its proper worth. Until there is a concerted effort by deer stalking proprietors in the Highlands, this superb resource, for which there is no equivalent anywhere else, will remain undersold and undervalued.

If deer managers have been slow to maximise the potential of woodland stalking, the law-makers in Brussels and civil servants in Whitehall have been quick enough to spot a comparatively unrestricted sport demanding regulation. Legislative ideas, drafts, and final statutes have appeared, and either stuck or disappeared, on a number of different items. Those referring to the hygiene of wild venison should be set against the backdrop of a completely clean slate for the wild venison industry in Britain to date; no contaminated wild venison is known to have ever entered the food chain. Legislation to upgrade larders has loomed without becoming effective for several years, and many deer forest owners spent large sums of money on lavish larders equipped with chill-rooms long before they needed to. The real culprits with poor larders were the fly-by-night game-dealers trading in poached venison, who put at risk the reputation of the legitimate trade.

At one point in 1989 a Brussels directive produced the astonishing idea that all carcases would have to be inspected by a vet on the hill: this was modified to veterinary inspection within twenty-four hours of death. This concept, which would have required the Highland veterinary service to be at least doubled, and on permanent standby for out-of-the-way carcase inspections, obviously arose from a committee quite ignorant of the way open hill stalking is conducted. Happily, it too has fallen by the wayside. British sporting interests, realising that impractical directives of this sort, or others which strike at British sporting traditions, may materialise out of the blue, have now created a watchdog organisation to appraise them of European whimsicalities.

UK legislation is equally unstable. In the course of 1989 the law affecting firearms certificates for stalking visitors from abroad changed twice. Firstly, foreign police forces were asked to verify and guarantee the characters of visiting sportsmen; then that dicey duty fell on deer forest owners or their agents as sponsors. The impracticalities of vetting each member of a foreign shooting or stalking party are self-evident. As a permit for each member of a stalking party costs £12, and all the burden of work falls on the sponsor, it looks as though the Home Office merely wanted to arrogate some sporting revenue to itself.

The great white hope of the 1970s for estates and farmers wishing to diversify management of their deer populations was deer farming. Already established with a good track record in New Zealand, the idea was that red deer would convert heather into meat more efficiently in the hills than sheep or cattle. The first government-backed deer farm venture was in Kincardine-shire, and it proved that deer became domesticated easily, maintained good health, and improved on their hill calving rate by two or three times. The research centre at Glensaugh gave the green light to deer farmers.

The message was acted on, not by Scottish hill farmers and estate owners, but mostly by English farmers in the south, who recognised in deer alternative grazing stock for their grass fields. The idea that was to save the heather laird became a challenging, enjoyable and profitable experiment for enthusiastic southern graziers, bringing to commercial perfection the old English tradition of deer parks. Scottish deer farms also are mostly on low ground or foothills. The poorer the herbage and the higher up, the larger the area that has to be monitored and enclosed, the less the natural shelter, and the higher the costs. Potential deer farmers in the Highlands found themselves faced with the same rigid equations which determined the viability of traditional hill farming. If winter feed needed to be bought in from outside, profits would evaporate. Deer farming had the added problems of high start-up costs, not being recognised by DAFS and therefore without grant aid, the illegalising of the trade in live velvet antlers (which had bolstered the New Zealand trade) on humanitarian grounds, and a British market stubbornly resistant to the charms of venison.

These disadvantages are fading away. Deer farming is now recognised and a few Highland proprietors have realised they can get round start-up costs by feeding hinds into hill parks then closing the gate. A few others have operated this ruse, then overcome the formidable difficulties of loading wild deer on to lorries and selling them to other deer farmers. We have been doing this successfully for a few years at Borrobol on ground from which the sheep have been cleared. A suitable situation is a natural surplus of breeding hinds, to avoid depleting the basic wild stock, a catching-up system into which the deer will readily feed, and a solid-sided race in which they can be sorted, tagged, and examined for ageing. The deer-catching system should be well away from estate marches to avoid disputes about whose hinds are being carted off; for the same reason intensive artificial feeding is undesirable — and unnecessary, if there is a genuinely top-heavy population.

The profit margins in this are attractive, but the herding of wild deer, which is done patiently and quietly, is a tricky business and should not be contemplated unless an able stockman is in charge. Separating out wild stags at the end of the rut is not a pastime for the faint-hearted. Attempts to catch up too large numbers of deer at once can lead to loss of control, mass break-outs, or the possibility of injury from crushing in the race. Deer catching codes of practice are already being discussed. Guidelines for newcomers to the business would be welcome. The danger is that, with insufficient evidence, these would be translated into statutory controls which took no account of the wide variety of circumstances of individual situations. Whatever controls materialise, they will be no substitute for intelligent stockmanship.

Into the volatile saga of British deer farming, typified by erratic price movements at the live deer sales in Perth, tuberculosis has burst onto the scene. Transferable quickly from animal to animal, particularly in crowded domesticated conditions, and even to humans, TB does not affect venison or anyone consuming it. But the TB outbreak occurred in early 1989 when the government's farm research programme was being sorely stretched by the salmonella scare and BSE in cattle. Aware that no positive test for TB in live deer so far existed, wary of funding expensive research for a marginal sector of British stock farming, yet keen to be seen doing something, the government created a health scheme for TB-free stocks, made TB notification compulsory, and introduced movement records for all live deer. Despite the illogicality of a health scheme without a conclusive test, and a compulsory notification without a compulsory test, deer farmers inured to bewildering public stances to their trade will presumably survive.

In the long term, venison will continue to carve out a niche in the national diet, and some Highland situations will find themselves more suited to deer farming than other activities. Those deer farms situated on the edge of deer forests will have the continuing advantage of a ready supply of fresh healthy stock on the hill with which to boost and reinvigorate farm stocks when necessary. There is every indication that venison is increasingly entering the consumer's consciousness, and if public knowledge about how to prepare a meat which is prone to dry out quickly were to be extended, venison might regain the popularity it enjoyed in medieval times. Deer farmers, who should be able to provide a continuity of supply and consistency of size and flavour, will be to thank for this.

The arguments against deer farming which denigrate enclosing a large and beautiful wild animal, which symbolises unfettered freedom, I cannot accept. All our domestic stock originated from wild beasts and some of them would have been extirpated if their tractability had not saved them in time. Deer have maintained a traditional presence in deer parks since very early times, and these parks kept in containment animals to be enjoyed as an amenity asset and as food. My only reservation about the long-term consequences of deer farming is that at some point in the future the objection will be put forward that to continue hunting an animal that lives side by side with man in domesticated state is unacceptable. Admittedly, mountain sheep in Canada and boar in Europe are hunted regardless of relations domiciled on farms in the vicinity. But wild sheep and boar bear little superficial resemblance to domesticated stock. More importantly, they are hunted in countries where their pursuit has no stigma of elitism. Also, the British mentality about animals is different, much more prone to sentimental attitudes and an anthropomorphic understanding of animal experience. It would be unfortunate if a deer farming concept devised to help out and expand an embattled hill farming economy in Scotland was ultimately transformed into a moral stick with which to beat the deer forest owner originally envisaged as its beneficiary.

Deer farming, more scientific wild deer culling, and wild deer capture, are complementary parts of a move towards better utilisation of our deer resource which is right and proper. At the other end of the spectrum — in random deer shooting and injury at night by poachers, in starving deer populations pushed onto farmland by the cruelties of winter, in deer drives in badly-designed forestry where the burgeoning numbers of animals have become a pest — lies waste, mismanagement, and abuse of the resource.

For some time now murmurs have been audible from the backwoodsmen in the stalking world articulating the necessity for the strengthening of statutory controls on deer management. What are perceived as tragic and unnecessary management errors, like heavy winter mortalities, add fuel to the controversy. What is required — private management by deer forest owners? Or a state body financed, staffed and properly empowered to enforce, not merely advise, deer culls, and resolve disputes on deer matters? Any conspicuous rogues amongst deer forest owners, rapacious landowners prematurely decimating stock, or indolent ones allowing hind populations to swell, give ammunition to the supporters of a beefed-up RDC.

A revised RDC role with the power of statutory culls for the whole of the Highlands would bring commissioners onto private property in a way which most deer forest managers would resent. There would be no precedent in Britain for such state involvement, although state management is practised in Europe. If landowners are alarmed at this prospect they should hasten to perfect their culling targets, form responsible management co-operatives, and ensure as best they can that wandering winter deer do not destroy farmers' and crofters' crops. The possibility of losing their unrestricted controls is real. The further sub-division of estates into smaller blocks on which the deer are not hefted transforms stalking from a carefully conducted cull into a haphazard, hit-or-miss affair based on opportunism. The unsatisfactory situation may exist where deer harassed for six months of the year are chivvied into a state of disorientation. It is the further subdivision of deer forests which will hasten more rigorous state management of our wild deer before anything else. The RDC itself has shown no enthusiasm for fortifying its remit. If it became necessary, it would be an indictment of private sector ability to shoulder adequately its responsibilities.

Chapter Twelve
Managing the Silver Harvest

If deer are integrally involved in the future of the Highlands, the salmon is equally so. The salmon's economic, social and symbolic importance has been recognised internationally. The North Atlantic Salmon Conservation Organisation (NASCO) was founded in 1984, and in it are represented all Atlantic salmon producing nations, including America and Russia. The creation of NASCO is one of the first occasions on which multi-state management has become recognised as essential for a far-ranging species valued for its sporting use; no bird species has ever successfully drummed up such a diverse assortment of supporters. The success and growing strength of NASCO, allied to powerful national salmon-interest groups, have resulted in a perspective for the 1990s in which for the first time for some years the future of salmon looks optimistic. Abuses may abound, and the discovery by the Icelandic coast guard of Danish drift netters illegally taking salmon under the camouflage of Polish and Panama flags of convenience as recently as January 1990 shows that some states are still willing to flout, or permit to be flouted, laws they have agreed to observe. The overall picture is nonetheless a safer framework for salmon, and a gradual tightening of protection over its migratory range.

One of the principles of internationally-agreed management of salmon on the high seas is that anadromous fish belong to the rivers in which they were spawned, and to which they return to spawn themselves. Catching them elsewhere interferes with the local management of fishing which is needed to protect the stock. This principle has strong support in NASCO and is the mainspring of the present initiative to buy off the netting rights of those nations which intercept salmon on their migration. The only non-salmon producers doing this are Greenland and the Faeroe Islands, and for several years NASCO has pressurised these two participants in the salmon fishery to restrict their drift-net and long-line catch; quotas have been lowered by agreement each year.

The depressed price of farmed salmon (Billingsgate prices in February 1990 were £1.60 a pound, compared to £3.00 a pound for cod and haddock) inspired an initiative from sporting and commercial salmon fishermen in Iceland to organise a buy-out of the salmon fishing quotas presently allotted to Greenland and the Faeroes. They have both been underperforming their quotas in a declining market, and the timing of the bid is perfect. At the time of writing, this idea is only three months old. It has been welcomed by NASCO members and the Greenlanders and Faeroese have accepted the possibility of a deal. Much needs to be sorted out — the value of their fishery and the size of compensation; each nation's share of the catch being bought out and the determination of national contributions to the buy-out fund; and the longevity of the deal (the Icelanders are stressing the importance of the restrictions being permanent). It seems that part of the Greenland catch which is local subsistence fishing will not be included. The interested beneficiaries of a buy-out are Iceland, Norway, Sweden, EC countries (primarily Britain, Ireland and France), Canada and America.

It is estimated that the initial benefit to British salmon fishing could be around 25,000 extra fish if the Faeroese fishery was suspended, and ten times as many if Greenland also stopped. A high proportion would be the larger fish that have spent two winters at sea, which British fishing waters so badly need. Again, very approximately, Britain's contribution to the buy-out might be £1,500,000, a figure which looks distinctly cheap at the price. With the public will to protect salmon already demonstrated, it is unlikely this sum could not rapidly be raised. The principle of richer nations buying out primary extraction rights of poorer countries is now accepted worldwide (American banks have cancelled debt in exchange for protection for South American rainforest). But it exposes the anomaly of a surviving drift-net fishery which is uncomfortably close to home, and has for some years cast doubt over Britain's commitment to sound domestic conservation. This is the English drift-net fishery off Northumberland.

The persistence of the Northumbrian fishery is an irritant in a number of ways. It annoys Scottish fishery bodies because the fish caught off Berwick are describing a loop in their migration run and heading north-west back into home rivers north of the border. Over ninety per cent of the catch is Scottish-homing. In Scotland, drift-netting is illegal, and has been since 1971. The Northumbrian catch is very big, comprising in 1989 some 47,000 fish out of a total catch by all methods in England and Wales of 110,000; the Northumbrian nets also extracted about a fifth (26,000) of all English and Welsh sea trout.

The Northumbrian fishery is obviously a blot on Britain's claim to be a responsible salmon producer. It weakens the British case against the Irish west coast drift-net fishery which, unlike the Northumbrian one, is unregulated and out of control, and it aggravates the Scots. Successive governments have declined to act and stop it, apparently because it is felt to do so would penalise local fishermen in order to gratify visiting anglers. Refusal to support the rod against the net is as inflexible with salmon as it is in the case of British sea anglers against commercial sea fishermen.

In Ireland the commercial netsmen have for years been hastening their own extinction. Huge numbers of cheap licences are issued (four hundred in Donegal alone in 1989), and countless more drift-netters deign to bother paying the nominal licence fee. Netting is conducted off the Hebrides, plundering Scottish-homing fish, and as far out as two hundred miles off the Irish west coast, unmonitored, unregulated, and unecological. Even the massive fecundity of the Irish salmon fishery has registered protest against this scale of maltreatment. During the 1980s the recorded net catch of an average 1,090 tonnes a year was fifty per cent down on catches in the previous decade. Rod and line catches are dropping; and fish sizes are dropping. Ireland is presently looking for EC funds with which to buy surveillance aircraft to monitor the offshore fishery.

The attempt by NASCO to buy off the Greenland and Faeroese nets signals a wind of change blowing through the salmon world. If these nets are bought off, the Irish free-for-all, the Northumbrian anomaly and the other small English and Welsh drift-net fisheries, will stick out like sore thumbs. Drift-nets take a toll on birds and mammals, as well as causing injuries to escaping fish. In terms of present-day knowledge they are simply crude, old-fashioned and illogical and, as such, doomed.

It is strange the way the gravity of an issue bears no relation to its exposure in the media, and thus to public awareness. While the drift-net fisheries were depleting the wild salmon stocks by thousands of tonnes a year, and the salmon was predated in its long migration by a plethora of illegal methods without much attention being paid, when salmon farming on the west Highland seaboard started making profits, the press grabbed the anti-salmon farming ball and ran with it as hard as they could go. No new industry that I can think of has been subjected to so protracted a barrage of criticism on more slender grounds. No wonder the salmon farmers are nonplussed. Offshore at Ullapool, dozens of East European klondikers offload fishguts and waste by the ton, dumping that goes quite unremarked by the environmental and salmon fishery lobbies. Meanwhile, without a shred of evidence, salmon farmers are accused of doing long-term damage to the sea bed, being profligate in the use of dangerous chemicals, and allowing the escapement of degenerate farmed stock which will hybridise with wild stocks and ultimately wipe them out. The ill-grace with which many environmental groups in the Highlands have greeted the only truly successful new farming-orientated industry of the 1980s is a warning. Following the salmon farming debate, it is impossible sometimes not to conclude that the only motivation of critics is envy or annoyance at someone else's success.

A success salmon farming has indubitably been. Production of a thousand tonnes in 1981 (roughly on a par with the wild salmon catch) had grown to 29,000 tonnes in 1989, making Scotland the biggest producer after Norway. Of the many projects financed by the Highlands and Islands Development Board, salmon farming is the flagship success story. The HIDB endorsed and supported salmon farming from the start, saw the value of the west coast's severely indented coastline offering sheltered saltwater sites, recognised the employment implications in a part of Scotland crying out for jobs, and spotted the marketing potential of a product that could justifiably parade tartan-wrapped. Never can it have occurred to the early pioneers that one day people could seriously demand that their mobile flotation rafts should be abandoned because they spoiled the view. The scenic point is generally raised by those who migrated to the Highlands for the scenery — a half-baked reason to change your domicile at the best of times. Most native Scots are delighted on the lonely sea lochs to see some sort of activity and enterprise being attempted. They have known the twin demoralisations of unemployment and shrinking communities for too long. At a fish farming conference in Inverness in 1988, a keynote speech was made by the HIDB's aquaculture spokesman referring bitingly to fringe conservationists as 'self-appointed custodians of the environment who want to preserve the Highlands in aspic'.

Naturally, there is more to the salmon farming debate than a consideration of the scenery. It is of proper concern that salmon 'cages', actually capacious weighted nets, do not accumulate beneath them decaying fish feed and fish waste-products that cause long-term damage. Solid waste filtering through the nets does indeed affect the seabed biosystem and sediment chemistry. But when solid wastes fall, biological activity speeds up to cope with it. Seabed nutrient states and phytoplankton growth change. The ability of a particular site to absorb change depends on the water-depth below the salmon cages and what is called the rate of tidal exchange, or the flushing powers of the high tide-low tide differential. The Scottish Marine Biological Association has examined fish farm seabeds and found that solid waste build-ups are very localised, affecting the seabed only below and around the cage. When the cage is moved the original seabed biosystem restores itself rapidly. Unless too many salmon farms were crowded into one sea loch, cages were not moved and tidal exchanges were abnormally weak, it is unlikely that salmon farms as presently constituted are doing any damage to the seabed. The spread of a deadly fish farm parasite in Norway, which resulted in heavy farmed fish mortalities, salmon cages being towed out of fjords to open sea, and wild salmon becoming infected, with fatal results, is not a probable scenario in west Scotland. The tidal exchange there is five times as strong as in Norway.

Many fish farmers now employ health specialists in recognition of their symbiotic relationship with the environment. For the salmon farmer a clean water state is a vital necessity. Research into the environmental impacts of medical treatments is not far advanced. The chemical Nuvan, used to treat sea lice, has been shown to damage lobsters and crustacean larvae if used in large doses. However, at present states of knowledge, Nuvan is imperceptible in treated salmon after only twenty-four hours, and is rapidly dispersed in the water with the flushing movement of the tide. The Scottish Salmon Growers' Association is trying hard to ensure Nuvan's use is responsible, and application kept to a minimum. The aim has always been to produce salmon as naturally as possible.

The most ticklish question, and the one which arouses most alarm amongst wild salmon interests, surrounds genetics. Salmon farming's critics say escaped farm fish (escapement is a common, probably ineradicable problem) will mix with wild stocks, interfere with their long-accumulated genetic evolution, and possibly displace them. This assumes that escaped fish will automatically head up rivers; normally they do the reverse, waiting a short time before heading for open water. Escaped fish which go into rivers tend to mimic the wild salmon they encounter there. The worriers also assume that competition with the wild salmon will be successful, unlikely in view of the re-acclimatisation farmed fish would need to undergo; and also that if farmed fish survived and spawned, their progeny would in their turn debilitate wild stocks.

Many of these suppositions are not thought out. Fishery scientists at Stirling University, where fish diseases have been studied for a long time, take a more sanguine view. They believe that in a mix of wild and farmed stocks there is no reason why natural selection should not operate normally, the smolts of the strongest stock returning themselves to spawn. In some rivers a system of multiple spawning populations has developed, with different growing and smolting periods, followed by different periods at sea. This spreads the risk of inclement conditions for reproduction of the species. There is no reason surviving escapees should not fit into this pattern.

Failure by farmed fish to locate winter feeding grounds, should this occur, would be part of this selection process. The only backward development would be escaped fish somehow lessening the genetic variability of different salmon populations. It is worth recalling that hatchery programmes have been mixing stocks of salmon in British rivers for a hundred years; few, if any, rivers have a pristine natural salmon stock. Some rivers, where original stocks became extinct, such as the Clyde, have been restocked successfully with non-native smolts. Some of the world's great fishing water (in New Zealand and the Falklands) was created by artificial stocking. So far no single proven case of wild and farmed stock intermixing in Scottish waters exists: the syndrome of perverted mutants is hypothetical. A study presently being undertaken is radio-tracking an assortment of wild fish and farmed fish after an escapement in Loch Eriboll early in 1989. Farmed fish were found in the River Polla apparently spawning alongside wild ones. Radio-tracking will give an idea of the survival rates of escaped farmed fish and, in a very small sample, a comparison of their performance with wild salmon.

It would be rash in the midst of pioneer research to state emphatically that the fuss over farmed escapees is alarmist. No-one would quarrel with the Atlantic Salmon Trust's (AST) recommendations that salmon farmers try and limit escapements, monitor any escapements as best they can, avoid using fish of foreign origin as a precaution, and possibly use sterile salmon while awaiting the refinement of knowledge about farmed and wild stock mixes. Too often, I feel, the rod fisherman has resented the arrival of the salmon farmer on his patch and used the genetic argument to raise a scare. It is forgotten that the last person wanting fish to escape is the fish farmer himself, with a vested interest in their security. (Ironically, as security in salmon cage construction improves a growing threat of escaped salmon comes from animal rights activists, who go on to vandalise onshore buildings into the bargain.) Where criticism could have been more fruitfully directed is at the present system of salmon farm licensing, and the role of the Crown Estate Commissioners responsible for the offshore side of development, in assessing new applications.

The Commissioners act as both maritime landlords reaping the benefit of seabed leases, and also the judges in the consultation procedure for fish farm licence applications. There is an obvious conflict of interest and the

Commissioners are not publicly accountable. If the Commissioners were bent on raising revenue they could, in theory, crowd a sea loch with more lessees than the natural cleansing processes could cope with. Appeal against Commissioners' decisions is permissible only from statutory bodies which emasculates the possibility of full and open discussion.

It is already evident that different local planning authorities take widely differing standpoints in their responsibility for the onshore part of fish farming's development. This makes for a confusion of regional policies inimical to the balanced development of the industry. The 1989/1990 winter has seen very low salmon prices, and small operators forced to close down as large producers have sold salmon at below production cost to avoid a log-jam. Britain is still not self-sufficient in farmed salmon; as the price recovers the pressure on new sites will resume. Salmon producers reckon the best sites were taken long ago and all eyes will be on the Crown Estate Commissioners to see what judgements are made after an upturn in confidence.

Most salmon farmers are in favour of this loosely-run, but heavily capitalised and high-risk, industry being tightened up. The role of the Crown Estate Commissioners is ambiguous. Planning authorities operate independently and outwith any nationally agreed policies, and there is no reasonable process of appeal. Responsible salmon farmers would welcome hygiene tests on farm stock being moved about as a form of self-protection, controls on the proliferation of salmon farms, and controls in the use of dangerous chemicals. It would also seem reasonable, as the AST has requested, that district fishery boards with responsibility for wild salmon stocks, should be involved in planning when fish farms are proposed in the vicinity of major salmon-run estuary mouths.

Despite its prevalence on the west coast and islands, salmon farming is still a young industry in the Highlands and the large east coast salmon runs, constituting three-quarters of Scottish fish, have not yet been encumbered with cages. Although the growth of salmon farming is expected very soon to level off, it will not be for want of new technology. The east coast is less suitable for salmon farming in a number of ways, but off western Ireland rubber-boom structures, developed from oil-extraction technology, are working well in completely exposed sites several miles out to sea and serviced by helicopters. Before this stage is reached it would be comforting to know the answers to some of the queries that salmon farming raises.

Atlantic salmon fishers should be grateful for the effect farmed fish have had on the economics of both estuary netting and poaching. The fish worth £6 a pound ten years ago is now cheap. Estuary nets in the early 1980s redoubled their efforts in order to compensate for lower prices. They were going against the current and damaging fisheries. One by one, netsmen round the Scottish coast are folding up or being bought out if they are lucky. Probably the total value of Scottish salmon netting is under two million pounds. With the value of rod fishing soaring it is clear that netting's days are numbered. The vaulting catches of rivers which own their nets and have suspended them spells it out: estuary netting is dying out.

Opposite: Megan Boyd, celebrated Brora fly-tier. Sadly she has had to give up, suffering diminished sight.

Top: Invernesshire forestry, with decorative hardwoods in grow-tubes. The water will probably have suffered altered acidity as a result of the conifer necklace.

Bottom: Alltnabreac in Caithness, flow country afforestation.

Opposite: Strathaird Salmon Farms near Glenelg. Harvesting marketable salmon from a salmon 'cage'.

Top: Lochdhu Lodge on Caithness flows, with bog-cotton foreground. Bog-cotton is a nutritious staple springtime food for grouse, sheep and deer.

Bottom: Forestry ploughing around Lochdhu. In twenty years not much of the house will be visible.

Previous page: This fish farm is situated on the north-west coast.

Top: Hydro-electric dam on Ben Cruachan, Argyll, with denatured river trickling in front of it.

Bottom: A crocodile of walkers, frequently a problem for stalkers.

What must certainly have irked netsmen and salmon farmers in these disputes was the holier-than-thou attitude of the rod fishing fraternity. These voices, after all, hailed from the parts of the river in which young wild fish look for congenial conditions in which to thrive. Research in Scotland has shown that the streamy riffles in upper catchments which chiefly support young fish are in trouble. The domestic problems of Scottish rivers in sustaining salmon runs have narrowed down to the period of development between egg and smolt. In this regard riverbank maintenance and artificial stocking policies have been unsatisfactory.

The floods of winter 1990 showed, on the big east Highland rivers which were not acutely affected, how progressive degeneration of riverbanks could result in appalling loss of banking from spates and subsequent damage to riverbeds. Critical bank revetment had been neglected. Government-induced agricultural improvements in the 1970s and early 1980s had bequeathed expanses of poor improved pasture where once there had been heather, a good binding dwarf-shrub, productive of insects which nourish young fish, and resistant to trampling hooves. Sometimes bank-firming scrub woodland had been cleared for reseeded pastures. Cattle and sheep had been wandering freely to the river to drink, only rarely provided with the fenced corridors and cut-away drinking-pools which are mandatory on properly-managed river-systems. Trampled banks, hollowed out by sheep seeking shade, and warrened by rabbits, were then torn away by the ripping swirl of spates. Boulders and clods filled the pools, making obstructions which pushed the river sideways towards newly exposed banking again. Rivers widened and shallowed, losing their productive capacity. Rueful riparian owners gazed at the damage in spring, and dread what effects will effects will show up when the young fish whose habitat has been destroyed are due to return again.

Artificial stocking is performed on Scottish rivers often with the slenderest scientific basis, by bumbling amateurs. How many river owners who have leapt into an artificial stocking programme stopped to analyse the present state of stocks, and particular deficiencies? Only one Highland river, the North Esk, even has a fish counter. What parr and smolt counts, done under controlled conditions, preceded stocking programmes on the rest? Very few. At the most blundering level, vendors of timeshare salmon fishing have written in assurances of artificial stocking effort as if, like with pheasants, the number of young fish introduced had a direct relation to the ultimate catch. The Freshwater Fisheries Laboratory had already shown that unnecessary stocking can actually compromise the survival of native fish. The best management tool of river boards and proprietors is the maximisation of conditions in which young fish have food and space. Too often dramatic and precipitate actions are harming the fish they are designed to encourage, where a more all-round environmental approach, costing less, and not needing repeating every year, would have served the objective better.

It is surprising for such a major salmon producer that the debate about management of rivers, artificial stocking, hydrology and water purity has not begun in earnest in the Highlands. Guidelines and ground rules have not been

Opposite: Early July salmon netting on Berriedale beach, Caithness, in 1980. The hut behind is made of fish-boxes. 150 fish were caught in one sweep later the same day. Now the netting is done in order to tag fish for research.

formulated, despite the useful scientific data already established. At root the problem lies with outmoded systems of ownership, and the relation of salmon fishing to politics. The right to salmon fish is a separate right in Scotland. Whole environment management, for a river encompassing the entire catchment, is therefore often impossible. Yet the nature of a river is determined by adjacent land uses; proper land and water management are bound together. The government has traditionally had a hands-off policy with regard to the salmon fishery, at any rate at home. This is despite the latest Salmon Act, which altered no fundamentals. The respected salmon authority, the Atlantic Salmon Trust, was formed by, and is funded by, independent individuals. It is looked to by government for information. Would we treat this grand resource so cavalierly if it was any other commodity than a sport?

An area of biological uncertainty in which government can shelter behind prolonged research programmes and delay action concerns seals. Seals are the enduring focus of heated debate between 'green' organisations, for whom the seal cause has become emblematic of their success in swinging public opinion, and a consortium of sea-using interests, including commercial white fish nets-men and salmon farmers, netsmen and rod fishermen, who believe burgeoning grey seal numbers are out of balance and a threat to the survival of other species. The question of the seal population's health was further confused by the herpes- and polio-related viruses which decimated common seals in 1988; a confusion not helped by the media which continued to muddle common with grey seals (which were unaffected) over three months after the story broke. The level of concern about the fate of common seals meant that all talk about the justice of a grey seal cull had to be damped down until reason could again do business with emotion.

It is unfortunate for salmon fishing that the British sea's best publicised inhabitant, the grey seal, is so closely connected with it; also, that seals are hard to count or cull (females only come ashore to calf for the first time after eight years), seldom land (calving and mating on land are combined), and prey on salmon for preference. Furthermore, they bite the throat and under-belly from one salmon, then move on to the next.

Almost everything about seals is disputed. Portrayed as cuddly puppies by conservationists, they are in truth hungry and powerful predators and probably the mammal with the most devastating impact on others in British waters. Their actual numbers are fiercely argued; a knockabout figure of 100,000, growing at five per cent annually, must suffice. Ninety per cent of these breed off Scotland, usually on uninhabited islands, and breeding colonies are expanding onto new territory, particularly around the Hebrides and the Orkneys. In the last few years grey seals have swum into estuaries and up into rivers further than previously recorded. The legal position is that the Secretary of State for Scotland may authorise a cull, but he has not exercised the right since 1978 on the Orkneys. Fish farmers and district fishery boards may shoot seals doing damage to fisheries, but only under licence. Grey seals are otherwise protected.

Crucially important estimates by the government-funded Sea Mammal Research Unit about the proportion of salmon in the seal's fifteen pound a day diet are controversial because the unit's technique of counting salmon ear-bones in seal droppings ignores the animal's preference for biting out chunks of the salmon's soft parts only. Researchers are nonplussed by the problems of accumulating hard data about a mammal which cannot, within practical bounds, be caught in the open sea, and leaves only a fraction of its waste product on land, peculiarly inaccessible land at that. The safest assumption is that grey seals are opportunistic carnivores, eating whatever is to hand; hence the vulnerability of estuary nets and salmon cages.

Plenty of assessments have been made about the numbers of fish needed to sustain our grey seals; their enormous disparity shows how conjectural these assessments are. The Marine Unit at Aberdeen University is attempting to put grey seals within a perspective of the overall ecology of British coastal waters, but their findings are incomplete. Even if the unit reports a top-heavy grey seal population, and despite the serious state of whitefish stocks, any government will blanch at the difficulties of persuading a public conditioned to view seals as eternal victims of the necessity for a cull. In all probability the present position, permitting limited controls only at the point at which seals are a pest, will prove a comfortable compromise for some time to come. Salmon fishing bodies will have to live with this, however uncomfortable it may become, until such time as conservation groups themselves acknowledge that grey seals have become a blight and need managing like other marine dwellers. The embarrassment of political action would then be removed.

The spread of salmon through so large a geographical range in its life history complicates its protection and bedevils research. Radio-tracking individual fish is perhaps the biggest step forward in a century of salmon talk in which speculation has sometimes run wild. Radio-tracking will be invaluable in throwing light on the behaviour of farmed escapees mixing with wild stock. Re-evaluation of the effectiveness of statutory close times for estuary nets, as well as re-evaluations of the actual close season for individual rivers, could potentially follow from a knowledge of salmon movements in and out of river systems. It has already raised some eyebrows to discover that up to ten per cent of salmon home into the wrong river first time, then swim back to sea and re-locate their true home-address. It has long been suspected by estuary netsmen that fish moving towards home rivers and hugging the coast as they travel have been caught up *en route* by nets along the way; now this is factual. If responsibility for and ownership of salmon accrues to home-rivers, estuary nets are, in part at any rate, unecological. Radio-tracking is also producing interesting and surprising information about migration routes which will aid salmon management in future. The discovery that a proportion of fish from the English Wye migrates round the notorious west coast of Ireland instead of along direct lines through the Irish Sea must provoke anxiety in the Wye riparian owners.

As salmon management becomes more streamlined new legal, institutional and international problems will arise. The EC open market of 1992 brings with it a host of regulatory inconsistencies regarding fish diseases and the transportation of live fish. Salmon farmers are concerned that Scotland's stringent controls on live fish movement will be relaxed under harmonisation; this will concern sport fishermen too. A European open market is advancing on British law which is inconsistent within its own regions. Differences between Scots law and English and Welsh law delayed the implementation of salmon dealer licensing, the purpose of which was to close loopholes in the sale of poached fish; the proposal has now been dropped. Drift-netting law, as mentioned, varies; so too does law regarding live fish movement. Game laws, stating when and where hunting and shooting, as well as fishing, are allowed, are a thicket of extraordinary complexity because of local inhibitions dating from the time of ecclesiastical involvement in the legalities of leisure. The sabbatarian sensibilities of Highland communities are matched in those parts of England and Wales where the Nonconformist chapels applied regional variants about Sunday sport to national game laws. Salmon fishing is not legal in Scotland on a Sunday, whereas trout fishing is; both are legal in England. To complicate the situation further, local traditions often overlay the actual legal situation.

Not only the law regarding salmon is changing, or likely to change: salmon fishing practices are changing too. Since the word 'conservation' loomed large over salmon management, a debate has started concerning the ethics of rod and line fishing, particularly with regard to the practice of what Americans have dubbed 'catch and release'. Whereas only a year or two ago reports of bonanza days were staple diet in the angling press, now concern has crept in about large catches, and the defensibility of criticising salmon netsmen for unecological behaviour while rod and line fishermen essay energetically to maximise their haul.

The two activities are not comparable in terms of scale. The rod and line fisherman will only deplete the number of fish in a pool to a limited degree, whereas estuary nets working long hours in dry summers when salmon are turning in huge shoals on the tide and waiting for high-water to run can, in optimum conditions, take the best part of an entire run. But the comparison has narrowed as salmon runs in rivers with afforested catchments and flashier spate-conditions have tended to become concentrated in shorter bursts. Fishing more than ever before is often a matter of being in the right place at the right time. This explains the bumper days recorded every year now on rivers suddenly flushed with rain after a dry spell. A fisherman exploiting his good luck to the full, and loading his car with fish he intends to sell, is frowned on. Sporting commentators, in shooting as in fishing, are referring more frequently to the quality of sporting experience, instead of bag-sizes.

Many rivers operate a catch and release policy for hen fish late in the season near spawning. There is anyway a reduced pleasure in catching a ferruginous, gravid fish on or near her redds. Probably large catches in grilse runs will also be partially released as time goes by. As nets come off, and are bought off, riparian management improves, and salmon numbers start to rise, fishermen will become more amenable to releasing some of their spoils.

It will always be a hard thing to enforce until it is shown conclusively that released fish, as the Americans claim, usually go on to spawn satisfactorily; if, conversely, it is demonstrated that the stress and physical injury of being played makes them inefficient reproducers, catch and release has no point. The Americans and Canadians who regard it as barbarous to keep more than a token of your catch, even of their massive runs of Pacific salmon, use barbless flies. They reckon that the absence of a barb loses the fisherman only one fish in ten that he hooks. (I have not yet heard the claim that a barbless hook makes fish more likely to take, but doubtless the fisherman's conjectural creativity will remedy the deficiency soon!) If the British fisherman can overcome his stoic adherence to tradition, barbless hooks would perhaps help resolve the problem of injury.

Catch returns annually submitted to DAFS are confidential. The Department publishes rod catches divided into sixty-two districts, big rivers generally being a district in themselves, but net catches divided into only eleven regions. This means that net and rod on the same fishery do not know, through official channels, what the other is doing. River proprietors responsible for the productive part of the fishery, should surely know catch impacts, the size and weight of grilse runs and so forth, area by area. The Department's non-disclosure of full and detailed statistics has a shakier legal basis since, in the 1986 Salmon Act, Parliament saw fit to delete the clause relating to the Secretary of State for Scotland's power to withhold statistics for an 'individual fishery'. Non-disclosure is looking increasingly archaic.

Gross under-reporting of catches (which is prevalent), or non-reporting of catches altogether, also plays no part in a future in which salmon management is a serious responsibility. Under-reporting of catches is usually to avoid rent increases. Tightening up on it is awkward, but it can be done, as has been shown by unscrupulous timeshare companies wishing quickly to inflate the value of their fishing. The privacy of good statistics is cherished by some river proprietors who don't want to attract unwelcome attention, either from the District Fishery Board preparatory to levying a rate, or from unofficial nocturnal visitors. In practice people living on rivers generally acquire catch information if they have a mind to. Without proper catch statistics being rendered, and made available river by river, river area by river area, and net by net, those who enjoy their salmon fishing cannot expect management over the salmon fishery as a whole to get better.

Care for salmon translates into care for our whole environment. Freshwaters are indicators of environmental health generally. Vigilance will be needed by salmon-interested parties so that developments such as electricity privatisation do nothing to imperil the salmon's environment (anxieties about private ownership encouraging the spread of smolt hatcheries in headwater reservoirs suggest the need to commence research into downstream impacts). Estuary barrages like those currently contemplated in England would certainly be detrimental to anadromous species. Much work is needed on afforestation of catchments before a balance of land use interests can even be usefully considered. Protection for the salmon itself is advancing healthily. The priority of the future is protection of its environment.

Chapter Thirteen
Looking at the Ground

The environment is not something of which land use must take account. It is the whole framework within which land use takes place. 'Environmental' is not just the buzz-word of the 1990s. It is the only standpoint to adopt, once pioneering agriculture, aquaculture and forestry has come up against finite frontiers, if the land is to be utilised for a sustainable yield. These frontiers have been reached. Genetic techniques in the future may be able to increase crop yields on arable farms, perhaps even to the extent of doubling them as is claimed, but lower gearings not higher ones are more likely to meet with public approval. Type of production not volume of production will be the criterion of the future. The Highlands is only a volume producer in one commodity — softwood timber. For the Highlands there must be a departure from conifer plantations over very large areas in which the sole aim is production of commercial timber.

It is now perfectly clear that timber production in Britain, as presently conducted, will never be commercial in the sense that it performs like other financial assets. It is hard fact that forestry, even with substantial public funds underpinning it, returns only between two and five per cent on capital in real terms. The more remote the location, the greater the distance from the processing plant; the more extensive the areas needed for low-grade timber grown on the hills, the higher the fencing costs and the lower the profit margin. No-one has tried to cost-account the risk of windthrow with reference to the cycle of winter gales recurrent since 1987.

Windthrow classes in the hills are disturbingly high. The uninsurability of many high-profile plantations speaks volumes. Had the gales in the south-east of England in 1989 and those of the south-west in 1990 struck the Highlands, which are more wind-prone, much more heavily planted, and with shallow-rooted and unstable evergreens, the irrecoverable losses would have pushed into the shade the millions of pounds worth of damage recorded in England.

The great advantages of native birch, in being deeper-rooted and leafless in winter, well recognised in Finland for many years, have been oddly ignored by forestry research in Scotland. This is despite birch's further benefits of growing straight and true (when not browsed by sheep and deer), of acting to suppress butt-rot in subsequent rotations of trees, and being an excellent cycling agent for nutrients. Birch is also a versatile hardwood with excellent utility value. Scots pine and birch mixes are being used around Speyside to improve per acre yields by volume, weight and value. Whilst the Forestry Commission admits it has had to act as a pioneer in rotational commercial tree-growing in Britain, it does seem strange that, with all the research finance and energy devoted to non-native spruces and pines, more attention was not given to the commercial and industrial possibilities of native trees with a proven track record. The forthcoming success of birch will make this a matter of retrospective embarrassment.

Forestry policies in the future should have a diversity of roles, achieving social and environmental objectives as well as those of timber production. The considerably greater potential of lower-down coastal-belt ground for growing good-quality timber of properly marketable calibre should be taken into account before more huge tracts of hill are commandeered by forestry companies. These smaller-scale plantings can work in harmony with other land uses, providing shelter, fencing materials, firewood, pallet wood and planking, in addition to enhancing the scenery. Plantations should be balanced ecosystems planned to harmonise with the objectives of neighbouring land users. The time will come too for re-evaluation of our clearfell policies. Already in the United States partial felling philosophies, mitigating impacts to the environment, and more sensitive to wildlife's habitat requirement, are being adopted. If necessary, relationships with neighbouring land uses should be quantified and commitments built into planting applications to mitigate damage indirectly caused by the forestry presence.

The Forestry Commission has toyed coyly with making planting permission of large conifer blocks conditional on a bottom-side belt of natural mixed hardwoods to act as a buffer between the conifers with their acidic run-off and sensitive freshwaters full of valuable fish eggs and fry. Equally, why should forestry planters not be responsible, at any rate partially, for controlling damage by vermin to neighbouring grouse moors? Impacts of forestry on good grouse moors should ideally be taken into account in locating woodland sites. Mixed land use in practice means a balance of considerations in the first instance.

Too often in the early days of deer/plantation problems, plantation owners with trees of a certain height were accused of letting weather-pressed deer into woodlands, and failing to provide or maintain adequate jumps for them to get out again. Forestry companies and the Commission were taking a hefty income from venison, the sheltering deer being slaughtered up against fences in a manner which no-one wanted to boast about. On unfenced plantations, where there were fewer deer in the vicinity, some came into the forest for shelter and settled down to a woodland existence never to re-emerge. The reverse also occurred; stags residing comfortably in the woods until the rut emerged to find hinds and meet bullets — the lucky landowner getting a stag which he had never had to support. No code of practice, formal or informal, has ever come into being to straighten out the matter of responsibilities in this grey area, resulting in neighbourliness between plantation owners and sporting proprietors generally festering at a low ebb.

Like all its predecessors, the February 1990 'Land Use and Forestry' report from the Agriculture Select Committee failed to consider sporting use. It was merely observed, seemingly with surprise, that financial returns could be obtained from sporting use in small woodlands, and this should be more widely known. Forestry's relationship to sporting use outside the perimeter fence was not referred to.

Nonetheless the report, in the subjects it does address, is a very interesting document. It is a keynote call, in a public atmosphere tuned to this wavelength, for a thorough re-examination of the objectives of British forestry. It calls for an end to the unrolling carpet of green monocultures. Multiple-purpose forestry, achieving social and environmental objectives, should be the aim, benefiting the communities where the trees are planted. The committee examines the fact of agricultural surpluses, consequent oversupply of good-class agricultural land, and calls for forestry to be brought down the hill. Without criticising too openly the status quo, and the legacy of some disastrous planting, the report refers to the FC's 'narrow, rather simplistic policy which has dominated the last seventy years'. Most importantly, open-ended *ad hoc* forestry proliferation is criticised: the report calls for planting end-targets to be set and related to a planned distribution of woodland and the identification of specific suitable areas for planting. Sensible suggestions are advanced for reforming forestry grants; paying out percentage cost grants, not gross cost ones, providing more support for broadleaves, and reintroducing management grants. The scandalous absence of the latter has resulted in much broadleaf woodland being left derelict.

The FC will have recoiled from a direct blow it must have been expecting for some time. It is proposed the Commission be properly split between the Forestry Authority, to oversee national forestry, and a separate Forestry enterprise with a remit to consider the potential for non-commercial forestry developments, in addition to its traditional tree-growing role, with a fresh identity as a 'state forestry service'.

There are two recommendations with special reference for the Highlands. One is the recommendation to introduce legislation allowing crofting forestry on common grazings, and the other that the RDC be given the powers and resources to reduce the number of open hill deer where necessary. The first idea has been knocking around for some time and is fraught with intricate legal and structural niceties, none of which is likely to prevail against it. The drift of change is already evident in Malcolm Rifkind's desire to return freeholds of government-owned crofts to community ownership. The second shows that rather than being seen as a valuable asset which spreading afforestation removes, open hill deer were regarded as a problem which needed to be shot out of the way. The groups representing stalking interests must have submitted some mightily unpersuasive material.

If conifer monocultures are an undesirable development for the Highlands, what chance is there for a start to the rehabilitation of native woodland which Sir Frank Fraser Darling so eloquently pleaded for? To know this it is necessary to understand Darling's prognosis.

He believed the Highlands had been subjected ecologically to damaging human assault for a thousand years. The steady burning down of wildwood, the leaf litter of which had maximised soil richness on the Highlands' acidic underlying rock, was succeeded by a cattle culture which in its short duration developed a wise and beneficial type of husbandry. Beasts were moved high up in summer to rest the woods which were their wintering quarters; sensible pastoralists maximised the fertility benefits of cattle-dunging in a controlled way, cattle being moved around arable areas in mobile wattle compounds. Darling laments the arrival of the sheep ranchers. Sheep nibbled off saplings and obliterated the chance for woodland regeneration, caused erosion where they rubbed out nestling-beds in the peat, and their selective grazing left behind rough grasses which spread and became rank. The agency of fire cleared off leggy, scrubby heather and set in chain a new wave of erosion of plant-life and then subsoils, usually peat. The ungrazeable colonist bracken finished the cycle by forming a canopy through which no other plant could grow. The introduction of the rabbit, a last-phase destroyer of badly eroded land, earns his most scathing tongue-lashing. To Darling, writing in 1955, the Highlands were a devastated countryside.

Darling is the colossus of Highland ecology, and his painstaking researches and passionate concern have laid the groundwork for future studies. However, in his harking back to the golden millenia of scrub forest cover over much of the Highlands is detectable the nostalgia of the pure scientist. Darling never evaluates the system of renewal he advocates, except to say that rejuvenated ecosystems will support again a higher human population. His assessment that the Highlands could support a maximum population of 60,000 red deer looks far too low, even accepting that his programme of woodland renewal would involve fencing deer out. His ultimate hopes for a ratio of one cow to one sheep have run up against the beef mountain and will never come to pass. Darling wrote before the age of conifer monocultures which spread to reveal their ecological handicaps. With his love of diversity of plant, animal and bird communities, he would surely have shrunk from the impoverishments of modern afforestation.

It is a sad fact that Darling's warnings about the dangers of growing hill sheep, red deer and rabbit populations, and the continuing disappearance of the few remaining patches of Caledonian Forest and native woodlands, went unheeded. It is only in the last few years, with the growth of environmental awareness, that such concepts are common coinage and have been taken on board at official level. The acceptance by government of the need for special protection for native woodlands, and especially old Scots pine stands, signalled a breakthrough, and legislation geared to encourage all forms of natural woodland will hopefully follow.

Attention since Darling has focused on a different area, a less conspicuous land use subject with insidious rather than dramatic effects — the effect of grazing patterns on plant diversity. As Darling pointed out, ecosystems on Scottish hills are complex and fragile; management of the ground is a delicate business made more problematic by the fact that the land is mostly unenclosed. The tools at man's command are burning regimes, mainly for heather maintenance, and grazing densities of both domestic stock and wild deer.

A superficial inspection of open hillsides in my part of Sutherland shows that mineral compositions often go through multiple variations between the top of a hill and the bottom. Man's involvement in cutting hill-drains, traversing slopes with roads, and creating a burning mosaic of heather age-groups, is superimposed on a mantle of peat of uneven depth covering variegated minerological bands, which sometimes alter many times in small areas. The object of management of this moorland is to sustain pasture in good heart for grazing or grouse-feeding, consistent with biological diversity. As the county of Sutherland contains nine hundred wild plant and fern species, over half the British total, the responsibility is a complex one.

A change of opinion about moorland management has resulted from research work done by the Institute of Terrestrial Ecology and the McCaulay Land Use Research Institute. This moves away from the ideas prevalent in the early 1980s, nursed on a philosophy of chronic overgrazing of hill pasture, which believed grazing animals reduced diversity and impoverished habitat unilaterally. This is now acknowledged as having been too simple. Different animals eat different parts of the sward; by chewing off fresh shoots they can strengthen the root systems and reinvigorate the plant. Moderate grazing increases plant diversity. Digestive systems of different animals (hindgut or ruminant) determine what herbage they select, in addition to seasonal and sex determinants, and the choice of vegetation available. The option to let land lie fallow in the vain hope this conserves what is there, implying nature is in stasis, is embodied in present agriculture policies. It is foolish and unlikely to last.

The old-time graziers and Highland shepherds today, had they been consulted, would have voiced in laymen's terms the ideas scientifically gaining credence about grazing patterns. Managing grazings was part of the cultural tradition of pastoral communities. Shepherds today know full well the necessity of moving stock up to high ground to prevent overgrazing on the lower, softer swards. They know too the uses of cattle with their wide mouths and unselective grazing pattern as mowers to remove rough and tussocky grasses, and as valuable fertiliser-spreaders through dunging.

The Nature Conservancy Council learnt about grazing values the hard way on Rhum, which they bought in 1957. Cattle and sheep were removed in order to concentrate on red deer studies. But the withdrawal of traditional grazing from conservation areas often leads to the development of stable or 'climax' communities of both plants and animals which are different from, and often less diverse than, those the nature reserves were designed to protect. By 1970 the grazing diversity on Rhum's maritime grasslands had declined dramatically. Red deer are selective grazers and in their natural woodland situation shrub browsers. The tussocky grasses were left behind and became dominant. Hinds ate heather in autumn and winter, grass in summer. Stags preferred the marshy grasslands. The NCC noted the declining ecology and introduced a herd of Highland cattle which rapidly reversed the loss of varieties on the grasslands. The complementary nature of the feeding habits of cattle and deer was augmented when it was shown that deer the following year preferred cattle-grazed ground. Even deer calving rates improved.

Cattle are generally beneficial grazers and, unlike sheep, goats and deer, do not eat tree saplings and dwarf-shrubs (heather) for preference. Their big bodies demand large daily intakes of herbage and the wide bovine muzzle is adapted to satisfy volume-feeding, whilst cropping close to the ground. Food being retained for a longer time in the rumen, cattle are able to digest more dry matter than sheep. Heavy cattle hooves are less suited to bogland, although trampling in other areas is a vital ground preparation for the establishment of pioneer plants.

Goat grazing patterns equate more to cattle than sheep. Goats are notorious omnivores and widely used in New Zealand to control the spread of scrub and weeds. Goats do graze heather but prefer the green top-shoots to green shoots at the base of the heather plant. They generally ingest more fibrous material than sheep and cattle and are of particular use in the Highland context in their willingness to eat the rushes which so quickly colonise re-seeded parks on the hill. Furthermore, they will eat rushes right to the base, preventing the development of seeds. Not being fond of clover, which is valuable for sheep, there are many areas in a sheep grazing regime where goats could, in theory, prove a useful grazing partnership.

Over-grazing by any one animal or any combination of animals is dangerous. When new shoots do appear they are pulled up by the roots and failure by plants to re-establish can lead to soil erosion. Protecting very young plant communities from intensive grazing is one of a shepherd's duties; in the case of roving deer, all that will save tender burnt ground is population control.

Grazing as a herbage management tool has many advantages. It replaces mechanical means of cropping herbage to keep it fresh (anyway impractical on open hill), it fertilises ground through dunging, is non-pollutant, and should produce a cash-crop in the form of sale stock. Whilst grazing on sown swards has been part and parcel of agriculture for a long time, the idea of a mixture of animals to keep rougher ground in good heart has not been practised since the early eighteenth-century cattle economy.

Organisations like the RSPB, the Wildfowl Trust, the NCC and its European counterparts use grazing animals to keep habitat in good trim. In some countries this aim is run in tandem with special variety breeds where herds and flocks need not be so large as those of ordinary commercial species. At the refined level this is a sophisticated science involving a knowledge of exactly what plants herbivores will graze at different times of year, at different times in their sexual cycle, and in what order of preference. The number of mouths has to be got right, in suitable complementary combinations with other mouths. In spite of all the research effort, this is bound to prove an inexact science and liable to considerable local variation. Even within these parameters, as stockmen know, animals are unpredictable in their feeding habits, more so when there is a choice. It seems strange to say so, but just as silviculturalists are dwelling in the dark ages about tree-growing (witness the volatile fashion-switching with regard to conifer combinations), so too are many ecologists in their efforts to preserve Highland flora and fauna. We have passed the point of looking for new ways to improve land to maximise its single-use potential; the future calls for a concentration on naturally-produced protein from the hills, consistent with general environmental good sense and the balance of mixed land uses.

Chapter Fourteen
Realities and Alternatives

Calls for the abolition of sporting estates, or 'the reform of the Highlands' landholding structure', as it is called, are an article of faith of left of centre political aspirants. It has been a plank of Labour policy in Scotland for most of the post-war period. Yet it has never been undertaken. The only times when reforms have been mooted, as mentioned earlier, have been when governments with wafer-thin majorities, or those trying to woo vital seats, have held out the carrot of statutory change. Mr Heath had a crofting amendment bill in preparation, containing some small carrots making it easier for crofters to purchase their holdings, when his government was toppled in 1974. Even these reforms, which would have given crofters the right of purchase only at prices reflecting at least some of the holdings' 'market' value, which they might not have been able to afford anyway, were essentially small beer. The real transformation, articulated by those furthest from the realities of having ever to carry it out, would be an appropriation of large areas by the state for redistribution in favour of the disenfranchised descendants of the victims of the Clearances. The greener departments of the left speak of huge national parks; government commissions are presently looking at the possibility of localised ones. Very wisely, none of the high-flown ideologies have embarked on analyses of cost. It does not take the wit of a political economist to realise that if most Highland estates are run at a considerable annual loss (a rough-and-ready figure might be £1 per acre per year), for the state to take on the burden of economic supports, with the extra increments inevitable in state-run organisations, would be an undertaking few taxpayers elsewhere would wish to contribute to — particularly if the only visible benefit was seen to be the despatch of the familiar figure of the laird in favour of a cohort of civil servants. The laird would not have survived if he were not so convenient.

It is often objected that landowners in the Highlands are a small collection of very rich people. It is not understood that they need to be rich, in order to offset losses on their estates against profits registered elsewhere. The charge of absenteeism is one that has been levelled at Highland landlords ever since the hereditary chiefs in the late nineteenth century began spending time further south. On the one hand, absenteeism can be seen as the saving grace of the lairds, who are busy spending their professional lives earning money which is remitted to the Highland economy; on the other, it is a pity that estate economies usually cannot, in present circumstances, support resident lairds. It is, however, in many ways a satisfactory redistribution of wealth that earnings gained in London's Square Mile should end up maintaining employment in the glens and straths of the north.

Furthermore, it is a traffic which has a long history. Much has been made by historians of the crofting movement of the unfairness of high rents levied by clan chiefs and landowners on their smallholders in the nineteenth century. Sir James Matheson on Lewis owned property with a rental income in 1872 of around £19,000; Lord MacDonald's rent on Skye at the same time was £12,000; MacLeod of Dunvegan on Skye received £8,000. The largest Highland landowner, the Duke of Sutherland, then earned from his 1.3 million acres about £63,000. Large sums indeed. What is less often recorded is the movement of funds the other way. In 1883 the Sutherland factorial agents informed the Napier Commission the family had spent £1.3 million in the Highlands during the previous thirty years, or about £250,000 more than its rental income. This money came from the family's interests in England in canals and railways, acting as aristocratic entrepreneurs in the Industrial Revolution. The Sutherland family has been much vilified by demagogues over time for its role in the Clearances, but the scale of these supports for the Highlands hardly suggests the hard-hearted exploiter of popular folklore. It is very doubtful if government funds on this scale, at the time they were made available, would ever have been forthcoming.

The situation of private subsidisation persists today, although no longer in the form of wagons full of potatoes. Private capital is swallowed up quickly on large areas of land far from major distribution centres. It would be inappropriate to pry into the scale of contemporary individual supports for Highland estates, but I know on good authority that a large estate sold in the mid-1980s was costing its proprietor over £100,000 a year to hold together. The new owner of Mar Lodge, one of the great estates of the Highlands, has spent several million pounds on the lodge alone. Such largesse is an extreme example of private investment in sporting assets which is widespread.

Given the present state of knowledge, it is hard to see how large financial inputs are not always going to be a necessity in a region of the country which is capable of supporting a marginal form of farming only with considerable public support. Approximately a third of hill farmers' incomes is subsidy. Without subsidies the whole sector would fold. There is no sign that the public consumer is anywhere near being prepared to pay this differential for meat produced in a natural way on heather and mountain grasses. Forestry is only practicable with gigantic public supports. That leaves land use alternatives, and the use for which the estates were created — sport.

It may be hard to understand at first glance why sport is not a paying proposition for the laird. Commentating journalists always quote the eye-catching figures. So-and-so may indeed have paid £35,000 for a week's grouse shooting. But the season is short; Highland moors where the numbers of high-quality birds justify this are few; the lodges kitted out to command this sort of rental as part of the package are also limited. Run-of-the-mill rents are in a very different category. Lairds in the northern Highlands are unlikely to see a return of more than £10,000 in a season shot over dogs. Stalking is presently selling at a top rate of, say, £250 per stag. Only a handful of forests can sustain an annual cull of 100 stags; the average might be between thirty and forty. Hind stalking lacks demand and is extremely cheap. The rents are received only for a few weeks a year. In the west, grouse shooting on most estates fails to enter the equation at all. If grouse populations are hit hard by disease or winter weather, or a deluge during nesting, shooting might have to be completely abandoned for stocks to recover. Those proprietors letting season by season to different clients will miss out on any income at all when there is a dearth of grouse. Shooting tenants who are asked suddenly to pay much higher rents when the stock is strong and birds are abundant object strenuously to the big price-hike. From the laird's point of view, unless money is made in the good years, management will suffer.

Management, and the employment of a keeper or keepers, continues through the year. Accommodation is provided, and in the modern day a wide range of vehicles — Land Rovers, hill bikes, all-terrain vehicles, tractors. Increasingly, keeping a kennel of pointing dogs for the shooting season has become too expensive. Where twenty years ago all good dogging moors had a kennel of no less than six setters or pointers, the modern solution is to keep one or two dogs of strong breeds which can jog along all day; or abandon dogging in favour of walking in line. To justify a full kennel, there has to be a reliable and productive moor and a client willing to pay a good premium for doing things stylishly in the classical way.

The extra source of income from game-meat itself has ceased to be the mainstay it once was. Grouse are supplied in sufficient quantities to markets in the south by the highly productive north English moors. They retain only a token value in the Highlands, where smaller numbers of birds and collection costs over long, winding routes cripple game dealers' economics.

Venison prices have languished for many years. In the 1970s they were approximately the same as today, which means a severe depreciation in real terms. Scottish venison suffers from lacking a home market; from late-season venison entering the market long after the rut has begun, when the meat starts to deteriorate; and from a general ignorance about how it should be prepared in the kitchen. With the growth of farmed venison it appears more frequently on menus in British restaurants, but the result is seldom what it should be. The trade in Scottish wild venison is still rooted firmly in northern Europe, especially Germany, and these markets are liable to flooding from other suppliers of ungulate meat from as far afield as Africa, and also from eastern Europe. Until the British develop a taste for their own venison, and learn how to cook it, and until demand becomes sophisticated enough — that is, makes a quality distinction between wild venison shot in the rut and the much better hind venison shot in midwinter, and between different types of venison — the venison cheque for Highland estates will remain a volatile asset. This is particularly unfortunate with reference to a wild game-meat, nurtured on untreated herbage, that is potentially as delicious as any protein that can grace a plate.

It may be observed that my encomium on the virtues of Highland sport is inconsistent with the relatively low market value it attracts when it comes to letting. If grouse shooting, salmon fishing and stalking in the Highlands, at their best, are as good as anything comparable elsewhere in the world, why is it that they cannot be let for prices which cover the cost of their production? Economics is vital in a consideration of land use in the Highlands because it explains the land ownership structure, and the failure of the sporting argument to play its part in the debate. Partly because sport is still anachronistically regarded as a pastime, not a business, its true place in the picture of land use alternatives has never been recognised.

Firstly, consider the economics of fishing. Surely if all that is needed to be done is to present an invoice to the man who stands on the bank for a week, seeking to catch a fish which returns of its own accord, free for the harvesting, riparian ownership should be profitable. On parts of the most famous rivers it certainly is, or should be; proprietors are in receipt of high rents for most of the summer, and possibly some of the spring and autumn. However, the picture is more complicated than it was at the start of the sporting era, when management was simply a decision about how much to amplify sporting income by netting income.

The highest charge on riparian owners is in protection of their waters. There are some river systems in Scotland on which one bailiff is employed for every mile of water; as a rough indicator, the fewer bailiffs per mile the fewer fish. In charge of such a team is a manager or head bailiff. The modern water bailiff is well equipped. Like the gamekeeper he must be housed, mobilised, kitted out with binoculars, walkie-talkies and two-way radios and, at critical times, replaced on his own beat in watches so that the water is guarded around the clock. This tedious day-round surveillance is particularly essential when fish are in the river in large numbers in low water conditions which favour netting.

Many, if not most, rivers operate hatchery programmes or restocking programmes of some sort. These are costly and labour intensive operations requiring constant attention. Bailiffs spend the less stressful winter months doing bank maintenance, replacing fallen-away revetments, cutting back undergrowth, building or repairing cruives (croys), footpaths, fishing-huts, boats and so on. Since land adjacent to river banks has often been developed for agricultural use, river-bank and river-bed maintenance have required much greater human input than in the old days of wild torrents pouring through untutored country. Where weirs, dams and fish passes have been put in place by man, these also have to be maintained. A further item on some river boards' list of expenditures is research into spawning rates, fry and parr counts, and general monitoring, using costly new scientific tools, of the health of fish stocks in the river. The same effort goes into monitoring the densities of predators — for example, trout and eels — and the occasional necessity to control them.

A traditional charge against riparian proprietors has been sporting rates, as for grouse and deer, levied on the size of the average bag. Where there is a properly-constituted river board, rates on fishing have recently been suspended. The money saved should be channelled by river boards back into management of the fishery. Few people in fishery management circles feel that rates will not be levied again in the future, although possibly under a different guise.

Fishing rents are thus offset by a wide range of expenditure items, outwith the cost of administering fishing lets itself. With the recent rise in the capital values of fishing, which is naturally related to rising rents, it is unlikely that any Highland river or fishing beat is rewarding its proprietor with a net return on capital comparable to orthodox financial instruments. Effectively, fishing proprietors pay a premium for the privilege of owning this form of asset.

The burdens of shooting and stalking subjects in manpower and time terms have already been gone into. For these activities letting seasons are considerably shorter than on major rivers. An assortment of home-bred sporting traditions restricts the main market in shooting and stalking lets to British clients. The favourable price comparisons with foreign sport fail to operate as an upward regulator in a market which is not in practice either very open or wide. Sport is therefore good value in the Highlands for the tenant, but offers a poor return to the proprietor. Frequently, rental income on a typical west Highland estate would accrue in a mere five weeks of the stag season. Probably such a place would have a single keeper. His wage and overall running costs would have to be met all year round; he might require seasonal help; and additionally, the crucial item in many estate finances, there would be the cost of maintaining the lodge.

Not only do sporting lodges tend to hold to rambling and cavernous stereotypes, with awe-inspiring expanses of roof and finicky turrets, they are also located in rough-weather sites with an abnormal quota of wear and tear from the elements. Rain, sleet, snow and gales lavish their magnanimous attention on the few buildings to be found in empty glens and bleak straths, themselves worn into sleek shapes by millenia of erosion. Keeping wind and water out is an expensive pastime, particularly when contractors are few and far away. One lodge owner I know has given up the unequal struggle, and drips coming through the roof are caught in suspended plastic gutters, which drain out off the topside of the window-frame. Insurance companies recognise the vulnerability of lodges to fire, in those cases dry enough to burn, and insurance premiums are pitched at specially painful levels for the laird stretched toasting his toes before his crackling fireplace.

Bearing costs such as these, it is understandable that estate owners, and factors pressed to justify their jobs, have looked to novel ways to raise money. At Borrobol I operate a bird-watching May–July programme directed at the American market. The seasonality of the spring migration fits in well with a sporting routine that gets fully underway only in August. The bird-watchers come in small parties and my wife and I have the benefit of their company over evening dinners derived from the produce of the estate. When bored with lamb, salmon, grouse and venison we serve the exotics — snipe, goose, roe venison, duck or trout. Piping in the haggis was abandoned when some of the guests, Highland blood coursing through their veins, became overcome with the emotion of MacCrimmon's lament. By day they circulate the counties of Caithness and Sutherland under the stewardship of a trained ornithologist, visiting selected sites which contain special treasures — a peregrine nest, a breeding colony, or whatever. The menu of interest is spiced up with historical-type ingredients, including viewing brochs, standing stones and castles. Trips to the Orkneys to see cliff-nesting colonies and ancient megaliths are an optional extra.

Having these parties from over the Atlantic has revealed many interesting things, apart from the charms of the dollar. In our itineraries we visit several types of habitat with different bird species in each. On the estate alone there are four distinct habitats: forestry, garden plus woodland, riverside and loch, and moorland. Of these the one they universally prefer is open moorland. The flow country elicits a powerful response. Furthermore, it has the advantage for naturalists that wildlife is eminently visible, and the long unspoiled panoramas are keenly appreciated. Then there is the agreeable lack of any unease in Americans over the fact that Borrobol is a sporting estate. They seem quite untroubled that a shooting season will follow a birding one. 'Feather-gunners', as some Americans refer to wing-game shots, are seemingly more an acceptable part of the rural mainstream in the USA than here.

This form of use for Borrobol gives me particular pleasure because the enthusiasm generated over a week for what the Highlands has to offer refreshes in me my own responses. I see as if for the first time the soft shadows crossing the hills, the passing mantle of the delicate pluvial light, and hear anew the buzzard's mournfully suggestive cry. Bird-watching is an attractive pastime which takes you into the heart of country matters, and understanding of the immense complexity of the symbiosis which underpins natural variety. The peace and quiet of the northern Highlands and the lightness of motor traffic suits an activity in which it is sometimes desirable to stop the car quickly and jump out and look at something. It is a happy time of year, when leaves are greening up the trees and lambs and calves are in the field. The northern Highlands have a superb concentration of seacliff nesting colonies and on Borrobol there are excellent densities of nesters such as golden plover, lapwing, curlew and oystercatcher. In the course of bird-watching experience I have counted on Borrobol itself a hundred species. This is a momentous total for a slice of nowhere in the flow country, and justifies the mixed land use policy which has been pursued. In many ways the bird-watching diversification is an ideal deployment of Highland resources. It has the advantage over ordinary tourism that the charms of the region are appreciated in detail; and bird-watchers get to grips with the countryside and enter the varying habitat the birds live in with a purpose.

Visitors appreciate the wealth of our historical monuments also. They find it surprising that such an ancient and dramatic heritage is so neglected. On Orkney, where energy and initiative have made famous landmarks of essentially routine monuments (in the context of all the Highlands has to offer), tourists get the full benefit of reconstructed history. Archaeological sites are manned and presented for elucidation in an imaginative way. The difficulty for other Highland counties is that they have neither the density of monuments nor the concentrated throughput of tourists from which Orkney so astutely reaps dividends. But the huge number of mouldering, unexcavated, sometimes unmapped monuments in my part of Sutherland are a sorry comment on the degree of local enthusiasm or academic interest. Proper presentation of a wider array of monuments would have the similar beneficial effect as bird-watching groups, of drawing people off the beaten track into rewarding byways. Whilst this is not an area intrinsically suited to development by estates, those with interesting monuments on them could possibly benefit. A few do. Encouragement of visitors would broaden public access, while focusing the impact on a specified site and therefore minimising general disturbance.

Estates face the same problem of widening public access as national parks, particularly national parks in foreign countries which also contain large wild animals intolerant of high levels of disturbance. The argument has gone on for many years about how to stream large numbers of people through ecosystems both fragile and remote. Access to deer forests is our own version of the problem. Disturbance is inimical to deer in the wild when twinned with seasonal culling programmes. Deer inured to public appraisal cease to be the wild animals people find it uplifting to see. The excitement felt by stalking people in close proximity to wild animals, and in a predator relationship with them, is unrepeatable on a large scale with quantities of people. Whilst deer do develop some degree of tolerance for human traffic on fixed routes, the problem becomes acute when walkers stray and take animals by surprise. Many game parks in the world have reluctantly accepted the principle of restricted access. The problem for sporting estates sensitive to the inevitability of growing demand for public access is, firstly, how to balance it with responsible wildlife management, and, secondly, how to tap the business dividend it must somehow provide.

Highland estates have on occasion been commendably entrepreneurial in doing this. As addenda to traditional activities, they have opened study centres, adventure schools, museums, antique shops, horticultural centres and private gardens, wildlife and safari parks, school visitor centres with craft shops, information displays, canteens and waymarked routes through the estate for walking. Estates have built golf courses, hotels, tweed mills, fish ponds, chalet complexes, caravan parks, shooting schools and fish smokeries. The last twenty years have seen Highland estates going public in many varied ways. Some shooting parties are personally hosted in a castle setting and resplendently entertained by night with the full flavour of Highland hospitality. Not all projects are visitor-related. One estate has its own hydro-scheme, another was a pioneer in private wind power generation: both contribute to the national grid. Several estates have an industrial role, commonly a sawmilling capacity for producing fence-posts.

The diversifications listed above may be divided into two categories. There are those which have an independent commercial function, as small businesses which happen to have an estate base; and there are those which have as their motive an attempt to draw the public into an understanding of what a traditional Highland estate is all about, catering for a multiplicity of visitor needs. It is the latter which is the greatest challenge, and has in many ways the potential to be the guarantor of the security of the estate as a land management institution into and through the next century. It is also the most difficult to achieve successfully. The basis of appreciation must be under-standing through education. If it is properly explained that there are certain times when freedom of access to the whole estate has to be curtailed it is likely to be accepted. Visitors can then be streamed to other less critical areas. It helps in making such strictures acceptable that the life cycle of the wild animals and birds is made comprehensible in an attractive and imaginative way.

Where there is greatest pressure on access, some estates have varied their approach, giving priority to visitor demands, and trying as best they can to channel them in a way compatible with sporting activities. Probably there is no practical alternative for landowners pressed by visitors in crowds, except to provide facilities for letting people do as they wish with a good grace. In this regard, the better the information material and the footpaths, the more congenial the public-private interface. Obviously, however, where footpaths are converted into miles of mush by pedestrian pressure it is unrealistic that landowners be expected to meet maintenance bills. No system at present exists for resolving this or similar issues. Arrangements are cobbled together *ad hoc* with whatever public body has the will and the means to assist at the time. An integrated land use system in the Highlands would have the means not only to facilitate public access with funding, and mitigate any damage, but also compensate landowners for loss of use. This would bring the system in line with the law regarding ordinary property rights.

Estates which make on-estate visits a positive aim of management generally use a visitor centre as a platform for information and explanation. At this point the public can justifiably be asked for a charge to assist upkeep for the area; a charge on access itself is obviously not feasible, irrespective of the land use restrictions it entails. Elucidation about the estate is initially a two-way process, both outwards to the curious public, and inwards to the estate staff who need to understand the necessities and possible benefits of having public incursions on what they may in the past have considered their own domain. Involvement of local schools in evolving programmes, such as a regeneration of natural woodland, is not only well-received locally but enables youngsters at an early stage to see the estate system acting as a steward for the common heritage. Local communities frequently welcome such public-spirited initiatives by estates because it brings passing traffic to a halt in their midst and prolongs stays there. The estate acts as a focal stimulus for a trade which benefits all. One estate owner in Caithness has gone to the extent of bequeathing parts of the estate in trust to the local community. The proportion of the property included in this trust is progressively increasing. It is an extraordinary act of public altruism which the owner, such is the nature of the man, has done nothing to publicise.

The future of public access in the Highlands is, as I have mentioned, the subject of keen debate. Estate owners who relish the privacy and remoteness of their Highland bases will have to recognise that the growing pressures of public access from groups ranging from butterfly collectors to hang glider pilots can only, ultimately, be accommodated gracefully within a positive management system. A tolerant approach to rural public access is the British way. Where this is accompanied by an information service, and a ranger service which replaces formalised codes with on-site explanation, the clashes between land uses are reduced. The means for private landowners to supply this are at present unsatisfactory. Between the land owner and the thronging public there may develop the need for a catalyst. This could take the form of local project officers, harmonising both parties' needs and interests. The Countryside Commission for Scotland is presently looking into this.

The situation is changing fast. The fell-walking brigade who raised the banner of public access fifty years ago have transmogrified into a diverse collation of special interests. There are many more foreigners, who do not understand the inherent dangers of high-altitude walking in the Scottish Highlands, and there are keep-fit enthusiasts for whom a strenuous ascent is a positive requirement. Some of these people strap on their hiking boots precisely to get away from footpaths, signposts and waymarked walks. With a tent in my pack I have done this myself and the memories are dear. A goodly proportion, luckily for the Highlands, just want to view from the car. In any event, the days of the burly gamekeeper barring the way are gone.

Diversification with a rather longer lineage is in farming alternatives. Wild boar, rare cattle and sheep breeds, goats, garrons, even South American camelids (llamas, alpacas, guanacos) have been, and are being, tried. As has been the case with that other more solidly-based diversification, deer farming, the economies of all these have been hard to read because of the artificially high and very volatile values of breeding stock. While breeding stock, the building-brick of the stock rearing enterprise, is still in short supply, and provided that enough media attention puffs up egregious ventures for their novelty value, returns from real trading of the animal's products are camouflaged. Breeding stock sales, disbursing the capital of the business, distorts its true trading base. This often has the effect of luring in outsiders to farming, as has happened through 1988 and 1989 in England and southern Scotland, who have more money than agricultural sense. It explains the frighteningly high implosion rate of fringe farming ventures and the reputation of the Highlands as the battlefield for more than its share of lost causes.

One of the problems has been the pathetic eagerness with which those who find the Highland landholding structure annoying or embarrassing seize on any new-fangled land use concepts which claim to have found alternative answers. Invariably, or very often, the parvenus who strut north proclaiming their freshly-fledged panaceas for the hills have completely failed to comprehend the vagaries of Highland weather. One such operator bought and wrecked an estate in Sutherland; its fall is an object lesson in the sort of group dementia with which the opinion-forming class greets new ideas, and the damage which their speedy collapse leaves in its wake.

The new laird, delighted with his large landholding purchased at so small a per acre price, decided to turn the rolling upland flow country into a prairie for grass growing. Selected parts of the estate were fenced off, rolled and levelled, fertilised, and sown-out with grass. The scale of this conversion from very rough undulating moorland, in a place notorious even locally for its inhospitable character, was astonishing. Earth-moving equipment carved enormous roads out of the rock and peaty topsoil. Preparing this rough boggy ground for cultivation, not on selected drained slopes where small-scale reseeding had taken place historically, but indiscriminately over a wide expanse, was a colossal undertaking. The grass crop was to be cut when still short three times a year, cured in an enormous drying shed fired by peat, and converted into briquettes for feeding to stock. This was in an impoverished farming area where the surviving farmers grow their own winter feed anyway.

Despite the extraordinary audacity and scale of the project (1500 acres were to be reclaimed in the first phase), this revolutionary concept was backed financially by every conceivable funding agency. Politicians of all hues fell over each other to lend their encouragement and make protestations of faith in its success. Television, radio and newspapers gave the mad-cap venture a rousing send-off, while local farming people watched in amazement as money was poured into an enterprise which denied all the lessons their hard lives struggling against the elements had taught them.

The scheme collapsed ignominiously in three years. Its backers at first suppressed their mounting doubts, then saw the project falling way behind schedule, and finally called in their debts. A very large sum of public money was wasted; over thirty jobs disappeared as quickly as they had materialised. In a very short time the county's farmers saw happening what they had predicted all along — the fields turned to rushes as water gathered on the surface turning the ground sour. Before long deer had jumped the electric fences and could be seen from the road grazing some of the most expensively produced grass ever to have been grown in Sutherland.

The project which had been hailed as a lesson to the laziness and conservatism of local lairds and farmers left an unfortunate legacy. For this estate's sporting potential had been sacrificed. When it came on the market it was bought by a forestry company. Now more gigantic tranches of public money are being spent covering this ill-starred landmass in little conifers nodding in the breeze. Deer forest and grouse moor have gone; whether the estate's excellent trout lochs will withstand the test of time and the acidic impacts of circumambient forestry remains to be seen. The estate's river is radically altered, with a much faster run-off.

The gross cost of this *folie de grandeur* was never, to my knowledge, computed. It certainly ran into many millions of pounds. Now more millions are being expended, again in a situation which is hostile to the land use plan for it. Local opinion is that the trees will blow over long before their time. As one man dourly put it to me, 'There'll never be a chain saw heard up there.' I agree.

This débâcle has many lessons to teach. It was a bad idea in the wrong place. The scale of the project was preposterous and it exhibited no understanding of the land on which its follies were forced. From the start, it ran behind schedule and the physical problems had been underestimated. It seems inconceivable that what was ultimately to happen to the green-grass briquettes was ever gone into at all. What was until a few years ago a happy estate, employing an inordinately large number of people, engaged in the only activity it was suited to — sporting and farming use — is now a dismal scene. The rusting hulks of big machinery still lie around, the hills are mostly ploughed, right up to the plateau. The employment generated is minimal. Neighbours are fearful for their grouse; a keeper on one side of the new plantations killed five times as many foxes in 1989 as he was accustomed to before. The ripples of the fiasco spread far and wide.

Chapter Fifteen
The Challenge for Sporting Use

The role of the laird is changing. He is being forced into the limelight in an environmental debate which has come to rest in the Highlands because the Scottish hills constitute some of the most dramatically recognisable environment we have left in Britain. The laird, roused from his reveries and the quiet contemplation of his resonant old gamebooks, peers over the battlements. Instead of an ever-dwindling population draining from the lonesome glens he sees an army of conservationists, mountaineers, cavers and fern-buffs, clamouring not only for access, which has never been denied them, but for special case treatment. From another angle, self-appointed groups of a quasi-political nature demand democratisation of land use decisions, in other words the entry into estate management decision-making of whoever has a voice and wishes to use it. Not all of these voices can be accommodated. But some estates, as I say, have advanced boldly to meet the tide of arrivals, sometimes consciously abandoning their traditional role as sporting properties and embracing a new one in which sport has fallen into a secondary position after people management. Shooting schools, stocked fish-lochs, rod-fishing classes can convey the image of a sporting estate, although the reality may have expired. Usually, sporting use is conducted on parts of the ground from which the general public has been led away.

The future of the sporting estate lies not in wholesale transformation into fun-parks and theme-reserves. Eventually everything comes back to the basics. No-one, to my knowledge, has devised a way to make opening an estate to the general public pay (the revenue from castle opening and historic building visits applies to a minority of places and seldom covers costs of maintenance). Generally speaking, estates which have developed a positively welcoming approach to public access subsidise their ranger service, footpaths, visitor centres, and provision of maps and information leaflets, from revenues earned elsewhere. Poorer proprietors might face difficulties apeing those who have gone public unreservedly. It would anyway be a thankless form of philanthropy unless there were some other aspect of the estate worth preserving. Usually this is sport. It is worth looking at the prospects for sport.

A report was published in March 1990 entitled 'The Economic Impact of Shooting Sports in Scotland'. It was commissioned by the Scottish Development Agency and the British Association for Shooting and Conservation from the prestigious Fraser of Allender Institute attached to Strathclyde University. The facts and figures which the institute comes up with make such a strong case for sporting use on economic grounds that it is hard to imagine prosperity for the rural parts of Scotland without it.

The database the institute used was comprehensive. Whilst the aim was to establish a picture of shooting in Scotland from the viewpoint of the providers of sport, information both statistical and informally yielded was garnered from sporting proprietors, game dealers, sporting agents and participants, retailers of sporting equipment, hoteliers in sporting areas, and anyone on whom sporting use had a direct impact. The report covers all Scotland, but those parts concerning red deer and grouse apply mainly to Highland areas, while pheasants and reared game apply to other areas.

Rounding up the figures, the report concluded that shooting sports provided direct employment for 12,000 people, mostly on a seasonal basis. The total revenue generated from sporting shooting in 1988–9 was £29 million, including the sale of game and venison. All except the largest concerns operated at a loss. Game dealers' sales were worth £8 million, nearly all of which was exported. The sporting people coming to Scotland are estimated to spend a total of £78 million in Scotland, a figure which includes VAT, travel costs, and agency charges. This expenditure is high when contrasted with other types of visitor. The significance of shooting sports to the Scottish economy was perhaps best illustrated by the figure for employment income generated of £53 million.

The report made several pertinent points about the nature of Scottish sport. Although most sporting assets were managed with negative cash flows, sporting use enhanced capital values of properties. Furthermore, the 'opportunity cost', or the income put aside in favour of sport, was reported as very low. The report records that sporting proprietors almost universally regarded themselves as conservationists; respondents felt sporting use had a better conservation record than forestry, agriculture, or letting ground go wild. The Fraser of Allender report summed up with an expression of concern over the lack of commercial viability for sport and a recommendation that sporting interests and the Scottish Tourist Board should co-operate in its development.

The report concerns only shooting and stalking, and not fishing. When the full complement of sporting uses are taken together, and excluding all-embracing general tourism, sport in the Highland area is a conspicuously vital linchpin in the nation's economy outwith the area of arable agriculture. Also the report studied sport as it exists within the present punitive frame-work, not as it could be. Some egregious examples of hill management show there is unrealised potential on selected sporting properties. On an estate near Inverness an energetic owner committed to grouse moor improvement, and willing to put up the venture capital necessary, converted a 200 brace a year bag to an average of over 1,500 brace in just a few years. The significance of this lies not only in the capital enhancement, but in employment. Five keepers are employed on 12,000 acres. This is a man to every 2,400 acres, not including shepherding manpower. No alternative land use, on ground climbing up to 2,000 feet, could begin to compare in employment terms.

Those who are opposed to all sport on ethical grounds should take fully on board the potential consequences of its disappearance in employment and national revenue losses. A scene in which Highland rivers flowed to the sea unfished; lochs sported no rowing boats on dreich days; keepering, ghillieing, shooting and stalking came to a stop with the attendant closing of hotels, tackle shops, letting agencies is unenvisageable.

The capital losses to the Highlands would be colossal. My earlier, very conservative, estimate for the capital value of Scottish salmon rod fishing was £800 million; sea trout fishing's value would add to the figure considerably. The annual stag cull of around 14,500 can be multiplied by £15,000 a stag to arrive at a capital value of stalking of over £200 million. This excludes the value of hind stalking, stalking other deer species, and those stags not shot for sport. Grouse, of which around 300,000 were shot in 1988, are difficult to assess for capital worth because the value of driven grouse far exceeds that of grouse shot over dogs, which in turn is greater than that of walked-up grouse. Rough shooting capital values are hard to guesstimate for other reasons.

However, the general picture over Scotland is one of very high capital values for sporting rights which generally yield low or negative returns. Fiscal penalties for sport fatally distort any comparison of economic performance between land uses. The time may come when environmental benefits will be written in to cost equations of comparative land uses, which would be of manifest benefit to the sporting case.

What becomes painfully apparent in a consideration of the land uses which presently take place in the Highlands is the haphazard nature of development. Not only are many interested parties at odds with each other, but no mechanism exists for evaluating the justice of opposite demands. Proposed land use changes get the green light if there is an absence of opposition which is considered reasonable, not on proven, positive merits. Occasionally councils are called upon to make judgements between one land use and another and they patently lack any model which could help consistent decisions.

Planning in the Highlands is in a mess. One little example is a mixed woodland planting scheme in three compartments at Borrobol for which I have applied for grant in the winter of 1989/90. None of the areas is over ten acres. Yet for a variety of tiny technical reasons each compartment will have a different sponsor. The NCC, the Forestry Commission and the Countryside Commission for Scotland will all be involved. Consider all the doubled-up human resources in time and effort processing applications in three different offices for small, almost physically adjacent schemes. It is a patently ridiculous situation.

Not only is planning within one land use department in a mess. Different land uses have no formal or defined relationship with each other. Development is *ad hoc*, opportunist. In a sensible world before the Sutherland grass-growing fiasco mentioned before was given over to wholesale afforestation there would have been an impact study with input from locals. The environmental consequences would have been analysed for the area itself, downstream in watercourses, and around the periphery. Employment and the volume of public financial support would have been looked at in the light of an overall objective for the harmonious management of the area. As it is, the forestry company has been assailed on all fronts, by local crofters, the NCC, the National Farmers' Union for Scotland, and a host of others. The raised voices of dissent did nothing to stop the relentless march of the forestry ploughs, working round the clock with their headlights on.

When forestry planting applications are considered, sporting use is not taken on board initially as an accepted primary land use of vital importance to the Highland economy: farming is, but not sport. Despite their major contribution to Scottish tourism, sporting opportunities are, in the main, absent from Scottish Tourist Board promotions. Sporting use nowadays has to fit in around land use alterations ordained in a forum to which it is sometimes denied admission. Highland land use conferences have been known to complete their programme without even mentioning sporting use, as if no such activity existed. The time is overdue when this attitude must change, once and for all.

Sport instead should be expanded where suitable. Loch and river fishing should be treated as first-class resources qualifying for top-priority protection. It would be desirable to see in place a scientifically formulated philosophy about management of the physical river, artificial stocking, and protection of the river habitat for juvenile fish. Codes of practice for productive fishing water relating to the disciplines of riverbank maintenance and revetment should be worked out. The protection of friable banks from trampling by cattle, deer and sheep, and the provision of fenced drinking corridors, and policies designed to shade and firm up vulnerable riverbanks and provide food for young fish by broadleaf tree-planting, should become agreed objectives in suitable situations. These are little-understood concepts in Britain, but widely-recognised objectives abroad. The maintenance of the Highlands red deer population should be regarded as an end in itself, not a sideline in the debate about the environmental value of deer forest as bog for breeding birds, a florally-rich wilderness or unique blanket peatland. Grouse moor management should be acknowledged as the most environmentally-friendly productive use of all moorland options. Debates about the creation of national parks, afforestation targets and public access should take place against this background.

The problem with a land use plan for the Highlands is it implies centralised planning, tending towards the sort of inflated macro-economic concepts from which the Highlands has suffered too much already. It need not. Contributions to the debate should be weighted in favour of those who live there and have a long-term financial stake in the area. The new local enterprise boards may go somewhere in this direction. Those resident in the Highlands too often feel they are pawns in bigger political manoeuvres, resulting in a fatalistic attitude towards fresh incentives. Highland people are fed up with being patronised by outsiders who claim to know better, and who hail from places where things are worse. If, as very often happens, the case for conservation seems a gross form of interference, it is because conservationists have made little attempt to understand the framework of communities on whom they wish to impose their ideas. Local opinion is important and based on longer experience. Landowners, if they feel left out, should join into local debate and make their case understood. They are the repositories of grand accumulations of knowledge on country matters and this is wasted in the wider community if they allow themselves to be excluded from the policy-making forum. The estate system has worked well and kept the Highlands in good repair. No remotely sensible alternative land use plan for the Highlands has ever been devised. The landowners' case is a strong one and they must ignore historic prejudices against the sporting option.

I have been fortunate. At the age of twenty-seven I inherited an estate which my grandfather bought in 1938. In all of Britain there was not a part of the country that could compare for me with Sutherland. I had handed me on a plate (along with a thought-provoking tax bill) exactly the sort of estate which, had I ever been able to, I would have sought to buy. Few people are lucky enough near the beginning of their working life to get given what others might dream of possessing at the end of theirs. As my mother was a Highlander, and as I had spent most of my working life till then in Scotland, I came to Sutherland not feeling a complete outsider. My job is to improve and protect as best I can a beautiful piece of country whilst simultaneously keeping on the right side of my bank manager. If this book has been motivated by anyone particular, it is to the county of Sutherland and its inhabitants that my interest and enthusiasm are attributable.

Bibliography

Anderson, Mark L., *A History of Scottish Forestry*, Nelson, 1967

Buxton, Anthony, *Travelling Naturalist*, Collins, 1948

Calderwood, W. L., *The Salmon Rivers of Scotland*, Edward Arnold, 1921

Clutton-Brock, T. H. and Albon, S. D., *Red Deer in the Highlands*, BSP Professional Books, 1989

Clutton-Brock, T. H., Guinness, F. E. and Albon, S. D., *Red Deer: Behaviour and Ecology of Two Sexes*, Edinburgh University Press, 1982

Colquhoun, John, *Salmon Casts and Stray Shots*, Blackwood, 1858

Colquhoun, John, *The Moor and the Loch*, Blackwood, 1840

Darling, F. Fraser, *The West Highland Survey*, Oxford University Press, 1955

Darling, F. Fraser and Boyd, J. Morton, *The Highlands and Islands*, Collins, 1964

Eden, Ronald, *Going to the Moors*, John Murray, 1979

'Ellengowan' (J. G. Bertram), *Out of Door Sports in Scotland*, W. H. Allen, 1889

Gilbert, John M., *Hunting and Hunting Reserves in Medieval Scotland*, John Donald, 1979

Haldane, A. R. B., *The Drove Roads of Scotland*, published by David and Charles, 1973. First published in 1952

Hall, Robert, *The Scottish Sportsman and Tourist*, J. Menzies, 1888

Hart-Davies, Duff, *Monarchs of the Glen*, Cape, 1978

Hunter, James, *The Making of the Crofting Community*, J. Donald, 1976

Hunter, Thomas, *Woods, Forests and Estates of Perthshire*, Henderson, Robertson and Hunter, 1883

Leslie, A. S. (Ed.), *The Grouse in Health and Disease*, Smith, Elder & Co., 1912

McConnochie, Alex, *The Deer and Deer Forests of Scotland*, Witherby, 1923

Mackenzie, Evan G., *In Grouseland*, Swan Sonnenschein, 1895

MacKenzie, Osgood Hanbury, *A Hundred Years in the Highlands*, Edward Arnold, 1921

Malloch, P. D., *Life History and Habits of the Salmon*, Malloch, 1910

Maxwell, Sir Herbert, *Memories of the Months*, 1897

Omand, Donald (Ed.), *The Grampian Book*, The Northern Times Ltd., 1987

Omand, Donald (Ed.), *The Sutherland Book*, The Northern Times Ltd., 1982

Orr, Willie, *Deer Forests, Landlords and Crofters*, John Donald, 1982

Richards, Eric, *A History of the Highland Clearances*, Croom Helm, 1982

Richards, Eric, *The Leviathan of Wealth*, Routledge and Kegan Paul, 1973

Ritchie, James, *The Influence of Man on Animal Life in Scotland*, Cambridge University Press, 1920

St John, Charles, *The Wild Sports and Natural History of the Highlands*, 1846

Scrope, William, *Days and Nights of Salmon Fishing in the Tweed*, J. Murray, 1843

Thomson, Derick S. and Grimble, Ian (Ed.), *The Future of the Highlands*, Routledge and Kegan Paul, 1968

Tomkins, Steve, *Forestry in Crisis*, Christopher Helm, 1989

Whitehead, G. Kenneth, *The Deer Stalking Grounds of Great Britain and Ireland*, Hollis and Carter, 1960

Index